The church that Christ built

D1340779

THE
CHURCH
THAT
CHRIST
BUILT

John D. Legg

EVANGELICAL PRESS

EVANGELICAL PRESS

Evangelical Press
Faverdale North, Darlington, DL3 0PH England
email: sales@evangelicalpress.org

Evangelical Press USA
P. O. Box 825, Webster NY 14580 USA
email: usa.sales@evangelicalpress.org

www.evangelicalpress.org

Originally published as *The footsteps of God* in 1986.
This revised edition 2006.

© Evangelical Press 2006. All rights reserved. No part of this publication may be reproduced, stored in a retrieval system or transmitted, in any form, or by any means, electronic, mechanical, photocopying, recording or otherwise, without the prior permission of the publishers.

Unless otherwise indicated, Scripture quotations in this publication are from the Holy Bible, New International Version. Copyright © 1973, 1978, 1984, International Bible Society. Used by permission of Hodder & Stoughton, a member of the Hodder Headline Group. All rights reserved.

Printed in the United States of America

British Library Cataloguing in Publication Data available
ISBN-13 978 0 85234 227 5   **ISBN 0 85234 227 6**

To Beryl

Contents

I will remember the deeds of the Lord;
*   yes, I will remember your miracles of long ago.*
I will meditate on all your works
*   and consider all your mighty deeds.*
Your path led through the sea,
*   your way through the mighty waters,*
*   though your footprints were not seen.*
You led your people like a flock
*   by the hand of Moses and Aaron.*

— Psalm 77:11,12,19,20

Many pious people among us are not aware that the ground on which they tread has, as it were, been hallowed by the footsteps of the Almighty.

— Archibald Alexander (1772 – 1851)

God moves in a mysterious way
*   His wonders to perform;*
He plants his footsteps in the sea
*   And rides upon the storm.*

— William Cowper (1731 – 1800)

Preface

This book has three aims. The first is to satisfy the legitimate curiosity of the average Christian about the history of the church. To do this I focus on some of the great men of God who are mentioned frequently in sermons and magazines but who are just names to many. I make no claim to original research or scholarship, although I have tried to be as accurate as possible. I am most grateful to those who have given me an entry into the riches of church history and thus provided the raw material for these pages. I hope that this will lead others to dig further and enjoy some more of these riches by following the suggestions for further reading. (An asterisk [*] indicates that a work is fairly basic and undemanding. Two asterisks [**] mean that the book is important and well worth the effort.)

The second aim links to the first. It is not enough just to know about and admire the heroes of the past; we must also emulate them. The purpose of the questions for discussion after each chapter is to stimulate both thought and action in this respect.

The author of Psalm 77 recalled the deeds of God in the past in order to find encouragement in days when it appeared as if God had 'forgotten to be merciful' and had 'in anger withheld compassion'. My third aim, therefore, is to provide such needed encouragement. My prayer is that by being reminded of the great days and great men of the past we might be stirred to hope and pray and persevere in our own day.

God led his people in the Old Testament by the hand of Moses and Aaron and has continued to lead his people by these more recent successors. However, it is God, whose footsteps are invisible, who enabled them to act as they did. It is in this God we too must trust; and all the glory will be his when he revives his work once again.

For further reading

For general help in reading and profiting from church history refer to the 'Appendix: The use and abuse of church history'.

The following books cover all of church history. The relevant sections from each book may be read after each chapter:

* S. M. Houghton, *Sketches from church history*, The Banner of Truth Trust, 1980.

** N. R. Needham, *2000 years of Christ's power*; *Part One: The Age of the Early Church Fathers*, Grace Publications, 1998; *Part Two: The Middle Ages*, Grace Publications, 2000; *Part Three: Renaissance and Reformation*, Grace Publications, 2004; *Part Four: The Enlightenment to the Twentieth Century* (D.V.).

* A. M. Renwick, *The story of the church*, Inter-Varsity Press, 1999.

Others were tortured and refused to be released, so that they might gain a better resurrection... The world was not worthy of them.

— Hebrews 11:35,38

I must needs be burned alive... The will of God be done.

— Polycarp (A.D. 69 – 155)

Thy saints in all this glorious war
*   Shall conquer, though they're slain;*
They see the triumph from afar,
*   And shall with Jesus reign.*

— Isaac Watts (1674 – 1748)

1

The blood of the martyrs

While Christians have no doubts about the truth and purity of the religion of the apostolic era covered by the New Testament, they are often in a quandary about the period that followed. For many the time from the apostle John to the apostolic Luther is one of unrelieved darkness, when the gospel was swallowed up by heresy, when the primitive spirituality of the church fossilized into ritualism and sacramentalism and when the missionary church was taken over by the ecclesiastics and finally by the state. The arch-villain of the piece was the Roman emperor Constantine and the resulting tragedy was the dead, gospel-denying, anti-Christian Roman church of pre-Reformation days.

How could the situation have deteriorated so completely and so speedily? We know that after some later revivals there were drastic slumps in life and spirituality within a few years, but for this to happen so soon after the apostles appears to cast doubt on the validity of apostolic and evangelical religion.

The answer to the question is that, although this picture has a lot of truth in it, this is by no means the whole truth. Our records of the church in those first centuries are very scanty and we must be very careful when drawing conclusions. What evidence we do have shows that in spite of all the failings of the church the gospel continued to spread in such a way that it overcame the world as well as turned it upside down. Christianity penetrated to the corners of the Roman empire, and when the state took over the church it was partly because it recognized that the church had taken over the world.

How then do we explain the impression of error and lifelessness that we gain from this period? A comparison with today may be helpful. The people who appear on television and whose speeches or sermons are reported in the press are usually the progressive clerics who deny the historic faith, the men with the gimmicks or the denominational leaders and ecumenically-minded church bureaucrats. Researchers in days to come will find little public record of the godly country pastor, the faithful Sunday school teacher and the isolated pioneer missionary. Yet these people are not only orthodox and zealous but also effective in the spreading of the gospel. In the same way there must have been thousands in the early days who, although not reaching the headlines of their day, laboured, prayed, taught and witnessed in the name of Christ. Even in the darkest days there was 'a remnant chosen by grace', and in the better times a multitude of genuine Christians engaged in the battle for the kingdom of God.

One thing above all demonstrates the reality of their faith: their readiness to die for what they believed and preached. There may have been uncertainty about some doctrines that, although clearly taught in the Scriptures, were only later stated and defined in formal confessions. We should not judge their orthodoxy by these standards. Instead we should ask ourselves whether we, with our far superior understanding and doctrinal awareness, are ready and able to make the same confession as them, the same as Christ made before Pilate (1 Tim. 6:13), a declaration of faith in and allegiance to the Lord and his truth.

As they 'attacked' the kingdom of this world in the name of Christ, so the world, in the shape of the Roman Empire, retaliated and the saints had to undergo a fiery trial. Many were arrested, tortured and, if they refused to deny their Master, executed. The ones brought to our notice must represent many more who believed and testified as they did. They died in varied circumstances and in widely spread places. Together they show how God's footsteps began to be seen throughout the world.

Emperor Nero

The king to whom Peter exhorted his readers to submit (1 Peter 2:13) was the emperor Nero (born A.D. 37, reign A.D. 54 – 68). Nero began a new stage in the persecution of Christians. Although we have many examples in the Acts of the Apostles of attacks on believers, both by Jews and pagans, there was no official persecution and Paul could generally rely on his Roman citizenship to give him protection from his enemies. The Jewish religion was a 'permitted' one and for a long time the followers of 'the Way' were regarded as a sect of Judaism. By the time of Nero it was becoming clear that this was no longer the case, and with the increasing number of Gentiles in the church Christians became both suspect and vulnerable. It was understandable that Jews, being foreigners, should have different religious customs, but there seemed to be no reason why others should want to be different and refuse to join in the ordinary activities of the rest of the citizens. Therefore, when Nero (whose empress, Poppaea, favoured the Jews) needed a scapegoat he turned on the Christians. As was so often to happen in the future, everything was treated as entertainment for the populace of the city. It is probable that the apostles Peter and Paul died in these persecutions.

In A.D. 64 a fire devastated much of Rome and rumour began to accuse Nero of having started it. (This was the occasion when he was alleged to have 'fiddled while Rome burned'.) Whatever the facts of the matter, Nero needed to divert attention from himself and, therefore, blamed the Christians. He had many arrested and tortured to make them implicate others. The victims were covered in the skins of wild animals so that dogs would tear them to pieces; others were made into living torches by being fixed to crosses and set on fire. Nero presided over the 'sport', which took place in his gardens.

'A vast multitude' was condemned to death, not apparently for starting the fire but for 'hating the human race' – in other words, because they were different and separate. Already Christians were seen to be different from other people; this is the reason for not only the world's hatred but also the success of the church's witness.

Emperor Domitian

Both Christians and pagans often regarded the emperor Domitian (reign A.D. 81 – 96) as a reincarnation of Nero; certainly he intensified the persecution. Domitian was a suspicious man who executed or exiled many of those nearest to him. Some of these seem to have been believers, including possibly his cousin and his cousin's wife (Domitian's niece) and others of noble birth. They were accused of a mixture of Judaism and atheism. Christians were considered by the pagans to worship no gods at all because they had no images and refused to acknowledge the many Roman gods; hence they were atheists! The charge of Judaism mixed with atheism probably means, therefore, that they were believers. If so, by the time of Domitian the faith had made great strides in the very capital of the empire.

Domitian also encouraged the cult of emperor worship that had been making progress for some time. He decreed that he should be addressed as 'our Lord and our God'. In general the state cult demanded only nominal acceptance of the deity of the emperor, and many of the emperors refused to take it seriously. Nevertheless, the acceptance of emperor worship was insisted on, and Christians could not give the formal worship and incense offering that it entailed.

In addition, Christians were suspected and accused of many abominable practices, such as cannibalism (probably a misunderstanding of eating the body of Christ in the Lord's Supper) and incest (possibly derived from their references to one another as brother or sister).

From every angle Christians were suspect and persecution followed. At this time and during the years that followed there were those whose faith was shown to be superficial because they conformed to the requirements of the state. However, others stood firm and paid the price.

Emperor Trajan

During the reign of Trajan (A.D. 98 – 117), Pliny was Governor of Bithynia in northwest Asia Minor. In a famous letter he consulted the emperor on the right way to deal with Christians. Trajan's reply was a mixture of moderation and injustice but leaves no doubt that Christians who remained obstinate were to be put to death. More significant for us is Pliny's unwitting testimony to the reality of the faith of these Christians. What he called 'stubbornness and unyielding obstinacy' and 'madness' we can only admire as faithfulness to the Lord Jesus Christ.

Pliny put supposed Christians to the test by ordering them to pray to the gods, to offer incense on the altar dedicated to the emperor and to curse Christ because, as he writes, 'I am informed that people who are really Christians cannot possibly be made to do any of these things.'

Pliny seems to have been very puzzled by these antisocial people who bound themselves together with an oath not to commit crimes but to abstain from all crimes and even from breaches of faith! He was very worried about the effect this would have on the worship of the gods and even on social and economic matters, and no wonder! Those who were ready to withstand his persecution must have been exceedingly powerful witnesses to the Christ to whom they sang hymns as God. Here, at least, we have no sterile Christianity, no dead and formal ritualism.

Polycarp of Smyrna

One of those put to death during Trajan's reign was Ignatius, the Bishop of Antioch, who was taken all the way to Rome to be thrown to the lions for the entertainment of the crowd in the Colosseum. On his way to the capital under armed guard Ignatius wrote letters to various churches and individuals, including Polycarp (A.D. 69 – 155), the Bishop of Smyrna. (The term 'bishop', at this time, seems to have meant something like our modern minister of a local church.) One of the letters from our Lord in the book of Revelation was addressed to the church at Smyrna (Rev. 2:8-11), and Polycarp, a relatively young man at this time, about

A.D. 115, had known and been taught by the apostle John himself.

Polycarp seems to have been a very different kind of man from the fiery, martyrdom-seeking Ignatius. He was gracious and peace loving, using his influence on the side of mercy in a difficult situation at Philippi. When he visited Rome to discuss the date for observing Easter, citing the apostle John in support of his own practice, he won great acceptance for himself, though not for his ideas, and ministered there to great profit.

He was nevertheless firm in his attitude towards heresy, writing to neighbouring churches to warn them against the false teaching that was threatening their lives. When the heretic Marcion asked Polycarp to acknowledge him, he did so as 'the first-born of Satan'! On another occasion he led his companions from the public baths lest they shared in the judgement of God on a false teacher whom he had seen in the building.

Many years later, probably in A.D. 155, this aged saint fell victim to the hatred of the mob. An outbreak of persecution occurred in the area around Smyrna and a number of Christians were thrown to the wild animals, accused of being atheists. Next, the crowd turned its attention to Polycarp and demanded that he be found. Friends prevailed on the bishop to withdraw to the hills where he owned a farm. There he passed the time in prayer. Eventually he was found and arrested. Three days earlier he had a vision of his pillow on fire and told those with him that he was going to be burned alive. The officers who took him were greatly impressed not only by his giving them food and drink but especially by his prayers.

When he was brought to the stadium the officials in charge, some of whom were well disposed to the godly old man, tried to persuade him to swear by the genius of Caesar and so save his life. Satan often uses our friends to lead us astray and Christians were often urged to comply with the regulations, just as a formality. To them, however, just as to Korean Christians of a later age, there could be no mere formality about the worship of another god. Therefore, in response to all of their pleadings Polycarp gave this memorable answer: 'Eighty-six years I have served him and he has done me no wrong. How then can I blaspheme my King, who saved me?'

To the end Polycarp was willing to instruct the proconsul in the faith, but he disdained to defend himself before the mob. He was threatened with wild beasts and then with fire, but he did not flinch. Once again his answer was memorable as well as moving:

> You threaten me with the fire that burns for an hour and in a little while is put out, for you do not know about the fire of the judgement to come, and the fire of eternal punishment reserved for the ungodly. But why are you waiting? Bring what you will.

And so they did. He was burned alive.

The issues were clear to Polycarp and to the rest of the Christians: 'It is better for you to enter life maimed than with two hands to go into hell, where the fire never goes out' (Mark 9:43). Immediately after Polycarp's martyrdom the local church wrote a letter describing the events, so eager were they for a neighbouring church to know of their leader's joyful and glorious end. To them and to the heathen around them such faithfulness was the best possible testimony to the truth of the gospel.

Irenaeus

The reigning emperor from A.D. 161 – 180 was Marcus Aurelius. During this time one of Polycarp's disciples at Smyrna was Irenaeus (A.D. 130 – 202). He later became famous as a theologian and a scholar and was the author of a five-volume work against the Gnostic heretics who troubled the second-century church. Irenaeus wrote with great ability, providing a link, as he was not slow to point out, between the apostle John, through Polycarp, and his own time. There were many links between the churches of Gaul (modern France) and Smyrna, and Irenaeus became bishop of the church at Lyons in 177. One of his first tasks was to restore the church in Gaul after some vicious persecutions in the area. The churches at Lyons and Vienne sent a letter to the churches of Asia Minor, including Irenaeus' home church at Smyrna, telling them about their trials.

Once again the persecution was a mixture of official trials and mob violence. The Christians had been accused of the usual offences and were ill-treated by the people, even being excluded from all public buildings. The mob's hatred of the Christians increased and they were eager for blood. Soon all the leading members of the two congregations were arrested and thrown into prison to await the arrival of the governor. Only too ready to grant the desires of the people, the governor began the torture of prisoners and their servants. Some broke down under the strain and recanted; a man who tried to defend them was himself arrested and condemned, and those who were so inconsiderate as to die in prison were replaced with new victims! Pothinus, the ninety-year-old Bishop of Lyons, was beaten by soldiers and died in prison.

The next stage was to take all the surviving prisoners to the amphitheatre (except those found to be Roman citizens, who were beheaded). This was what the mob was waiting for. Ever since a gladiator had been accidentally thrown to the lions and torn to pieces, no public games had been regarded as complete without some victims being given to wild animals for the entertainment of the crowd. A festival at Lyons provided just the occasion for a trial, torture and execution.

Blandina

Blandina was a slave girl. Both she and her mistress were believers and people feared that the young girl would be unable to stand firm. It was she, however, who amazed the pagans with her courage. She resisted all the soldiers' efforts to make her deny her Lord. When torture failed she was thrown to the beasts but survived the first day of the terrible sport. Steadfastly she maintained her profession of faith in Christ and denied that the Christians practised wicked customs. Far from proving frail under trial, she strengthened others by her courage, including a fifteen-year-old boy called Ponticus. Ponticus died under torture still refusing to deny Christ, and Blandina was at last killed by a wild bull.

The persecutors spared no one: young or old, male or female, high rank or low. By the same token Christians from all walks of life gave evidence of the grace of God. When a despised slave girl could resist the combined power of officialdom and the mob, it is no wonder that the world was impressed. As a result the gospel spread throughout Europe.

We may be able to find fault with the theology of Irenaeus, by our later standards, but there cannot have been much wrong with a gospel and a faith that produced Blandina.

Tertullian

During the reign of Septimus Severus (A.D. 193 – 211) the gospel very quickly reached Egypt and the North African coast where some of our earliest New Testament documents come from. When the Christians of the town of Scilli were tried for refusing to sacrifice to the gods in A.D. 180, one of them, Speratus, brought to the trial not only a copy of the Old Testament but also Paul's letters.

Tertullian (A.D. 160 – 225), a lawyer born in Carthage, was one of the most famous Christian authors of those days. He was a brilliant advocate responsible not only for scathing attacks on paganism and skilful defence of the faith but also for penetrating theological statements. There are many varied estimates of his standing as a Christian because he sympathized with and may have joined the extreme Montanist sect. In view of his hard-line attitude and violent language one might have expected him to be one of the martyrs, but in fact he died peacefully at an advanced age.

MONTANISM

Montanism arose when a young convert named Montanus, together with two women, Priscilla and Maximilla, began to prophesy, asserting that the Paraclete (the Holy Spirit) was speaking through them in a new way. This was accompanied by claims of visions and speaking in tongues. They asserted that all this heralded Christ's imminent return. Today they would probably be called Pentecostals or Charismatics. Indeed, some in these modern movements have claimed the Montanists as their spiritual ancestors. However, they would not favour the Montanist's emphasis on fasting, celibacy and martyrdom. Some fell into heresy on the doctrine of the Trinity, which gave the establishment a further excuse to condemn the whole movement.

It may have been Tertullian who edited an account of the martyrdom of some Carthaginian Christians, including Perpetua, in
about the year 202. In one of his writings Tertullian describes how
the Christians were blamed for everything: 'If the Tiber rises to
the walls, if the Nile fails to rise and flood the fields, if the sky
withholds its rain, if there is an earthquake or famine or plague,
straight away the cry arises: "The Christians to the lions."'

Perpetua and Felicitas

The story of Perpetua, a young wife from a noble family in
Carthage, and Felicitas, a slave girl, was told in part by themselves.
Perpetua had only recently been baptized, in the face of her father's
opposition, when she was arrested with several others. She was
twenty-two with a baby boy whom she was allowed to have with
her in prison. As the result of a vision she was convinced that she
was going to die. Neither her father's threats nor his pleas could persuade her to give up her faith. Among the other prisoners was
Felicitas, a slave girl who gave birth to a daughter in prison. The
baby was taken away and cared for by the local Christians.

Although the group had to put up with a lot of ill-treatment in
prison, conditions improved after the governor was converted.
Nothing, however, could prevent the climax. Once again the
amphitheatre was the scene for the end as all the prisoners were
thrown to the animals. Once again the unity of the faith, as well as
its strength and glory, was demonstrated to the watching heathen as
free woman and slave girl stood hand in hand encouraging one
another to stand firm in Christ.

Summary

The accounts that we have lay great stress on the actual physical
sufferings and the courage and endurance of the martyrs; these
can hardly be overstated. The records also emphasize the tremendous effect that these deaths had on the attitude of the unbelievers
who witnessed them. We should also take notice of the reasons
the Christians gave for suffering. When Justin Martyr was executed
at Rome in A.D. 165, he asserted that he did not just *think* that he

would ascend to heaven, but that he was *convinced* of it. The Christians were quite sure that to give up their faith would be, as Polycarp put it, to exchange the better for the worse. The manner of their dying, with confidence and even joy, proved that for them earthly fire was not as terrible as eternal fire and that heavenly bliss was more glorious by far than worldly happiness. It was, therefore, no little thing, as both friends and enemies often asserted, to swear by the genius of Caesar or throw incense on his altar. It was worshipping another god, serving a different king and so betraying Christ.

Through this kind of testimony the church made clear the issues of the gospel and the infinite worth of eternal life. Through men and women such as these the kingdom of Christ gained many glorious victories throughout the world. In this we rejoice and glorify God who enabled them by his grace.

If we want to see the same kind of victory in our world the question has to be asked whether we are ready to give the same kind of testimony. God's way of blessing is often the way of suffering. Are our lives so different that we arouse interest and provoke opposition by our godliness? Do we stand firm for the gospel among our friends and neighbours? Are we ready to suffer ostracism, loss of job or earnings and even torture and death for the sake of our Saviour? If not, we need not expect God to use us as he did those early Christians.

Questions for discussion

1. *How can we keep the proper balance between orthodoxy and godly living, between being naïve and hypercritical? Does 1 Corinthians 13:1-3 apply here?*

2. *Is it still true that 'The blood of the martyrs is the seed of the church' (Tertullian)? Can you think of New Testament evidence that this is so? How does this work?*

3. *Consider Polycarp's martyrdom in the light of Mark 9:43. How would you respond in such a situation? What considerations should help you to persevere in faith in lesser trials today? (Read 1 Peter.)*

For further reading

Read the relevant sections of S. M. Houghton, *Sketches from church history*, The Banner of Truth Trust, 1980; N. R. Needham, *2000 years of Christ's power*, Grace Publications, 1998, Part One; and A. M. Renwick, *The story of the church*, Inter-Varsity Press, 1999.

* R. Alderson, *The early Christians – a taster*, Day One Publications, 1997.

H. Bettenson, ed., *Documents of the Christian Church*, Oxford Paperbacks, 1999.

** M. A. Smith, *From Christ to Constantine*, Inter-Varsity Press, 1971.

In the beginning was the Word, and the Word was with God, and the Word was God.

— John 1:1

We believe ... in one Lord Jesus Christ, the Son of God, begotten of the Father, only-begotten, that is of the substance of the Father, God of God, Light of Light, true God of true God, begotten not made, of one substance with the Father.

— The Creed of Nicaea (A.D. 325)

Thou art the everlasting Word,
*   The Father's only Son;*
God, manifestly seen and heard,
*   And heaven's belovèd one.*
Worthy, O Lamb of God, art thou,
*   That every knee to thee should bow!*

— Josiah Conder (1789 – 1855)

2

Athanasius against the world

It is in the fourth century that we plunge into the morass of acrimonious debates, divisions, councils and creeds that deter so many from reading church history. Yet it was in the midst of these often unspiritual and unpleasant events that Christian doctrine was defined, error condemned and foundations laid for the future. Instead of judging these arguments by the standards of later orthodoxy we should realize that without these battles and victories the later developments would have been impossible. Without Athanasius and Augustine in these early days the wonderful confessions of the sixteenth and seventeenth centuries would never have been given to us. God was building his church and in some measure we can trace his footsteps.

Emperor Constantine

The Roman empire was in a poor state, both socially and economically, and the church seems to have been little better. The persecutions had, on the whole, ceased and Emperor Constantine (born A.D. 274, reign A.D. 306 – 337), as a result of a vision in A.D. 312, took the church under his patronage in the hope, naturally, of enjoying the patronage of the Christians' God. How genuine his Christianity was is a matter of some debate, but he certainly took it seriously. Although he showed little understanding of Christian doctrine and was not baptized until he was dying, he interfered constantly in the life of the church. Therefore, the favour of the emperor became an important factor in church politics as church leaders descended to deceit and intrigue in order to gain or maintain prominent positions. Constantine became involved when, in order to give presents to his new friends, he had to decide between different groups claiming to be the true church. Disputing parties asked for his help as an independent arbitrator, and soon the church, which had resisted persecuting emperors to the death, began to do what the friendly emperor told them.

Too often the doctrinal debates were merely part of the power game instead of a search for the truth. The creed became a hedge against error, a weapon used against enemies as well as heretics, instead of a vibrant declaration of living faith in the gospel of Christ. However, some men stood out in the history of the first half of the century because of their concern for the truth of God for its own sake. One such man of principle was Athanasius.

The Arian controversy begins

In A.D. 318 a dispute arose in the church in Alexandria in Egypt. This church and its bishop were recognized as having authority over all the churches of Egypt; therefore, the trouble soon spread throughout the country and then beyond. The bishop, Alexander, appears to have been giving a rather ambitious lecture to the surrounding ministers on the doctrine of the Trinity, laying stress especially on the unity of God. Suddenly he was interrupted by a young presbyter named Arius from one of the outlying churches. Arius, who has given his name to the controversy that followed, asserted that Alexander was undermining the distinctions in the Godhead, and in opposition to him maintained that the Son of God was not the same as God but definitely an inferior being.

Arius (A.D. 256 – 336) was, in fact, accusing Alexander of Sabellianism, which was a fourth-century theological swear word. Sabellius (who lived around A.D. 220) had laid such stress on the unity of God that the three persons came to be regarded as different ways of appearing of the one person. The church rightly rejected this view and although Alexander, in common with many in the east, may have emphasized the unity of God too much, he was certainly not a Sabellian.

Arius, on the other hand, had developed the ideas of the great but erratic theologian, Origen. He had held that the Son was subordinate to the Father. Arius went much further than this, saying that the Son was a distinct and inferior being, created and non-eternal. He foreshadowed the modern idea that Christ had divinity but not deity, and his teaching was very similar to that of modern day Jehovah's Witnesses. In a letter to his friend and former fellow student, Eusebius of Nicomedia (not to be confused with the church historian Eusebius of Caesarea living at the same time), Arius wrote, 'Before he was begotten or created or appointed or established he did not exist, for he was not unbegotten. We are persecuted because we say that the Son has a beginning, but God is without beginning.'

Immediately Arius began to spread his teaching with great zeal and ability. He and Eusebius organized their forces, enlisting the support of many bishops who had been students with them at the theological school at Antioch. Arius, we are told, was a great favourite with the ladies and used his charm to gain support in the churches. He also composed doggerel verses containing his ideas, which he set to music and taught to the people of Alexandria. He and Eusebius used every kind of intrigue to win over the church to their way of thinking. Indeed, Eusebius, who was described by Arius as 'his dearest lord, the man of God, the faithful and orthodox Eusebius', seems to have been not only unorthodox but also a most unsavoury character.

The Council of Nicaea

Bishop Alexander also took steps to gain support. He called together his clergy to discuss the matter and then summoned a council of 100 bishops, which debated and then condemned Arius' teaching. The whole of the east was taking sides, and as the dispute began to affect the rest of the empire Constantine took a hand, in the interests of imperial unity and security. He called a council at Nicaea at which he would take the chair. This took place in A.D. 325.

Nicaea was a pleasant town conveniently near to Constantinople, or Byzantium, the capital of the eastern part of the empire, of which Constantine was now the sole ruler. About 300 bishops gathered for the council, but the most important person there, theologically and spiritually speaking, was not a bishop at all.

Athanasius and the Council of Nicaea

Athanasius (A.D. 296 – 373), a deacon in the church at Alexandria, was present merely as secretary to his own bishop, Alexander. We know almost nothing of his family and early life, but he was clearly the protégé of the bishop, who had made himself responsible for the boy's education and training for the ministry. Athanasius had showed great promise in theological matters, but Alexander very wisely also kept him occupied with pastoral affairs. It is generally agreed that Athanasius helped Alexander to draft the circular letter that he sent to the clergy opposing Arius. Although he would not be able to play an audible part in the council's deliberations, probably the young secretary provided much of the ammunition used at Nicaea by Alexander and his orthodox colleagues.

Already Athanasius had published two works: *Against the Nations* and *Concerning the Incarnation of the Divine Word*. They do not specifically mention the Arian controversy and were probably written before it arose, but they show quite clearly not only the author's early commitment to the full deity of Christ but also his awareness of the importance of this doctrine for the whole issue of salvation. They are evangelistic works aimed at showing the heathen the true nature of the gospel. Therefore, in the second of the two treatises we read, 'For being the Word of the Father and above all, it followed that he alone was also able to re-create everything and to be ambassador for all men with the Father', and again,

'Thus, taking a body like ours, because all men were liable to the corruption of death, he surrendered it to death instead of all, and offered it to the Father.'

Christ alone, because he is the eternal Word, is able to redeem or restore man from his lost condition. We must not suppose that Athanasius had a full understanding of the atonement as later explained and defined; he thought in terms of restoration through union with Christ in all that he did as man, rather than satisfaction and substitution in our sense. Nevertheless, he taught clearly that we are saved only through Christ's work and especially through his death and resurrection.

Perhaps the most important fact that we need to grasp about this whole debate is that the issue is really the nature of the gospel and salvation. For Athanasius and for us the person of Christ is basic to his work. Only one who was truly God and truly man could be our Saviour.

Arius' teaching was defective, not only on the deity of Christ but also on the subject of man's lost condition in sin. If man's condition was not as serious as the orthodox teachers insisted, then there was no need for such a radical salvation or for such a great Saviour. On the other hand, if these teachers were right about man then they were also right about Christ. Similarly today those with an optimistic or humanistic view of the essential goodness of man are often those who regard Christ as a mere man, his incarnation as a myth and his deity as an outmoded idea. An Arian Christ could not save man as the Bible describes man; as has been said, a second-rate god could only provide a second-rate salvation. Athanasius fought his battle over the gospel he was to preach all his life to the lost around him.

After much argument the council produced a creed that was essentially the same as what we know as the Nicene Creed, defining orthodoxy and deliberately excluding Arianism. Much of the discussion centred on one word, the Greek *homoousios*, translated as 'consubstantial' or 'of the same substance'. Many were unhappy with this word, which had had a chequered career, because it was associated with the notorious Paul of Samosata. They would have preferred to substitute a slightly different word, *homoiousios*, 'of similar substance' (to the Father). However, it seemed that no other word could so effectively shut out Arianism as *homoousios*. Therefore it was eventually adopted, together with expressions like 'true God from true God', which unmistakably asserted the full and eternal deity of the Son. An appendix was added, just to make sure, specifically condemning certain expressions used by Arius, such as 'there was when he was not'. (Arius was careful not to say 'a time when' because according to him the Son's beginning was before time.)

MORE THAN JUST AN IOTA

It is ridiculous to represent Athanasius as a narrow, doctrinaire man haggling over one letter, the tiny Greek iota. Apart from the obvious fact that one letter, such as the 'i' in 'maid', can mean a world of difference to the sense, this charge ignores the spiritual and evangelistic motive behind Athanasius' whole campaign.

The battle continues

Nicaea was not the end of the controversy; indeed, in one way the struggle was only just beginning. Arius and his friends did not take their initial defeat lying down. Even though Constantine had chaired the Council of Nicaea and approved of the creed, they knew that political intrigue and ecclesiastical power politics could achieve a lot. So for the next forty years Athanasius was at the centre of a running battle, attacked in various ways and from all sides, criticized, deposed, exiled and hunted around the east and Europe. His preservation through all of this and his eventual triumph show again the providence of God at work in the decisions of heathen emperors, in the hearts of the ordinary people and in the labours and sufferings of godly bishops.

In A.D. 328, three years after the Council of Nicaea, Athanasius succeeded Alexander as Bishop of Alexandria and almost immediately had to face pressure from Constantine. Anxious to preserve the peace that had descended on the empire, at least superficially, the emperor suggested to Arius that if he was to recant he might be allowed back into the church. Athanasius, who was still young and impetuous as well as a man of principle, knew what a slippery character Arius was and refused point-blank to receive him back. This was hardly tactful and from that time on Constantine regarded the awkward bishop with suspicion.

Knowing this, Athanasius' enemies continued to attack him and tried to have him removed. Some of his troubles he brought on himself. One blot on his reputation was his harsh treatment of a group called the Melitians. They had opposed his predecessors at Alexandria and continued to cause trouble to the new bishop. It may be no coincidence that Arius had once been a follower of their original leader, Melitius. Athanasius had some of these dissidents imprisoned and beaten in an attempt to crush them. The only result, however (and this should be a lesson to us), was to drive them into the arms of the Arians. Together they brought charges against Athanasius, not only the justified ones about his treatment of the Melitians but also many others, ranging from his allegedly illegal consecration as bishop to murder.

This last charge of murder concerned a man called Arsenius, whom Athanasius was accused of murdering so that he could cut off his hand to use in black magic ceremonies. Athanasius and his supporters scoured the country, found Arsenius and produced him in court alive and complete with two hands. 'Has any man more that two hands?' enquired the bishop triumphantly.

Some of the slander inevitably stuck. Athanasius appealed to Constantine, but when he was reported to have threatened to cut off supplies of corn from Egypt for Constantinople, the emperor lost patience and exiled the fiery bishop to Trier in Gaul. This first exile lasted only one year because Constantine died and one of his three sons, Constantine II, who controlled the west, declared an amnesty for those exiled by his father. So in A.D. 337 Athanasius returned to Alexandria to a hero's welcome.

One of those who welcomed the returning bishop was Antony, the eighty-year-old hermit from the Egyptian desert; he was both famous and highly respected and his support for Athanasius was very important in the east. When Antony died he bequeathed his most valuable possessions, a sheepskin cloak and mantle, to the bishop, who later wrote his biography. From our standpoint Athanasius' admiration for hermit life is a weakness, but we must remember that Christians of that day regarded such men as spiritual warriors, the successors to the martyrs. Taken in historical context this indicates an awareness on the part of Athanasius of the spiritual dimensions of the battle in which he was engaged with Arius and Eusebius.

Emperor Constantius

The east, including Egypt, was under the sway of Constantius (A.D. 337 – 361), another of Constantine's sons. He favoured Arius, and when Eusebius approached him he readily deposed and exiled Athanasius. The citizens of Alexandria were so angry that imperial troops were needed to enforce the decision. When Athanasius left once again for the west he was accompanied by two friends of Antony, whose presence helped him to gain support from the western bishops. This was to prove invaluable later on.

Council followed council and creed followed creed as one faction after another gained the ascendancy. After A.D. 346 the empire settled down a little and Athanasius was able to return to his people, still as popular as ever. He spent the next ten 'golden' years preaching the deity of Christ around Egypt, even to the Coptic-speaking peasants who had previously been pro-Melitian. Support grew for the orthodox teaching all over the empire in spite of pressure from the pro-Arian Constantius. Although Athanasius' determination aroused hatred in his many opponents it also provoked great devotion from those who shared his love of Christ and his gospel.

Victory

This support for Athanasius was more than Constantius could stomach and he decided on drastic action. One after another the bishops were ordered to agree to Arian creeds or face exile. Many in the west refused and were exiled to the east, where some of them joined forces with Athanasius. Hosius of Cordoba, the last survivor from the age of persecution and now over 100 years old, had the temerity to rebuke the emperor and his favourite bishop, Valens, who responded by threatening him with torture. In the end they compelled him to sign an Arian statement, but even then he maintained, 'I won't condemn Athanasius.'

Next Constantius turned his attention to the east and Athanasius. By now Egypt was solidly behind the bishop, so when the soldiers came to arrest him he slipped away and hid in the desert. For the next five years he was on the run, occasionally visiting his flock in Alexandria but spending much of his time writing, including his important *Letters to Serapion on the Deity of the Holy Spirit.*

While Athanasius was in the desert it seemed as if Arianism had triumphed. The creed produced by one synod was so heretical that the orthodox Hilary of Poitiers nicknamed it 'The Blasphemy of Sirmium'. Another, supposedly a compromise, produced at the Council of Rimini allowed the Arians back into the church. 'The whole world groaned', wrote Jerome later, 'and marvelled to find itself Arian.'

As so often, however, the devil had overreached himself. The power of the emperor had brought about this situation, and when Constantius died in A.D. 361 things began to change.

Emperor Julian the Apostate

The extreme heresy of some of the creeds the Arians had produced had provoked a reaction not only among those who had been orthodox all along, even though a little dubious about the Creed of Nicaea, but also among others who had regarded Athanasius as at best wrong and at worst a troublemaker. Then, in the mysterious providence of God, the successor to Constantius was not even a Christian in name. Indeed, he is known to history as Julian the Apostate (reign A.D. 361 – 363). His teachers in his youth had been Arian court bishops whom he had come to hate and when he became emperor he proclaimed his unbelief openly and set about destroying the church.

Julian's idea was to allow all the exiled bishops back into their sees and then to sit back and watch the divided church tear itself apart. In practice this meant that the orthodox bishops returned to the fray. Hilary went back to the west and organized the defeat of Arianism there, while Athanasius was able to resume at Alexandria. Contacts and friendships that had been made in exile now bore fruit as Athanasius, learning wisdom with age, united with others to gain the final overthrow of Arianism.

Athanasius still had to face two more periods of exile: one when Julian, who was trying to revive paganism, was angered by Athanasius' conversion of some heathen in Alexandria and the last when the Arian Valens became emperor in the east. Together with the great Cappadocian teachers, Basil the Great, his brother Gregory of Nyssa and their friend Gregory Nazianzus, Athanasius preached and wrote until Arianism was finally beaten. Athanasius was able to spend his last seven years in peace in Alexandria, dying in A.D. 373 just a few years before the official end of Arianism in the church, which took place at the Council of Constantinople in A.D. 381.

Summary

It is hard to discern the important elements in the life of Athanasius from the multitude of emperors, councils and bishops. There is, however, one golden thread running through all the debates, exiles and failures. His ability, learning, determination and courage were consecrated to one thing: the exaltation of Christ, the honour and glory of the Son of God. He was concerned with the Son, not as a philosophical idea or theological symbol but as the only possible Saviour. His aim was not to gain prestige or power but to preserve the gospel that he preached all his life to the lost.

Such was the man whom God used against the world. If he was too concerned with his own isolation, that was perhaps inevitable in a life that included five periods of exile. God certainly had his 7,000 who had not bowed the knee to the Arian Baal, such as Hilary of Poitiers. However, few of them, if any, were ready to fight as Athanasius had; few had the ability to teach as he did. In any case it was Athanasius whom God had prepared and placed in Alexandria and raised up at the appropriate time to resist the onslaught of Arius. His doctrine, viewed from our century, was by no means perfect; his policies and methods were too often those of his day, although there is a world of difference between him and, for example, Eusebius of Nicomedia. Nevertheless his zeal for truth and his determination, courage and perseverance should stir us to greater efforts for the same Lord Christ whom he served.

The battles of our own day may be different; although modern Arians and others still deny the Son of God, the arguments and methods have changed. The battle for truth, however, still needs people like Athanasius; God still works to raise up those who can stand for his truth against the tide. We must be ready in our day just as Athanasius was in his.

Questions for discussion

1. *Jehovah's Witnesses have been described as 'your friendly neigh-bourhood Arians'. What does this mean?*

2. *In what ways is it essential to have a correct doctrine of the person of Christ if we are to have a true faith in his work? See John 8:23-25; Colossians 1:15-20; and Hebrews 2:14-18.*

3. *What use should we make of the example of Athanasius? What are the dangers as well as the benefits?*

For further reading

** M. Haykin, *Defence of the truth*, Evangelical Press, 2004.

A. McGrath, *A cloud of witnesses*, Inter-Varsity Press, 1990, pp.7-22.

** N. R. Needham, *2000 years of Christ's power*, Grace Publications, 1998, Part One, pp.201-230.

** S. Olyott, *Jesus is both God and man*, Evangelical Press, 2000.

For it is by grace you have been saved, through faith — and this not from yourselves, it is the gift of God — not by works, so that no one can boast.

— Ephesians 2:8-9

Give what you command and then command what you will.

— Augustine of Hippo (A.D. 354 – 430)

'Tis done! The great transaction's done!
   I am my Lord's and he is mine;
He drew me, and I followed on,
   Charmed to confess the voice divine.

— Philip Doddridge (1702 – 1751)

3

Give what you command

The words that head this chapter, addressed to God by Augustine of Hippo in his *Confessions*, sparked off one of the greatest and most important controversies in the history of the church. The ideas and doctrines implied by Augustine's prayer have been argued over ever since his day and have divided Christendom and, sadly, even genuine Christians. Augustinianism enshrines much of the essence of the gospel and especially the doctrines of the grace of God that have been the great strength of the church since the Reformation. The hero of the debate (not to be confused with the later and inferior Augustine of Canterbury) was one of the greatest men of the early centuries in the church. His life and work provide an instructive and often inspiring example of how the Lord prepares and uses his human instruments for his glory.

It is often said, with much truth, that orthodox creeds and confessions cannot safeguard the gospel or protect the health of the church if the actual teachers and preachers at any given time are not orthodox and spiritual men. It is quite easy to affirm publicly and deny privately, as many have unscrupulously done with the Anglican *Thirty-Nine Articles* or the Presbyterian *Westminster Confession*, or simply to relegate the awkward creed to a shelf of interesting but irrelevant antiquities, as is frequently done today. Nevertheless, once a battle for the truth has been fought and won, its results can be stated in a clear form that provides a useful foundation for those who follow.

Thus, although the truth about God's sovereign grace, asserted and vindicated by Augustine, lay hidden and ignored, if not utterly denied, for many generations, the preachers of the Reformation era found in it a ready-made weapon that they could and did use against error and for the gospel. The battles had been fought and the issues clarified; the arguments had been refined and criticisms answered by one of the church's greatest theologians. Although the Reformers appealed only to Scripture for the truth of their doctrine, at least the great name and reputation of Augustine saved them from the charge of teaching a novelty. Although for a long time it seemed that Augustine's fight had been in vain, as councils denied or watered down his conclusions, we can see how God prepared the way for the later spread of the same doctrines though the great Reformers.

Augustine

Augustine (A.D. 354 – 430) was an intellectual giant whose gifts the Lord used in debate and writing, but we must begin by looking at his Christian experience of the grace of God working in his own life and conversion. Only a man with his kind of practical knowledge of the Holy Spirit's power could have written the books that made clear to others the nature of that power.

Augustine and Monica

Augustine was born at Tagaste in North Africa in 354, but in upbringing and culture he was entirely Roman. His mother, Monica, had become a Christian as a young woman. One day she had rebuked a servant, who had retaliated by calling her, with much justification, a drunkard. She was convicted of her sinfulness and soon became a believer. Later she married a pagan, Patricius, and therefore her two sons were not baptized. Like so many modern children in the same situation, Augustine followed his unbelieving father rather than his godly mother and grew up apart from God.

Patricius was a bad influence on the young man. Augustine records in his autobiographical *Confessions* that his father and his friends were concerned only for his intellectual and material advancement, and his mother's advice, which was more spiritual, was rejected as old wives' tales. However, even his mother was determined that he should become famous for his learning; therefore, it is no surprise to find that her son's life at this time was dominated by this ambition.

One incident that later was to affect him greatly and which gives considerable insight into his subsequent teaching on the nature of sin was the theft of some pears from a neighbour's orchard. We might not regard this as a great sin. Some would consider his concern grossly exaggerated, just as they do John Bunyan's attitude to the sins of his youth. However, Augustine, writing from his later Christian viewpoint is in no doubt as to the seriousness of the offence: 'I did it', he writes, 'not because I was forced to it by any misery or poverty, but because I was weary of doing well and because of my great sinfulness. I had better ones at home and I gathered these only for the sake of stealing.' In fact he and his friends stole a huge amount and then threw them away to the pigs! It was by such experiences and his sensitivity to the awfulness of sin that Augustine understood something of the depth of human depravity that his later opponent, Pelagius, never appears to have grasped.

Augustine's father was eventually converted a year before his death, in 371, largely because of Monica's gracious dealings with him. In the spirit of 1 Peter 3:1-6 she was subject to him, refusing to resent his sharp words and never answering back.

After his father's death the wayward youth went even further astray into gambling and immorality. It is true that he had some idea of the right way and even faint desires to be better, like his mother. The shallowness of such desires may be judged from his notorious prayer uttered around this time: 'Give me chastity and continence … but not yet.'

Therefore, at the age of eighteen he fathered an illegitimate son, whom he rather strangely called Adeodatus ('Gift of God'), and continued to seek only pleasure and entertainment.

After living for a time in a separate house from his mother he left for Carthage to study rhetoric. There the theatres, the race-course and the amphitheatre further corrupted him. However, one important turning point in his life occurred at this stage: he became fascinated by philosophy, largely through reading a book by Cicero, and began to study various systems of thought. He rejected the Bible because of what he regarded as its poor literary style and was attracted instead by Manichaeism.

MANICHAEISM

Manichaeism was part philosophy and part religion, a mixture of Christianity and the Persian religion of Zoroastrianism produced by Mani. This dualistic teaching maintained that light (God) and darkness were both eternal and bitterly opposed to each other, and that the aim of religion was to release souls, which belong to light, from the prison of their material bodies.

Although Augustine found the teaching superficially attractive he never committed himself wholeheartedly to it. This was partly because Manichaeism denied, or at least seriously doubted, the historical existence of Jesus Christ. In addition, when a prominent Manichaean visited Carthage, the young student questioned him and found his answers unsatisfactory.

Meanwhile Monica was longing for her son's conversion. She asked the advice of various bishops and urged one to visit Augustine and convince him of the error of his ways. The bishop wisely counselled her that her son was not yet ready to listen, but that she should 'wait the Lord's good time. Meanwhile,' he added, 'you should go on praying, for the child of so many tears cannot perish.' In due course a sovereign God confirmed his words and heard Monica's crying and prayers.

In 383 Augustine moved on to Rome to teach rhetoric. Monica pleaded with him not to go and thought that she had persuaded him, but while she spent the night in prayer he left. In Rome he lived with the Manichaeans until their life of ease and pleasure shocked him into leaving. Their dualistic system made ease or asceticism equally acceptable! After a year he moved again, to Milan, where he lived with his friend Alypius, his brother Navigius and his son Adeodatus. Monica also went to live in Milan, still longing and praying for her son's salvation. Here she was influenced and encouraged by the bishop, Ambrose.

In 373 Ambrose had been given the responsibility for arranging the election of a new bishop; at the time he was only a civil servant and, although apparently a believer, not yet baptized. In the middle of much argument a cry went up: 'Ambrose for bishop!' and so it was. He soon proved his fitness for the task, preaching with great power and resisting the encroachments of the civil authorities with great determination in the name of Christ.

Monica added witness to prayer and persuaded Augustine to give up swearing. He also gave up his liaison with one woman but soon entered into another. In spite of this lapse it is evident that God was now working in Augustine; he was not happy and he knew it. One day he saw a beggar laughing and commented, 'That poor wretch is happy and has what I cannot attain to.' As dissatisfaction grew stronger in his heart, so his mind began to be influenced by the gospel until he became convinced of the intellectual truth of Christianity.

His conversion

Augustine was attracted by the reputation of Ambrose and went to see him. Ambrose received him graciously and courteously and so began to win his heart. Augustine began to attend church in order to hear Ambrose preach, although part of his reason for going with Alypius was to hear and study the rhetoric of the noted orator. He wrote later, 'I was careless and despised the matter which he delivered, but I was attentive to and delighted with the sweetness of his speech… Salvation is far from sinners such as I was then and yet, by little and little, I grew daily nearer to it, though I knew not how.'

Soon he began to see some truth in what was preached and resolved to become a *catechumen* and receive instruction in the gospel until he could be certain where truth lay. Being a deep thinker he had many problems to sort out, and his mind was in great turmoil as he wrestled with issues such as the being of God, the origin of sin and evil, immortality and the nature of Christ's person.

In his search he turned from 'Christian' philosophers to the Bible and especially to the writings of the apostle Paul. He also consulted an old minister called Simplicianus, who was the spiritual father of Ambrose. He told Augustine about Victorinus, at one time a teacher of rhetoric in Rome whom he had known. Victorinus, a proud scholar like Augustine, had been converted in his old age and publicly professed the name of Christ in spite of the shame and rejection it brought from his academic colleagues. Thus, Augustine began to see not only the truth of the gospel but also something of the practical cost of becoming a Christian.

Another influence on the seeker was Pontilianus, an African officer in the emperor's household. One day he visited Augustine and noticed that he had been reading Paul's letters. He began to speak to him about his own faith and particularly about Antony, the Egyptian hermit and friend of Athanasius. He related how two of his friends had been converted through reading the life of Antony, and this story had a tremendous effect on Augustine. Addressing Christ, as everywhere in the *Confessions*, he wrote,

> You, O Lord, turned me inward upon myself, taking my soul from behind my back, where I had placed it so that I might not see it, and setting it before my face so that I might see myself, how deformed I was, how sordid, how full of spots and sores. I saw and in so doing I abhorred myself, nor was there anywhere I could fly from that odious spectacle.

Augustine was now in great distress and ran out into the garden, closely followed by his friend, Alypius. An inner conflict tore him as he debated with himself whether he should turn from his sins or not. Eventually he moved away from Alypius and wept bitterly under a fig tree – bitterly because he could not make up his mind to leave his sin. Here was no easy passage for Augustine because he realized very clearly that there was no way to Christ and salvation apart from repentance; if he was to be joined to Christ he must be separated from his life of sin. Quite evidently he was not free but bound by sin and unable to turn to Christ unless God enabled him to do so by his grace.

Just then Augustine heard a child's voice repeating some words, which at first he took to be part of some children's game. The voice said, 'Take and read. Take and read.' He interpreted this as a divine command to read the Scriptures and went back to the copy of Paul's letters that he had been reading earlier:

> I took it quickly into my hand, opened it and read in silence from that chapter on which my eyes first fell: 'Not in orgies and drunkenness, not in sexual immorality and debauchery, not in dissension and jealousy. Rather, clothe yourselves with the Lord Jesus Christ, and do not think about how to gratify the desires of the sinful nature' (Romans 13:13-14). I would read no further, nor was there any reason why I should, for instantly with the end of the sentence, as by a clear and constant light infused into my heart, the darkness of all former doubts was driven away.

The Word of God applied to the heart and conscience by the Holy Spirit had now freed Augustine from the bondage that had kept him from Christ. Now he could leave sin to serve the Saviour, and he was determined to do so. Augustine told Alypius what had happened to him and the latter joined him in his resolve. Together they told Monica who, we are informed, 'rejoiced and triumphed and praised God'.

Augustine in A.D 386, now a true believer, gave up his lecture-ship and began to prepare for baptism. He read deeply and learned quickly. The Psalms were his first love, and he delighted in them as he studied them in depth. His mother was a great help to him, but he turned naturally to Ambrose for advice on which books to read. He recommended Isaiah, but Augustine, like many others before and since, found this too difficult and set it aside until he knew the Lord better. He was baptized at Easter in 387, together with his son Adeodatus and his friend Alypius. This was clearly a time of great blessing for him, and he wrote the following,

> Nor was there any end in those days to the unspeakable delight I had in considering the depth of your counsels concerning the salvation of mankind. How copiously I wept during those hymns and psalms, being touched to the very quick by the notes of your church so sweetly singing. Those words flowed into my ears and the truth contained in them distilled melting into my heart, causing my feelings to overflow in devotion to God so that my tears ran streaming down and I felt a great sense of happiness.

Augustine was certainly a great intellect, and his writings are full of deep thought. However, passages such as these from the *Confessions* show that he was also a deeply emotional man and that his conversion was no mere change of philosophy.

Back in Africa

Soon he decided to return to Africa with the rest of the family, but he had gone no further than Ostia at the mouth of the Tiber when his mother died. Just before this the two of them had stood one evening overlooking a garden and talked of the life to come. Monica had confided that there was nothing now to keep her on earth; her one desire had been to see her son become a Christian, and now she saw him happy to be God's servant. A few days later the godly Monica died, her prayers fully answered. If she had known what he would achieve for the church of Christ, she would surely have considered that God had done exceeding abundantly above all that she had asked or thought.

Conflicts and controversies

The Manichaeans

For a while Augustine returned to Rome where he wrote against Manichaeism. Although he seems to have retained a few ideas or influences from his own Manichaean period he answered them strongly, placing stress on the unity of the Old and New Testaments and particularly on the incarnation, the ultimate contradiction of Manichaean claims that God could have nothing to do with a material world. Then he returned to Africa where he began a semi-monastic life at Tagaste with Alypius, reading and writing. Thus he was prepared for his future life as a defender of the faith. Before his death in 430 he had written over 100 works, excluding sermons and letters, against five different opponents of the truth.

The Donatists

Four years after his conversion he was ordained by Valerius, the Bishop of Hippo. Although Augustine had hoped for a quiet life, Valerius had special reasons for ordaining him against his will! The bishop had tried to found a monastery, but the monks spoke Latin and Valerius did not. Augustine's task, as a Latin scholar, was to preach to them and, when his great gifts were recognized, to preach in the cathedral. Indeed, Augustine's job was to do any-thing that Valerius found to be beyond him, whether in governing the church or in controversy with the Donatists.

THE DONATISTS

The Donatists were followers of Donatus who died in A.D. 355. They were schismatics in North Africa who rejected all cooperation with the state and existed in many places along-side the Catholic Church, which had the backing of the Empire. They believed that the church should always be a besieged and persecuted minority; the martyrs were regarded as the great leaders of a holy, separatist congregation. So all collaborators with state authorities were denounced as traitors to the cause of Christ, and the battle against the Catholic Church went on for many years.

Into this controversy Augustine was inevitably plunged. The Donatists were not always, or even often, as spiritual and pure as they claimed. The methods of the Donatist terrorist band, who ravaged the rural areas of North Africa, would hardly commend them to some who have claimed these separatists as their spiritual ancestors.

All this Augustine could point out, and he was easily able to show that historically they were largely in the wrong. However, he does not appear at his best in this controversy. His view that the church will inevitably be a mixture of true and false Christians, with which we can agree, does not justify his conclusion that we should do nothing about error. The Donatists were certainly overly optimistic about their prospects of purifying the church, but that did not mean they were wrong to try. Further, they always regarded Augustine as the symbol of the persecuting church and this, regrettably, he became. At first his attitude was 'that no one should be compelled to the unity of Christ; he must be won by word, convinced by argument, satisfied by reasons, lest we should have disguised Catholics instead of open heretics.' Sadly his awareness of imperial support and the obstinacy of the Donatists led him in exasperation to use force against his opponents, quoting 'Make them come in' (Luke 14:23) in support of his actions.

Augustine and Pelagius

Augustine's controversy with the Donatists continued after he became Bishop of Hippo in 395, at the age of forty-one. While at a conference with them in Carthage he first met his most important and dangerous antagonist, Pelagius.

Pelagius, who has given his name to the theology of free will just as Augustine has to the theology of free grace, was a moral and decent man from Britain. He was shocked by the appalling condition of the churches in Rome and used his opportunities to preach there to rebuke their immorality.

The concern for holiness that Pelagius possessed is, of course, worthy only of praise, and there is no doubt that the situation in Rome and many other places deserved his rebukes. The trouble was that the earnest moral preacher was basing his appeals on the assumption that man is basically good and free to live a good life if only he will make the effort. It is true that he spoke of the grace of God, but by this he meant only external influences for good, such as the teaching and example of Jesus.

Pelagius took special exception to a statement found in the *Confessions*: 'Give what you command and then command what you will.' To Augustine these words signified a humble but confident dependence on the grace of God; to Pelagius they were an insult to man and a denial of the justice of God. It would be unjust, maintained Pelagius, for God to command what man could not perform; man must be free and able to repent, obey and be holy. Grace is limited to making known to man his duty and encouraging him in performing it.

Augustine was horrified at this low view of grace and opposed it with all his might. He knew from the Bible and from his own experience the enslavement of sin. He remembered his delight in sin, his inability to reform or to turn to Christ. He had been fully aware of his duty but had been unable to carry it out until the grace of God freed him. Therefore, he taught that our free will, by which he meant our freedom to act as responsible beings, is a slave of sin; we must be born again before we can repent and believe.

Thus Augustine's deep experience of the grace of God in his own conversion prepared him to defend the doctrine in the church. Starting from this aspect of scriptural teaching, he went on to assert the rest of the doctrines that are usually associated with his name, such as human depravity, predestination and final perseverance. Pelagius was condemned as a heretic, but many continued to hold his ideas in a modified form, often known as semi-Pelagianism. Other church leaders, although agreeing to the condemnation of Pelagius, often refused to go all the way with Augustine's teaching. Nevertheless, in God's purposes, Augustine was responsible for preventing a wholesale abandonment of the gospel of the grace of God. Without him the church could have yielded to the persuasive arguments of Pelagius and, in the name of justice and holiness, adopted a man-made, man-centred message instead of the glorious and God-glorifying truth of the Scriptures. Not only is the promise of salvation in Christ the gift of God but also our faith itself; God calls whom he will, not according to our merit or worth but according to his eternal plan.

It is true that there are many passages in Augustine's writings that show traces or more of sacramentalism, which Roman Catholics seize on in support of their own doctrines of grace mediated directly through the sacraments. There are also aspects of his teaching on salvation of infants and prayers for the dead that later theologians have condemned. Overall, however, he remains the great theologian of grace, and the longer he went on the more consistently biblical he became. The church of Christ owes him a great debt for the way in which he expounded, clarified and defended the faith of the gospel, far more thoroughly than anyone had done before. Augustine clearly not only believed the truth, he rejoiced in it. He valued it above anything else because he had seen the sinfulness of his own heart and the bondage of his own will and had experienced the grace of God in his own life. God had prepared his servant most thoroughly for his task.

The City of God

Augustine contributed to theological thought in many areas, but he wrote one of his greatest works, *The City of God*, to be directly useful to the church of his day. In the providence of God it has also been of service to succeeding generations. He wrote it in the dark days when barbarian hordes were sweeping down from the north on a weakened Roman empire and a relatively defenceless capital city. Since Constantine's day Rome had become for many in the church virtually the city of God. Paganism was still far from dead and its supporters seized their opportunity to attack Christianity. Some interpreted the many defeats of the Roman armies as a judgement by the old pagan gods on Rome for adopting Christianity as its official religion.

When Rome was finally captured in A.D. 410, Augustine, still safe in Hippo, again rose to the occasion and began to write his *magnum opus*. In it he was not content just to point out that in the mercy of God it was Christian (Arian) armies that had taken Rome, but he also dealt with the whole matter theologically, distinguishing between the city of Rome and the city of God.

The church is not to be identified with the empire or its capital even when it has become officially Christian. The city of God is not even to be identified with the visible church on earth because this, as he had already argued against the Donatists, will always be mixed.

He was in many ways breaking new ground and was frequently inconsistent in working out the implications of his teaching. The problems of church and state relations, which trouble us today, simply did not occur to him. Nevertheless, even in our day it is important to be reminded that the nation is not a modern Israel, the industrial society is not the city of God and the visible church of today is not necessarily to be equated with the people of God.

For his own day, by dissociating Christianity from the empire's defeats he ensured that the church would not sink with the city of Rome but battle on as the city of God. All his previous controversies were fought over again in this work, and the results of his disputes were used in defence of the church. He defended the God of the Bible against the Manichaeans and others and pleaded for a realistic view of the church against the Donatists. Above all he denied a merely formal and outward Christianity and asserted that the God of grace will have a real people for himself, redeemed and delivered from sin through Christ. He then looked forward to the glorious day when the city of God will be triumphant and God himself will be all in all. Augustine died while the Vandals were actually besieging Hippo in 430, but he had already ensured that their victory over the Empire would not destroy Christianity.

Summary

Augustine's times were not ones of spiritual prosperity or doctrinal clarity. There is much to object to in his teaching, practice and attitude, but everything must be tested by Scripture. Nevertheless here was a giant of the church, a man who stood in the forefront of the battle when the truth of God had many and powerful enemies. Prepared by God from his earliest days (and even before, when we remember the part played by Monica), Augustine stood firm and laid the foundation for later Reformed orthodoxy and the world-wide spread of the gospel. While the world was in turmoil and the Roman empire falling to pieces, God was building his church. Though darkness was to increase for several centuries, a light had been lit that was to illuminate many; although the superstructure of the church crumbled, a foundation had been laid on which the church of the Reformation was to be built. We should be ready not only to believe what Augustine taught but also to fight as he fought, to face the enemies of the truth, to trust God and so to lift our eyes up to him in days of worldly darkness and disaster, confident that the city of God will be victorious.

Questions for discussion

1. *Discuss Monica's role both as a wife and as a mother. What encouragement can you find in the fact that she did not actually want her son to go to Rome?*

2. *What lessons may we learn from Augustine's dealings with the Donatists? Do we have their equivalent today?*

3. *How would you answer the charge that Augustine's prayer, to which Pelagius took exception, was a denial of human responsibility? Can you distinguish between free will and free agency?*

For further reading

* Augustine, *Confessions*, trans. Sir Tobie Matthew, Fontana, 1959.

H. Chadwick, *Augustine*, Oxford University Press, 1986.

* F. W. Farrar, *The life of St. Augustine*, ed. R. Backhouse, Hodder & Stoughton, 1993.

A. McGrath, *A cloud of witnesses*, Inter-Varsity Press, 1990, pp.23-35.

** N. R. Needham, *2000 years of Christ's power*, Grace Publications, 1998, Part One, pp.240-254.

** B. B. Warfield, *Calvin and Augustine*, Presbyterian and Reformed Publishing Company, 1956, pp.305-383.

Prepare the way for the Lord, make straight paths for him.
— Matthew 3:3

Therefore, if there were a hundred popes, and all the friars were turned into cardinals, their opinions in matters of faith should be believed only in so far as they are founded in Scripture.
— John Wycliffe (c. 1329 – 1384)

A glory gilds the sacred page,
    Majestic, like the sun;
It gives a light to every age;
    It gives, but borrows none.
— William Cowper (1731 – 1800)

4

Before the dawn

For many years it has been customary to refer to John Wycliffe as 'the morning star of the Reformation', the herald of the real dawn, which only arrived with Luther. It is important that we bear in mind constantly this preparatory aspect and do not exaggerate either his achievements or his significance. There has often been a tendency to see Wycliffe as a great hero of the faith, a fully-fledged evangelical with understanding, experience and practice on a level with those who came nearly two centuries later. In fact we have little personal information about Wycliffe and we must avoid the temptation to overstate either the advanced nature of his ideas or the extent of his activity. Nevertheless it is agreed, even by those who are no friends of reform, that Wycliffe made an outstanding contribution in preparing the way for the real Protestant Reformation, and it is right that we should trace his influence in England and on the Continent. It is even more vital that we trace the hand of God in his life and work.

Already the Lord had raised up individuals like Thomas Bradwardine to call the church back to the Scriptures and movements like the Waldensians on the Continent to maintain a simple and spiritual, if somewhat unorthodox, Christianity. Now he prepared a man whose ideas and attitudes were to challenge the very foundations of Catholic orthodoxy and who, though he apparently achieved little at the time, made possible the successful attack on the Catholic establishment, which we know as the Protestant Reformation.

John Wycliffe

The scholar

We have little information about the early life of John Wycliffe (c. 1329 – 1384). He is traditionally linked with a village bearing his name near Richmond in Yorkshire, but probably the most we can say is that he was a member of the Wycliffe family living in the area. Indeed, where he lived would not be important but for the fact that John of Gaunt (1340 – 1399), the Duke of Lancaster, was the feudal overlord of the area and was later to advance and defend the rebellious scholar.

We have no record of godly parents, no account of a youthful conversion or even of any unusual religious tendency. We may, however, assume that he grew up familiar with the ways of popular religion in the countryside. The corruption of the church and priests at that time is well known, but in spite of this religion flourished. Ordinary people flocked to church on Sundays and holy days, and special events such as dramas and carol services were very popular. Wycliffe would have gathered with the rest of the villagers on the village green to hear the sermons of the friars and pardoners, urging the superstitious people, by means of threats and legends of the saints, to buy their relics and papal indulgences. He was later to condemn the friars' practices out of hand, but his followers used open-air preaching to spread their master's teachings.

Historically speaking we first meet the future reformer as a graduate at Merton College, Oxford, in 1356 and then as Master of Balliol in 1360. These brief details are a sufficient reminder that he would have begun his academic career as a lad of fourteen, having received the tonsure, which marked him off from the unlearned of the world. Both of these colleges had links with the north of England, and it may be that even at this stage he was a protégé of John of Gaunt. Nine years of study, reading and public disputation, together with some lecturing in the later stages, completed his arts course. Only then was he allowed to specialize in theology, which would have taken a further nine or ten years. In fact Wycliffe must have had some interruptions in his course for he was over forty when he finally emerged as a doctor of divinity in 1372.

By this time Wycliffe had a thorough grounding in the system of medieval thought, which he was to attack at its foundations. He knew how to think and argue with the best minds of his day. Even opponents admitted that he was 'the flower of Oxford, in philosophy second to none, without a rival in the discipline of the schools [i.e. the scholastic method of disputation].' Oxford University had a reputation beyond even that of Paris at this time, which meant that Wycliffe was widely regarded as the foremost scholar in Europe. God had thus prepared a supremely sharp tool for his hand because even at this time Wycliffe did not conform to the church's conventional orthodoxy.

No one really worried about Wycliffe's different ideas at this stage because it was customary to advance new or unusual ideas and then defend them in public disputations within the academic world. This was considered perfectly safe, for it did not disturb the common people or in any way affect the state of the nation. Wycliffe favoured new philosophical ideas, against the traditional ones on which most of the contemporary theology was based. He was able to use these ideas to counter not only the dominant theories of authority but also to undermine the whole Roman dogma of transubstantiation. Others criticized the many abuses evident on the surface of church life, but it was only when Wycliffe and others delved deeper that anything close to reformation began. It is instructive to see how a training that appears at first sight to be utterly unspiritual and quite unpromising was in fact God's way of preparing one of the greatest English scholars for his appointed task of fighting medieval religion on its own ground.

Already Wycliffe had begun to attack abuses in the church, not only regarding priests holding political offices but on moral matters also. He wrote an exposition of the Ten Commandments, apparently a novel idea in 1372! It was, he maintained, not unusual for a man 'to call God Master forty, sixty or even eighty years, and yet to remain ignorant of his Ten Commandments'.

He attacked the belief held by all, but practised mainly by the wealthy, that if men 'give a penny to a pardoner, they shall be forgiven the breaking of all the commandments of God'. Instead of this, he referred his readers to Christ's 'death upon the cross, to buy man's soul out of hell, even with his own heart's blood, and to bring it to the bliss of heaven'.

We must not read too much into Wycliffe's position at this juncture. Although critical of faults in the church he was himself guilty of some of them. Thus while attacking pluralism, the practice of holding more than one church office at the same time, he held livings at Fillingham in Lincolnshire and at Westbury-on-Trym near Bristol without moving from his lodgings at Queen's College at Oxford! Up to this point he acted simply as a scholar, concerned only to advance himself in the scholarly and ecclesiastical spheres where he was already quite eminent. Apparently he was passionately fond of Oxford's river and woods, as a rare personal reference in a later letter revealed. Now, however, the time had come for him to enter the wider world of politics and diplomacy, for which his studies were regarded, in those days, as the ideal preparation. Now in the purpose of God his ideas were not only to be developed further but also to be introduced to non-academics as a basis for action.

The politician

A career in politics may not seem to us a very likely way to produce a reformer, but we must remember that in Wycliffe's day church and state were very closely linked or rather locked together in combat as they fought for control over the battlefield of the nation. In particular there was a constant warfare between the pope and his leading clergy on the one hand and the king supported by Parliament on the other. The pope claimed the right to tax the clergy within the king's realm and to appoint his nominees to the higher offices of the church in England. Although the king controlled the actual country and had the final say, there were complicated matters of treaties with other countries involved, not to mention the spiritual sanctions that the pope could apply; therefore, much was decided by discussion ending in some sort of compromise.

Wycliffe became involved in these discussions in two ways. His patron, John of Gaunt, Duke of Lancaster, virtually controlled the council that ruled England during the senility of Edward III and the minority of Richard II. When Parliament debated the issue of papal taxation Wycliffe was present and later he was a member of two diplomatic teams that negotiated with the pope at Bruges. He does not appear to have been a great success in this role, but this activity led to a more important contribution to Lancaster's cause, which had great significance for the cause of reformation. Wycliffe was now required by his patron to produce a theoretical and theological justification for the council's continuing opposition to the pope. In working this out Wycliffe inevitably developed a system that also provided a basis for spiritual resistance to the pope, that is, for the Reformation.

To attack corruption in the church and so limit its authority, Wycliffe adopted the teaching on lordship or dominion formulated by Archbishop FitzRalph of Armagh. Wycliffe then developed the teaching to provide a justification for the lay ruler, the king, to deal with abuses within the church. It may seem strange to us to defend this teaching by arguing that although the pope was the vicar of Christ, the king was superior because he represented God the Father, but it sufficed! From this base Wycliffe proceeded to attack corruption in the church, where he had no shortage of targets, especially in the riches and possessions of the religious orders. Thus the secular clergy, the parish priests and others like Wycliffe joined forces with the laity in resisting the claims of the pope. They asserted that dominion depended on being in a state of grace, and, therefore, sinful popes might even be resisted. In such a situation it became the king's duty to reform the church. The conclusion of this was to put power into the hands of Wycliffe's patron and his noble friends.

For his earlier assistance the scholar had been rewarded with the rich living of Lutterworth, where he was to end his days. His attacks on the pope, however, brought him trouble from the hierarchy of the church in England.

On 19 February 1377 he was summoned to appear before the bishops at St Paul's. John of Gaunt employed four doctors of divinity to defend Wycliffe and even attended in person in an attempt to intimidate the enemy. The duke tried to take charge of the trial but failed, partly because of the firmness of Courtenay, the Bishop of London, and partly because he was unpopular at the time with the people of London. The mob caused the hearing to be abandoned amid great uproar. Wycliffe appears to have kept silent and, although the whole business was a disgrace to the name of Christianity, at least he was preserved for future service for both Lancaster and the Lord.

Next an attack against Wycliffe was prepared before the pope, who was now back in Rome. Eighteen propositions drawn from Wycliffe's writings were condemned, more for anarchy than heresy, and their author's arrest was ordered with a view to confession and recantation. However, he was not arrested because the university authorities, who tentatively supported him, persuaded Wycliffe to submit to a voluntary confinement, although they agreed that the propositions sounded 'ill to the ear'. Then, when he appeared before the bishops at Lambeth Palace, once again the London mob broke up the proceedings.

Wycliffe was, however, ordered to keep his ideas to himself to avoid upsetting the laity. This, of course, was the real issue. Nobody minded Wycliffe discussing his ideas with his clerical friends and scholarly colleagues, but if the common people got hold of these ideas who knew what might happen! The church could lose its authority in the eyes of the people and anarchy would follow.

Meanwhile Wycliffe was once again delivered from his enemies. Pope Gregory died and the so-called Great Schism began when two rival popes were elected. This schism ended twenty-five years after Wycliffe's death, and when it did the 'heretic's' bones were not left long in peace. For now, however, neither of the claimants to the papal throne dared risk losing English support by laying a finger on Wycliffe, so he was left alone. This, writes one historian, 'was not the only piece of luck that attended the birth of the reform movement'. We may rather describe this once more as the hand of God who was still preparing a tool for his work.

Wycliffe at this point in his career was at the crossroads. He could withdraw from his dangerous position and probably receive a bishopric in return, or he could persist. He chose to do the latter. It was certainly an act of intellectual defiance; how spiritual it was at this stage we have no means of telling.

The heretic

Wycliffe's most prolific and important writings came from his last years, 1378 to 1384. In these works he developed the ideas that were to be maintained and propagated by his English followers and which sowed the seeds of destruction for the medieval church. He now followed the logic of his own position and began to spread his views among the uneducated laity. This was what his opponents feared most and which produced the effects they most dreaded.

One of these works was *On the Truth of the Holy Scriptures*. He had already demonstrated in his earlier writings his thorough knowledge of the Bible in Latin and had constantly annoyed his critics by taking the practice of the early church as the norm rather than the tradition of the fathers. Now he asserted not only the truth and authority of the Scriptures but also the right of all to read them: 'All Christians and lay lords in particular ought to know holy writ and defend it.' If the nobles have the Bible in French, then why should the common people not have it in English? So he writes, 'No man is so poor a scholar but that he may learn the words of the gospel according to his simplicity.'

In addition he insisted, in theory if not always in practice, on a common-sense, literal interpretation of Scripture within the grasp of the ordinary reader, in contrast with the involved methods of his contemporaries that successfully avoided the force of the Word of God. All this implies the necessity of a translation of the Bible into the language of the common people.

Having raised the Scriptures as a positive authority, Wycliffe went on to deal another blow to the power of the pope and priests. In his treatise, *On the Church*, he took over and developed the doctrine of predestination that he had learned from the great Thomas Bradwardine, Archbishop of Canterbury, who had died in 1349. The usual idea of the church was of an association of clergy, bishops, monks, friars and so on. For this Wycliffe substituted the concept of the church as the body of the elect, those chosen by God in his grace. According to this teaching, which is found in the Bible and the writings of Augustine as well as Bradwardine, man's salvation depends not on whether he submits to the priests by means of the sacraments but on whether God has determined to be gracious to him. Wycliffe does not seem to have worked out properly where faith fits into this scheme or even to have been very clear about the necessity for righteous living, but this was probably because he was preoccupied with the negative implications of the doctrine. By this teaching men were freed from bondage to the church, that is the clergy, and brought into direct dependence on God in Christ. Further, because the priests and even the pope might not be elect, they could not insist on the obedience of ordinary men who might be predestined to salvation! No wonder the clergy feared the common people knowing these ideas!

However, they had one strong support left. In the eyes of the congregation the power of the clergy rested ultimately on their ability to turn bread and wine into the body and blood of Christ in the mass, the doctrine of transubstantiation. Wycliffe's philosophical basis for opposing this was his philosophy of Realism. He was also able to prove that it had not become officially the teaching of the church until the thirteenth century and further that it was contrary to the plain sense of the Gospel record. He was not quite so definite as to what should replace the offensive teaching but appears to have leaned increasingly towards receptionism, the idea that it is the faith of the one sharing in the sacrament that gives reality to the presence of Christ. If the layman is not dependent on the priest to work this miracle for him, then the last chain of his slavery is broken and he is brought into direct contact with his Saviour. Thus, another essential element in the foundation of the Reformation had been laid.

REALISM

In this context Realism is not the same as our modern usage, which says that someone is a realist because he is not a dreamer but one who takes the real situation into account. It was a medieval philosophical movement, influenced by Plato, which asserted that universal concepts, like 'humanity', were more 'real' than individual ones, such as 'Wycliffe'. The opposite view was known as Nominalism. Some, of course, held to a middle path.

It was this particular 'heresy' that broke the camel's back. Criticizing abuses in the church was commonplace, and the doctrine of predestination had been orthodox, at least in theory, since Augustine. However, to deny the sacrifice of the mass was quite unthinkable.

Even John of Gaunt called Wycliffe's teaching 'that detestable opinion on the sacrament of the altar'. Most of Wycliffe's supporters now deserted him, even the friars who had liked his earlier attacks on the monks. Worn out by overwork and opposition Wycliffe became seriously ill during 1379. His enemies, including representatives of the various orders of friars, gathered at his supposed deathbed. As they gloated over his condition, he listened quietly. Then, as his servant raised him up in bed, he answered them confidently: 'I shall not die but live, and again declare the evil deeds of the friars.' And so he did.

A young Augustinian friar in Cambridge, Adam Stockton, copied one of Wycliffe's most violent attacks on the pope into his notebook, ascribing it to the 'venerable doctor, Master John Wycliffe'. Soon after, he crossed out the first two words, substituting 'execrable seducer'! He was not alone in changing his opinions and loyalties at this time.

An Oxford commission considered and condemned Wycliffe's ideas in 1380 to 1381, threatening anyone holding them with suspension from their university posts and even with excommunication. The 'flower of Oxford' was now regarded as 'a venomous snake' to be fled from. He was actually seated in the university teaching when the verdict was read to him. One of his opponents records, 'On hearing this condemnation he was confused, but yet he said that neither the Chancellor nor any of his accomplices could in the least weaken his opinion.' John of Gaunt hurried down from London to appeal to him to submit but he refused. Not only did Wycliffe appeal to the king, though without success, he also published a defiant *Confession* in May 1381 in which he defended the condemned opinions. All this seems to indicate more than a merely intellectual stubbornness; it was certainly not a bid for popularity.

Apparently defeated, he soon retired to his rectory at Lutterworth. During these last years he wrote various works and also some 'unpolished sermons for the people' in their native English. The first of these works to be printed was the *Trialogus*, though it was not published until 1525. He suffered a stroke in 1382 and died on the last day of 1384 after a further attack. It would be presumptuous to pronounce on Wycliffe's spiritual state, but although there is nothing to indicate that he had penetrated the heart of the gospel of justification by faith, he clearly taught men to rely directly on the work of Christ, not on the work of the priests. Further, his increasing consistency and understanding towards the end of his life indicate a firm spiritual commitment to his intellectual convictions.

In 1407 one of his staunchest followers and defenders appeared before the Archbishop of Canterbury and asserted that men had regarded Wycliffe not only as a great scholar but also 'a passing ruly [virtuous] man and innocent in his living'. To this the archbishop is alleged to have replied, 'Wycliffe your author [founder] was a great clerk and many held him a perfect liver.'

According to some, Wycliffe had missed his last opportunity of achieving moderate reforms in the church by alienating his friends in high places. This may be true, but such a reformation may not have been worth having. It would have meant that his more far-reaching ideas would have remained undeveloped or hidden, but, although the superstructure of the church might have been cleansed from its worst abuses, the foundations would have remained unshaken. As it was, he took several steps nearer the day when a radical reformation could take place. The people, freed from bondage by the understanding of justification by faith only, would be able to withstand all that Rome could do to change their minds. Often when God holds his hand, it is in order that he may make deeper and better preparation for a greater and more glorious work than would otherwise have been the case.

Wycliffe died in apparent failure, even ignored by the authorities because they considered him no longer dangerous. They were utterly mistaken because Wycliffe always had what has been called 'the dangerous gift of inspiring academic discipleship'. Previously it had been troublesome to him; now his opponents would find it so. We must now turn our attention to his disciples, academic and non-academic, known as the Lollards.

The Lollards

The word 'lollard' is Middle Dutch for a mumbler and was already in use as a term for heretics, especially on the Continent. It was applied to the followers of Wycliffe at least as early as 1380 and continued in use for two centuries. We should probably be cautious about the traditional picture of Wycliffe spending his time at Lutterworth translating the Bible into English and sending out his 'apostles, clad in russet gowns and barefoot like pilgrims on missionary journeys round England'. On the other hand there is no doubt that it was Wycliffe and his ideas that were responsible, directly or indirectly, for translating the Scriptures and for the existence of the so-called 'poor preachers' travelling the country.

The first Lollards were the academic disciples who Wycliffe left behind at Oxford, and they may have been responsible for sending out the preachers. In 1382 the Blackfriars Council was called to deal with two clearly related matters: the formal condemnation of a selection of Wycliffe's opinions (although he was not named) and the suppression of unlicensed preaching, 'not only in churches and churchyards, but also in markets, fairs and other open spaces where people greatly congregate'. Although the opinions were easily condemned as heretical the bishops seemed powerless to halt the lay preaching. The council ended with a minor earthquake, which was claimed by both sides as indicating divine support; it was probably more symbolic of subsequent happenings in the church as foreshadowed in the events of the council.

Some of the academic Lollards made brave but rash gestures in support of their master by preaching in English and distributing handbills in the streets of London even while out on bail on a charge of heresy. Some were excommunicated and others fled. Nicholas Hereford optimistically went to Rome to convert the pope! Many recanted and submitted, like Philip Repton who later became the Bishop of Lincoln and then persecuted the Lollards. The movement, however, continued to spread, involving uneducated lay people more and more. Trials and burnings continued for many years, but after abortive rebellions in 1414 and later in 1431 under the leadership of Sir John Oldcastle, one of the few nobles to be involved, the Lollards went underground. This did not mean inactivity nor did it bring immunity from persecution, but from that time it was essentially a lay movement without any educated leadership and was denied access to the newly introduced printing press.

The Lollards persisted and in places even flourished. There were many notable missionaries who, if anything, outdid the romantic traditional image. They did not merely preach on the village greens, ousting friars from their positions, they organized cells of simple but devout believers. Lollard strongholds were found in places as far afield as Leicester, Bristol and Amersham, with informal but effective intercommunication between the groups. A missionary at Windsor found a group of Lollard fugitives from Amersham who were 'a godly and great company which had continued in that doctrine and teaching twenty-three years'. John Aston, a Lollard from Oxford who at one time submitted to the bishops, was later found evangelizing on the Welsh border, and William Swinderby from Leicester seems to have covered most of the country in his itinerant preaching, making converts everywhere, including the young Sir John Oldcastle.

We are reminded of the apostle Paul tent-making with Priscilla and Aquila when we read of Nicholas Belward who: 'hath a New Testament which he bought at London for four marks and forty pence and taught the said William Wright and Margery his wife and wrought with them for the space of one year and studied diligently upon the said New Testament.'

The Lollard Bibles

What New Testament version did Nicholas Belward use? There were two Lollard Bibles. The first was a word-for-word literal version of the whole Bible, which was not very serviceable for ordinary reading but was probably prepared for a different purpose. There were many, including the ill-educated clergy, who had some Latin but found great difficulty reading the Bible in that language. They were thus provided with a translation that supplied a source of proof-texts for use against the pope rather than a book for continuous reading. The first part of this was produced by Nicholas Hereford, whose contribution ends abruptly in the middle of the Apocrypha, possibly because he fled to avoid persecution and death.

The other version was a free, idiomatic translation probably by John Purvey, the companion of Wycliffe's last years at Lutterworth. Purvey was also responsible for the popular expositions of Wycliffe's teachings in English that circulated among the Lollards. This second Bible, which appeared about 1395, is both accurate and readable, a proper translation, not a mere polemical document. It was often found in the possession of those who were not Lollards, and over 100 manuscripts survive today. It was a worthy forerunner of Tyndale's New Testament and its successors, as we may judge from the following extract from John 1:10-14:

> He was in the world and the world was maad bi hym, and the world knew hym not. He cam in to his own thingis and hise resseyveden hym not. But hou many ever resseyveden hym, he gaf to hem power to be maad the sones of God, to hem that bileveden in his name, the whiche not of bloodes, nether of the will of fleische, nether of the wille of man, but ben borun of God. And the word was maad man, and dwellyde among us, and we han seyn the glorie of hym, as the glorie of the oon bigetun sone of the fadir, ful of grace and of treuthe.

The Lollards, or Bible-men as they were sometimes known, may have had little appreciation of the finer points of Wycliffe's theology and often expressed their simple faith in somewhat crude terms, but we can find in their words the echo of true religion, a personal encounter with God that was to characterize the later Reformation. John Badby, a tailor from Evesham, denied transubstantiation before his Catholic judges by asserting picturesquely that 'John Rakier of Bristol [presumably a Lollard preacher] had as much power to make Christ's body as any priest.' Badby sealed his faith with his blood; in spite of the pleas of Prince Hal himself to recant, he persevered and was burned at the stake. The same spirit is evident in the words of a young cloth worker from Dewsbury who defended his refusal to attend confession before a priest claiming, 'If I confess directly to God, calling to God with a sorry heart for my offence, God will forgive me.'

Records of similar trials and defences are to be found in many parts of the country over the next two centuries, and when Lutheran ideas began to enter England in the sixteenth century they found the ground prepared to receive them. The enemies of Lutheranism called it 'the foster-daughter of Wycliffe' and one complained, 'New arms are being added to the great crowd of Wycliffite heresies.' Wycliffe had little, if any, direct influence on Luther, who only knew of those selected opinions that had been condemned. There was, however, an intermediate link via John Hus, whose writings and life made a deep impression on the German Reformer.

John Hus

In the fourteenth century Bohemia was a very important country. From 1346 to 1378 its king was also the Holy Roman Emperor Charles, one of whose achievements was to found the University of Prague, which he aimed to put on a level with Paris and Oxford. His successor on the throne of Bohemia, Wenzel or Wenceslas, arranged a marriage between his sister Anne and Richard II of England. These two events provided significant links with the philosophy of Realism and Wycliffite ideas in Oxford, which thus spread to Bohemia by the turn of the century. (Ironically the marriage was at the instigation of the pope, the one in Rome!)

Further, Peter Payne, an Oxford Lollard, wrote a letter in praise of Wycliffe and sent it to Prague, having somehow attached the official university seal to it. He later became Principal of St Edmund's Hall but had to flee to Bohemia to escape persecution. There he played an honourable part in the religious struggles of the next forty years.

Wycliffite influences were certainly important in the movement towards reform in Bohemia, but that movement had begun much earlier. Stimulated partly by Waldensian ideas and by popular opposition to German domination in the church, many pietists and mystics had denounced abuses during the earlier years of the century. Largely as a result of this, in 1391 Bethlehem Chapel was founded in Prague for the public preaching of the gospel as they understood it. Their authority was the Bible: their aim was the reform of the church. It was here that John Hus (1371 – 1415) was appointed preacher in 1402.

THE WALDENSIANS

The Waldensians in many ways anticipated the views and practices of the Reformers. Valdes their founder, later often referred to as Waldo, came from Lyons in France. He took Matthew 19:21 literally, gave away all his possessions and began preaching. The church authorities opposed him and his followers, known as 'the poor men of Lyon'. Soon they were expelled from the church but grew and spread into Spain, Austria and Germany. They replaced the authority of the pope with that of the Scriptures, making and studying the Bible in translations in their own languages. Many were martyred at the hands of the Inquisition, but the movement survived in northern Italy.

Born of peasant stock in 1371, Hus had to contend with poverty and other difficulties as a student, but when he was ordained in 1401 he soon became known for his reforming zeal and preaching ability. When the German masters in the university attacked Wycliffe, Hus was chosen to defend the English scholar, and he began to study his writings in earnest. Although he was selective in what he adopted of Wycliffe's teaching, never for instance denying transubstantiation, he found much with which he heartily agreed. Over the next few years Hus defended Wycliffe and continued to work for reform, being himself defended by the queen. In 1410 one of the popes, in an attempt to crush the reformers, ordered the burning of Wycliffe's books and forbade preaching in private places, including the Bethlehem Chapel. Hus refused to surrender Wycliffe's writings and to stop preaching, saying, 'I will defend to the death the truth God has vouchsafed me especially the truth of the Holy Scriptures.'

It was about this time that Hus opposed the sale of papal indulgences, like Luther after him. Since King Wenceslas had given his approval to this unholy traffic Hus's condemnation of it lost him the royal favour. Consequently the preacher had to withdraw from Prague. He spent his time away from the capital in preaching in the towns and villages and in writing. His great work, *On the Church*, which so impressed Luther, dates from this period.

Matters came to a head at the Council of Constance in 1414. This was called chiefly to deal with the scandal of three rival popes but also to stamp out Wycliffite heresy. Hus was summoned before the council, but instead of being allowed to defend his opinions he was imprisoned despite a safe conduct from the emperor. He became seriously ill in his island dungeon and was for a time transferred to a healthier prison. When he still refused to recant he was sent to another dark hole where he remained for seventy-three days, sleeping on two boards to which he was chained.

Eventually when the council had finished condemning Wycliffe's writings they ordered that his remains be dug up and scattered. Hus himself was then put on trial. For weeks he was alternately argued with and threatened to no avail. He refused to recant 'lest I give offence to the souls of so many to whom I have preached and to others who proclaim the Word of God'. He was condemned to be burned at the stake and died commending his soul to 'my gracious Lord Jesus'.

Summary

Although his ideas were in some ways less advanced than Wycliffe's, in others Hus went beyond the Englishman. He began a movement that, although it was ultimately crushed, for a while successfully challenged the authority and power of the Roman church. The more he was opposed the more he asserted the right of every man to make his own decisions based on the Bible and to find salvation in Christ alone.

Full light had not yet dawned, but God was clearly preparing the way for the one who would take up the torch of the gospel. Using men from all walks of life, from scholars to tailors, God was calling the church back to the authority of the Word of God, to the salvation found in Christ and against the sacraments and indulgences of the priests. The spark had been kindled.

Questions for discussion

1. Discuss the comment: 'Often when God holds his hand, it is in order that he may make deeper and better preparation for a greater and more glorious work than would otherwise have been the case.' What encouragement does this give us today?

2. What sort of criteria should we use when assessing those who lived before the full light of the gospel dawned again?

3. What do you think was the most important contribution of Wycliffe and Hus to the Reformation? Does this have anything to teach us today?

For further reading

* V. Budgen, *On fire for God*, Evangelical Press, 1983.

** D. Daniell, *The Bible in English: its history and influence*, Yale University Press, 2003.

* J. M. d'Aubigné, *The Reformation in England*, The Banner of Truth Trust, 1962, pp.79-106.

** A. G. Dickens, *The English Reformation*, Fontana, 1974, chapter 2.

N. R. Needham, *2000 years of Christ's power*, Grace Publications, 2000, Part Two, pp.382-395.

A man is justified by faith apart from observing the law.
— Romans 3:28

Those who assert that a soul straight away flies out of purgatory as a coin tinkles in the collection-box are preaching an invention of men.
— Martin Luther (1483 – 1546), *Thesis No.27*

A safe stronghold our God is still,
 A trusty shield and weapon;
He'll help us clear from all the ill
 That hath us now o'ertaken.
The ancient prince of hell
 Hath risen with purpose fell;
Strong mail of craft and power
 He weareth in this hour.
On earth is not his fellow.
— Martin Luther (translated by Thomas Carlyle, 1795 – 1881)

5

Here I stand

The Reformation is the most important event since the New Testament. It was not 'a mistake' or 'a tragedy', as some misguided Christians have recently been asserting, but a glorious work of God restoring the gospel and reviving his church. It is correct, in one sense, to date this as beginning in 1517, when Martin Luther burst on the international ecclesiastical scene, but God had begun his work long before. Hus had been preceded by Wycliffe and the Lollards, and even before that there had been Bradwardine, the Waldensians and the less orthodox Albigensians, all of whom had a large element of reform in their beliefs and practice, especially in opposition to Rome. The darkness of centuries was beginning to pass; the gospel of Christ was once more becoming known, albeit not very clearly. William Farel, an important figure later in our story who was born at a time when the Waldensians were targets for a persecuting papal crusade, could find believers in Paris who were able to direct him to faith in Christ. Nevertheless, it was with

Luther that Protestantism really began, and the edifice of Catholicism started to topple before the power of the gospel. To understand this power we must go back before 1517 to Luther's search for peace of heart and conscience.

Martin Luther

Early years

Although Martin Luther (1483 – 1546) was always deeply religious and sensitive to spiritual matters, it would be wrong to think of him as morbid and dull. Born at Eisleben in Germany in 1483, Martin had a normal and happy childhood. His parents were peasants by birth, but Luther senior became a miner and then a prosperous mine owner, a man of some standing in the town who had a large house on the main street and later attended his son's ordination with fifty horses. Martin was fond of music and played the lute well. He loved the countryside and enjoyed his youth. Although discipline at home and school was harsh, if not cruel, he was a brilliant scholar who was expected to bring credit to his family by becoming a lawyer.

The religious atmosphere of the time was one of fear. Martin grew up in a land and church dominated by the devil, demons and terror of God's judgement. The priests continually played on the fears of the ignorant, and not so ignorant, to keep them in submission to the church and dependent on the clergy who administered the sacraments, the only source of hope. In all this the young student shared and suffered. Later pictures of the jolly and even rather coarse Luther must not blind us to his tremendous intellect or to his sensitive soul. His tender conscience soon became an instrument of torture, removing hope and inducing a desperate search for peace.

At the age of twenty-one, already a bachelor and master of arts, he was returning to the University of Erfurt when he was overcome with fear of the judgement of God during a violent thunderstorm. Overwhelmed by a sense of his own danger he vowed to become a monk because the so-called 'religious life' was popularly regarded as the safest way to save one's soul. Typically, Luther considered this impulsive vow to be binding, and he soon entered the Augustinian monastery at Erfurt. His father naturally regarded this as a waste of the money he had spent on his son's upbringing and education. After all, he had hoped for some recompense by Martin's caring for him in his old age. In spite of his father's protests Martin entered the monastery in September 1505. When some of the monks tried to persuade his father of the rightness of Martin's decision, the blunt Hans silenced them with a few well-chosen words: 'Haven't you read the fifth commandment?' He became reconciled to his loss only when two of his other sons died of the plague, which he took to be a chastisement from God for his rebellion.

The monk

Once at Erfurt Luther entered conscientiously into the disciplined life of a monk: services, confession, Bible reading, domestic chores, outward humility, begging in the streets and a gloomy external appearance. According to Luther the devil leaves a monk alone for the first year and the novice seemed to have enjoyed relative peace of mind during his probation. In September 1506 he took vows of poverty, chastity and obedience and in May of the following year was ordained as a priest.

Nevertheless, below the surface all was far from well. In spite of his diligent obedience Luther could not find peace of conscience. He could never be certain that all his sins had been confessed and therefore forgiven, and although his confessor was kindly and wise, Luther remained convinced that he lay under God's condemnation. He was no rebel; he was too good a Catholic. He fasted, prayed and afflicted himself well in excess of what was stipulated by his spiritual advisers, but he could never be convinced that he had done enough to satisfy God.

After his ordination Luther resumed his studies, both because this was how he was expected to serve the church and because Dr Johann Staupitz, the vicar or head of the Augustinian order, wisely considered that this was the best way for the young scholar to resolve his problems. Although his early studies provided only questions without answers, it was through study that Luther was to discover the truth or rather, more accurately, the truth would be revealed to him. However, that time was not yet.

The professor

In 1508 he was appointed professor of moral philosophy at the elector's new university in Wittenberg where he was to lecture as well as complete his own theological education. There he would undoubtedly become aware of the vast army of relics that the Elector Frederick had gathered together. It was claimed that by worshipping them, saying the appropriate prayers and making the appropriate payments a person could secure a remission of 1,902,202 years 270 days in purgatory. These treasures included such wonders as pieces of Moses' burning bush, nine thorns from Christ's crown of thorns, thirty-five fragments of the cross, a whole baby from those slaughtered at Bethlehem and many more.

Even greater indulgences were available in Rome, the 'Eternal City', and soon Luther was given an opportunity to go there. After a rather sudden recall to Erfurt, where his fellow monks treated him somewhat coolly because they did not recognize his degree from Wittenberg, he was sent to Rome with a colleague in 1510 to represent the Erfurt chapter in a dispute within the Augustinian order. Here was a wonderful privilege, a pilgrimage not to be missed! He would have time, after his ordinary devotions, to visit shrines, venerate relics and say masses, thus appropriating the immense spiritual benefits to be obtained in the holy city. The result of his diligent and wearying efforts was utter disillusionment. At every level and in every aspect he found ignorance, irreverence, unbelief and immorality among the Roman clergy.

According to Luther's son, Paul, he crawled up the Scala Sancta (the staircase which Christ was supposed to have gone up to face Pilate, now miraculously transported to Rome) saying a paternoster (the Lord's Prayer) on each of the twenty-eight steps. This was supposed to release one soul from purgatory immediately. Luther could only think of one person he knew in this position, his grandfather, but when he reached the top he asked himself, 'Who knows whether it is so?'

So Luther was left in even greater turmoil; not only was his own holiness inadequate, but the church's means of grace and even the treasury of the saints, providing indulgences for the less godly, were also in doubt.

The visit to Rome settled nothing, not even the dispute. Soon, perhaps to avoid further conflict, Staupitz transferred Luther to Wittenberg. There, under a pear tree in the garden, Staupitz persuaded him to become a preacher and a doctor of theology and to take Staupitz's place as professor of Bible. So in 1512 Luther took over Staupitz's room in the tower as his study and began his new work with lectures on the book of Genesis. The wise vicar-general, who seems to have been a good example of Catholic piety, was counselling Luther at this time. He became very impatient with his overscrupulous confessions, urging him to come with something to forgive – like blasphemy or adultery! He directed Luther's attention to sin as a whole, to the sacrifice of Christ and to the mystical approach of seeking direct communion with God, but nothing really helped. He seems never to have understood Luther's problem. Nevertheless it was Staupitz who provided the cure by directing Luther to the Scriptures. As the teacher of others he would have to solve his own problems.

The meaning of righteousness

In 1513 Luther turned to the book of Psalms after having completed his lectures on Genesis. Beginning with Psalm 31, 'Deliver me in your righteousness', Luther came to a new understanding of God's righteousness. Until then he had seen this only as justice, the punitive righteousness of a judge who Luther confessed to hating rather than loving. Looking for other scriptures to cast light on this more hopeful concept he came across Romans 1:17: 'For in the gospel a righteousness from God is revealed, a righteousness that is by faith from first to last, just as it is written: "The righteous will live by faith."' He describes what happened:

I clung to the dear Paul and had a great yearning to know what he meant. Night and day I pondered until I saw the connection between the justice of God and the statement that 'The just shall live by faith'. Then I grasped that the justice of God is that righteousness by which through sheer grace and mercy God justifies us through faith. Thereupon I felt myself to be reborn and to have gone through open doors into paradise. The whole of Scripture took a new meaning, and whereas before the 'justice of God' had filled me with hate, now it became inexpressibly sweet in greater love. This passage of Paul became to me a gate to heaven.

Luther spent the next four years teaching at Wittenberg. After completing the Psalms he expounded on Romans (1515 – 1516), Galatians (1516 – 1517) and Hebrews (1517 – 1518), according to the prescribed order. What more useful topics could he have had to clarify his own thinking on the great issues of sin, righteousness, justification and the person and work of Christ? As well as teaching he preached. He was, in effect, the parish priest for Wittenberg as well as professor, and it was in this function that led him into open conflict with Rome. Already he was having a tremendous influence on the rest of the faculty, the students and the townspeople, many of whom were converted. Then he became known at the court of Frederick the Wise, the Elector of Saxony, through his friend Spalatin, the court preacher.

Tetzel

In 1516 he published his Ninety-Seven Theses against scholasticism to make his theological views better known. These quite startling statements had no effect at all! However, on the eve of All Saints Day, 1517, the day the university as such came to the Castle Church and when the town was flooded with crowds venerating the relics that Frederick had gathered there, Luther nailed his Ninety-Five Theses against indulgences to the church door. These did cause a stir, one that is still with us today.

In theory this was merely the opening gambit of an academic theological debate. In practice it was a declaration of war on the system of issuing papal indulgences.

INDULGENCES

It is widely supposed that medieval man lived in terror of hell, but this was not exactly the case. He was, in fact, quite confi-

dent that the church could and would, through its sacraments, take care of eternal punishment. Proper contrition (or even attrition, sorrow for sin, based solely on fear) guaranteed absolution from eternal punishment. What really bothered him was purgatory, whose torments, extending possibly to thousands of years, were scarcely less terrible than hellfire and quite certain. So when the church began to issue documents that promised, on the pope's authority, that the period in purgatory was lessened by so many years or even abolished altogether, the people were naturally more than interested. These documents could be used immediately or kept until needed, either for one's own use or for that of a relative. Of course contrition was required, at least in theory, but what better way of showing penitence could there be than a payment, carefully graded according to status and means? Confession, contrition and contribution procured consolation!

In 1514 Prince Albert of the house of Hohenzollern, who already had two lucrative bishoprics, decided that he would like to become Archbishop of Mainz, primate of all Germany, although he was actually too young even to be a bishop! This cost him 10,000 ducats, which he had to borrow from Fuggers, the bankers, to pay the pope. The pope kindly offered to help him in his financial difficulties by issuing a plenary indulgence, guaranteed by the papal seal, the proceeds from which would be shared: half would go to repaying the bankers and half would go to the pope to fund the rebuilding of St Peter's in Rome. (This pope, Leo X, has been described by a Catholic historian as 'one of the most severe trials to which God ever subjected his Church'. He was so inconsiderate of the feelings of the faithful that he even wore long hunting boots, which made it impossible for them to kiss his toe!)

The sale of these indulgences was entrusted to a Dominican monk called Tetzel. He ignored the subtle theological qualifications of contrition that might have hindered his business and soon began to earn a huge salary. Accompanied by the beating of a drum, his sales talk represented the appeals of the dead from purgatory:

'Pity us! Pity us! We are in dire torment from which you can redeem us for a pittance... Will you leave us here in flames? Will you delay our promised glory?'

As soon as the coin in the coffer rings
The soul from purgatory springs.

Frederick the Wise would not allow him into Wittenberg, not because he disagreed with the practice but because he would have diverted attention from the Castle Church's relics, his own source of revenue. In spite of this, Luther's parishioners could easily slip over the border to purchase indulgences, which they did, bringing back tales of Tetzel's excesses. Tetzel assured them that his indulgences even guaranteed absolution for one who had violated the Virgin Mary. Luther took up the cause with the words: 'I'll knock a hole in his drum!' His reasons were pastoral rather than theological at this stage; he rightly considered that indulgences diverted attention from true repentance and faith in Christ.

The Ninety-Five Theses

The Ninety-Five Theses, which Luther nailed to the door of the church, revealed the theological basis of his antagonism. This was not as dramatic a procedure as we, in our day, might suppose; he was simply following the customary method of publishing a set of topics for academic discussion. No one responded to his invitation to dispute publicly, but the popular press seized on these theses and spread them abroad, more or less accurately, so that within four weeks they were known throughout Germany and Switzerland. Many were sympathetic and the artist, Albrecht Dürer, sent him a woodcut in appreciation. The Dominicans were enraged but took comfort in the thought that he would soon be burned!

Luther wrote to his bishop explaining the theses, going much further in the process, and eventually the archbishop was compelled to report 'the rash monk of Wittenberg' to Rome. Another Augustinian, Gabriel della Volta, was sent from Rome to soothe (and silence) Luther, while the Dominicans set up Tetzel, whose trade had been ruined, to ruin Luther in turn. Tetzel, having been made a doctor of theology for the occasion, was put forward to defend 106 theses written by a university professor attacking Luther's position. These he had printed and sent to Wittenberg. There the students, without Luther's knowledge or approval, but one imagines much to his amusement, burned hundreds of copies. Meanwhile Luther was busy on his own account; he prepared more explanations of the Ninety-Five Theses and also wrote and published a sermon in German aimed at the man in the street. This was a notable step as Luther bypassed the academics and ecclesiastics and appealed to the people.

Disputations

In April 1518 Staupitz sent Luther to the triennial gathering of the Augustinian order in Heidelberg. There he took a leading part in a disputation, not about indulgences but on the classic Augustinian doctrines of sin and grace. He journeyed there on foot, had a personal triumph and returned in a wagon as a guest of the scholars of Erfurt. Among those impressed by his performance were several who were to be important in the development of the Reformation, including Martin Bucer who attended as a Dominican guest! Bucer wrote at the time,

> Although our chief men refuted him with all their might, their wiles were not able to make him move an inch from his propositions. His sweetness in answering is remarkable, his patience in listening is incomparable, in his explanations you would recognize the acumen of a Paul, not a Scotus; his answers so brief, so wise, and drawn from the holy Scriptures, easily made all his hearers his admirers. On the next day I had a familiar and friendly conference with the man alone and a supper rich with doctrine rather than with dainties. He agrees with Erasmus in all things, but with this difference in his favour, that what Erasmus only insinuates, he teaches openly and freely.

Erasmus was the great humanist scholar who gave Luther vital help by publishing his edition of the Greek New Testament, but who confessed that he was not cut out to be a martyr and, accordingly, compromised.

On his return from Heidelberg Luther wrote a reply to another attack by Tetzel. Also, hearing that he was under 'the ban', a form of suspension from church privileges that was another valuable source of papal revenue, he preached against it. The Dominicans, who were by now after Luther's blood, reported this sermon to Cardinal Cajetan, chief theological adviser to the pope and himself a Dominican. As a result Luther was declared a notorious heretic and the Elector Frederick was required to hand him over to Cajetan for arrest. In case this failed another Augustinian 'mediator', della Volta, was ordered to seize him and send him to Rome. Of these days Luther recorded, 'I clearly saw my grave ready and kept saying to myself, "What a disgrace for my dear parents!"'

At this point political interests interfered with the pope's plans. Suddenly Frederick the Wise, Elector of Saxony and thus Luther's prince, became important in the manoeuvrings over the succession to the dying emperor, and the pope began to seek Frederick's favour. So when the elector demanded that Luther's case be heard in Germany, not in Rome, he gained his point; the hearing before Cajetan would be in Augsburg. This, as Luther realized, lessened but did not remove the danger, and he was prepared for suffering. To a friend he wrote,

There is one thing left, my weak and broken body. If they take that away, they will make me the poorer by an hour of life, perhaps a couple. But my soul they cannot take.

I know perfectly well that from the beginning of the world, the word of Christ has been of such a kind that whoever wants to carry it into the world must necessarily, like the apostles, renounce everything and expect death at any and every hour. If it were not so, it would not be the word of Christ. By death it was bought, by deaths spread abroad, by deaths safeguarded. It must also take many deaths to preserve it or bring it back again. *Christ is a bloody partnership for us.*

Luther set out for Augsburg on foot but travelled the last three miles in a cart, not in honour but in exhaustion and illness. Still he was confident that Christ ruled 'even in Augsburg in the midst of his enemies'. The hearing before the cardinal was a failure from every point of view. Cajetan was authorized only to accept a complete recantation and Luther wanted to debate, saying that he had taught nothing contrary to Scripture. After some hedging and recrimination he denied that the pope was above councils and Scripture. Believing that the pope was badly advised, Luther wrote an appeal based on a true statement of his position but received no reply. As the situation became increasingly unfavourable his friends hurried him out of Augsburg, 'without breeches or boots', to the safety of Wittenberg.

He published an account of the interview and wrote an appeal to be heard by a general council. Cajetan instructed Frederick to send Luther to Rome or banish him from his territory. Luther was willing, as he put it, to go 'under the open sky' and wrote to Spalatin that he would be like Abraham, 'not knowing where I am going. Yet I am most certain where I am going, for God is everywhere.' At the last moment the elector, whose only concern was to do his duty as a Christian prince, changed his mind and Luther was allowed to stay, at least until the pope had formally declared him a heretic.

Cardinal von Miltitz, a relative of Frederick, made another attempt to get him to Rome using various bribes. When this failed he turned on the unfortunate Tetzel, accusing him of embezzlement and immorality, which was true but hardly fair. Tetzel then retired to a convent where he soon died, comforted only by Luther, who declared that he should not blame himself as he was only being made the scapegoat.

John Eck, a German theologian who had formerly been a friend of Luther, now came forward as the champion of the University of Leipzig under the patronage of Duke George of Saxony. When the two came face to face in June 1519 Eck cleverly insinuated that Luther was nothing more than another Hus. This was a very clever move as not only had Hus been burned for heresy, but his followers were much feared in that area. Under this provocation Luther averred that Hus had taught much scriptural truth and alleged that even councils might err: 'A simple layman armed with Scripture is to be believed above a pope or a council without it.'

Eck was convinced that he had won the debate and proved it by staying on in Leipzig to indulge his worldly, not to say immoral, tastes. Luther and his colleagues were disappointed but returned to Wittenberg to work and, above all, to write. Luther was rapidly becoming known throughout Europe as the leader of the Reformation, and his writings spread to Rome and to Zwingli, the Swiss Reformer. Ulrich von Hutten offered the help of a hundred armed knights, but he wrote to Spalatin, 'You see what Hutten asks. I am not willing to fight for the gospel with bloodshed. In this sense I have written to him. *The world is conquered by the Word, and by the Word the church is served and rebuilt.*'

The Word, however, had to be proclaimed and explained so Luther wrote more and more. His books dealt with a vast array of subjects, such as simple devotional works written at the request of Frederick, theological treatises on the sacraments and good works, a commentary on the Psalms and his *Open Letter to the Christian Nobility of the German Nation concerning the Reform of the Christian Estate.* His two other great 'Reformation writings' of 1520 were the *Prelude on the Babylonian Captivity of the Church*, addressed to the clergy, and *The Freedom of a Christian Man.* (For the remainder of his life he produced books at the rate of one a fortnight!)

Excommunication

This last work he sent to the pope with an accompanying letter, which destroyed the last vestiges of hope of reconciliation, if indeed any remained by then. Meanwhile a condemnation was drawn up in Rome and the pope issued a bull (a papal edict sealed with a lead seal or bulla) in the intervals of hunting wild boar at his hunting lodge. In this crucial document the heretic Luther is described as being himself a wild boar in God's vineyard (and a serpent!) and is given sixty days to submit or be excommunicated. The bull took three months to reach Luther, and the bearer was not well received in many places. Various bonfires of Luther's books were arranged, but frequently his student supporters saw to it that the illiterate hangman appointed for the task burned other volumes, especially anti-Luther tracts, instead.

On 10 October 1520, the bull actually reached Luther, and the sixty days of grace began. Two months later Luther's younger colleague, Philip Melanchthon (1497 – 1560), issued an invitation to all the university to assemble at nine o'clock. Just outside the old city wall volumes of works by Eck and others, together with copies of the Roman Canon Law, were burned. Then Luther himself threw the pope's bull into the blaze.

The Diet of Worms

Schoolchildren learning about the Reformation have frequently been amused by the occasion of the next and final confrontation, the Diet of Worms. There was, however, nothing amusing about this national gathering of the German Parliament at Worms. After the issuing of the fatal bull and Luther's failure to retract, his condemnation, arrest and execution by the emperor, as the secular arm of the church, should have followed automatically, as indeed the church authorities expected. However, Frederick, supported by the imperial constitution signed by the newly elected Emperor Charles, insisted that Luther must have a fair hearing in Germany. This was arranged for April 1521 in Worms. The diet discussed the case, with some members coming to blows in the process, and eventually, again at the insistence of the elector, the emperor personally summoned Luther to appear before him and granted him a safe conduct for the purpose.

After some hesitation Luther went, resisting all attempts by both friends and enemies to keep him away, with the words: 'Even if there were as many devils in Worms as there are tiles on the roofs, I would enter anyway.'

He was given an enthusiastic welcome by 2,000 of the common people and the next day appeared before the great assembly. Strangely, when challenged to acknowledge and renounce his books, he asked for time to reply, possibly on the advice of his friends. The next day, after a night spent preparing his statement, a very different Luther faced the emperor. Fearlessly he talked about his writings, once again asking them to show from Scripture if he was wrong. He was answered by a demand for a plain answer to a plain question: 'Will you retract?'

His answer 'without horns or teeth' was, 'Unless I am convinced by Scripture and plain reason – I do not accept the authority of popes and councils, for they have contradicted each other – my conscience is captive to the Word of God. I cannot and will not recant anything, for to go against conscience is neither right nor safe. God help me. Amen.' The famous words, 'Here I stand. I can do no other', though not recorded on the spot, occur in the first printed version and certainly represent his attitude.

Having repeated his statement in Latin he was ordered by the emperor to leave the hall. Although some people around the doorway thought that he had been condemned and shouted out, 'To the bonfire!', he had in fact survived for the moment.

The next day the young emperor took the initiative and, asserting that a single friar who went counter to all Christianity for a thousand years must be wrong, demanded that the six electors support him in condemning Luther. Two, one of whom was Frederick, refused to sign the edict. Charles was going to honour his safe conduct, but his advisers became terrified at the prospect of an armed rising by the peasants on behalf of Luther, so the emperor gave them three days to try to persuade Luther to give in. This attempt also failed, so when Luther's supporters had left Worms the emperor and those who remained issued the Edict of Worms. Luther had twenty-one days to return to Wittenberg, after which he was to be regarded as a convicted heretic. No one was to harbour him or his followers and all his works were to be destroyed.

Both the ecclesiastical and civil authorities had now condemned Luther, but the universities largely supported him. The English Bishop Tunstall, who had attended the diet, reported to Henry VIII that 100,000 Germans were ready to lay down their lives for Luther, and de Vales, the emperor's secretary, saw Worms not as an end but as a beginning. How right he was!

In Wartburg Castle

Luther left Worms the next morning, escorted by twenty nobles. After visiting and preaching in several places, Luther was 'ambushed' and 'kidnapped', together with his Hebrew Old Testament and Greek New Testament, and taken to Wartburg Castle for his own safety on the instructions of the Elector Frederick. For almost a year he disappeared from view; many thought, feared or hoped that he was dead, but soon his friends began to hear from him. Out in the world his books continued to be burned, but, in spite of all that Rome could do, the truth spread far and wide. Meanwhile, in his lonely refuge Luther concentrated on the Scriptures, particularly on translation; the first draft of his version of the New Testament was completed in an astounding time of three months. This was to be a vital foundation stone for the new evangelical church that Luther could see must be established and which would, in due course, change the face of Europe.

For the last twenty-five years of his life Luther was confined to Saxony and was unable to have any direct influence on many of the consultations and conflicts that made those days so stirring and complicated. However, in the providence of God it meant that he could study and work out the many problems that he faced. Many lose interest in Luther after the dramatic stand of the Diet of Worms, but it is a mistake to think that his work was done or that everything would now move on smoothly to perfection. The young church faced many problems and Luther heard of alarming developments in Wittenberg in his absence. A secret visit enabled him to assess the situation; the difficulties, which continued to bedevil the work until the end of his life and afterwards, were in two opposite directions. Led by Carlstadt, Luther's senior colleague in the university, some were rushing ahead with practical reforms that Luther agreed with in principle but felt should be proceeded with more slowly. Others, notably the Elector Frederick himself and the court preacher, Spalatin, thought that nothing should be changed at all.

After Luther's return to Wartburg things went from bad to worse. Carlstadt had already preached against monasticism and demanded the rewriting of the mass along the lines of the original Last Supper. Now he put much of this into practice by denouncing images, distributing both bread and wine to the lay people and, with great publicity, marrying a peasant girl. Moreover, several fanatics from Zwickau, who claimed to be prophets with direct revelations from God, soon joined him. In this situation Luther considered that he had no alternative but to return to Wittenberg without the emperor's permission, which he did at great personal risk.

On the way, disguised as the bearded knight Sir George, he stayed overnight at an inn in the company of two students on their way to study theology at the University of Wittenberg. He was able to assure them that Professor Luther was not there yet but would certainly be there soon. We do not know what the students thought or said when they met him in Wittenberg the following week! However, once back in his pulpit Luther preached eight sermons in a week and the 'prophets' and disorder departed. There were many other enemies to be faced, however, and Luther did not shirk his responsibilities.

DEFENDER OF THE FAITH?

One of the first opponents to be surprised and angered by Luther's blunt treatment was King Henry VIII of England. He had earned the title of Fidei Defensor *(Defender of the Faith) from the pope for writing an attack on one of Luther's books. (English monarchs still claim this title, though with a rather different connotation, which is indicated by the initials F.D. on current English coins.) He can hardly have been pleased to see a reply addressed by the 'minister of Wittenberg by the grace of God' to 'Henry, King of England by the disgrace of God'!*

Bible translation and books

Although there were other Catholic adversaries to be answered, it was Erasmus the humanist, once a half-hearted reformer and timid supporter of Luther, who provoked the real Reformer to write one of his masterpieces of theology, *The Bondage of the Will*. Nevertheless, Luther was by no means merely negative, and he spared no effort in his attempt to set the evangelical church on a sound footing.

His most important achievement was his translation of the Bible, which has dominated German thought, theology and language since that day. He published the New Testament in September 1522 and the whole Bible in 1534 but was constantly revising it until his death. Indeed, the last pages he read were proofs for a new edition of his Bible.

He was also responsible for writing a liturgy for the German non-sacrificial mass, preparing catechisms for the instruction of young and old and writing hymns, both words and music, as well as lecturing constantly and preaching three or four times a week as pastor in Wittenberg. Add to this numerous tracts and considerable correspondence and you get the fifty-two volumes of Luther's works, of which the larger part consists of commentaries on Bible books.

As his teaching spread, additional cities and provinces adopted the Reformation, and, under the protection of evangelically-minded rulers, the infant church began to be established, even though outside these boundaries the pope held sway and persecuted evangelicals through his agent the emperor. For fifteen years after 1530, the emperor was busy defending his empire against the Turks with the help and support of the 'heretics', and so for a while the Reformers were left alone and the pope was unable to enforce his edicts. Luther has been criticized for accepting the help of the Protestant princes, such as the successive electors of Saxony and Philip, the Landgrave of Hesse, and others. However, he never sought their protection and often took their help unwillingly because he recognized that rulers have a duty to allow their subjects to live peaceable and godly lives (1 Tim. 2:2). He did come to accept the idea of inferior rulers resisting a tyrannical emperor, but his attitude remained one of non-violent resistance, preferring to trust in his sovereign God.

Later days

Marriage

In the midst of all this Luther married. In 1523 he responded to a request for advice from some converted nuns by helping them to escape from their convent. This was a capital offence that Duke George, Luther's old enemy, treated with absolute seriousness, but that was not Luther's only danger! Three of the nuns went home, but nine arrived in Wittenberg and the task of finding them husbands fell to Luther. When only one was left, Katharina von Bora, various jokes about Luther marrying her himself turned into reality. So, in 1525 the forty-two-year-old Reformer began a new life with his twenty-six-year-old Katie.

There is no evidence that he had fallen in love, but in fact the marriage was singularly successful. Katie brought happiness and order to Luther's home. Indeed, when we read of everything she did for him we wonder how he survived without her. 'Before I was married', he wrote, 'the bed was not made for a whole year and became foul with sweat. But I worked so hard and was so weary I tumbled in without noticing it.' Katie changed all that and much more.

They had six children, as well as bringing up several orphaned relatives, and Luther revelled in the family atmosphere. He loved to play with the children, to teach them and to make music with them, for he was a gifted musician. When his daughter Magdalena died aged fourteen he said, 'Darling Lena, you will rise and shine like the stars and the sun. How strange it is to know that she is at peace and all is well, and yet to be so sorrowful!' This Luther is too often forgotten – the loving father, the caring pastor, the lover of music and the arts, the gardener and the dog owner.

The man of faith

This background must have been a great strength to Luther in the midst of many trials, but his greatest resource was, of course, in God himself. In 1527, a time of great turmoil when he was ill and under attack on many sides, he wrote perhaps his finest hymn, '*Ein feste Burg ist unser Gott*' (variously translated as 'A mighty fortress' or 'A safe stronghold is our God'). The same faith that took him to Worms, no matter how many devils were there, kept him to the end. We know little of his praying because his students, who were always with him in his home, were not allowed to invade the secret place. But pray he did! In fact, the busier he was, the more he prayed.

His servant once wrote to Luther's colleague Melanchthon,

I cannot sufficiently admire Dr Luther's remarkable constancy, his joy, faith and hope in these miserable times. But in these graces he grows daily by means of a most diligent use of the Word of God. Not a day passes on which he does not devote at least three hours, which are the most convenient for study, to prayer. On one occasion I heard him pray. What a spirit, what faith in his words! He prays as devoutly as one who is actually talking with God and with such faith and hope as one who is speaking to his father.

Luther himself wrote, 'If I should neglect prayer but a single day, I should lose a great deal of the fire of faith.'

Problems and divisions

Naturally Luther was far from perfect and the difficulties of beginning a new church virtually from scratch can hardly be overestimated. Typically, when Luther made a mistake it was a big one and all his enemies seized on it. Through the years he has been accused of many faults and errors, some of which should be mentioned, although this is not the place to expand on them. His great failure concerned the unity of the Reformation, but this was not all his fault. While his treatment of the Anabaptists was inexcusable, he was not alone in overreacting to the horrors of one section of this movement which instituted the 'reign of the saints' at Munster, with terrible results both for the population and for the Reformation in that area.

There were other divisions as well, notably with Ulrich Zwingli, the Swiss Reformer, and his followers. Luther, in fact, persevered in attempts to find a basis for unity with the Zwinglians at Marburg and at Augsburg in 1530, although he could not be present in person. However, it was his obstinacy in holding to his incomprehensible doctrine of the real presence of Christ in the Lord's Supper (that is, bodily but not locally) as well as Melanchthon's fear of further alienating the Catholics that prevented an agreement from being reached.

He also had problems of a political kind, not just with the emperor who had outlawed him, but whom Luther did his best to support, but with the German peasants. Without doubt, they were oppressed and had many legitimate grievances against the princes and landowners, which Luther recognized. Soon their political and economic protest gained religious overtones as they also demanded the right to choose their own Protestant pastors. They began to invoke the name of Luther, and he became afraid that the whole of the Reformation movement would be brought into disrepute. His fears were realized when the Peasants' War began and the undisciplined hordes ravaged the countryside, looting and murdering indiscriminately. Luther counselled peace to the peasants and justice and tolerance to the rulers but all to no avail. In the end he came down on the side of law and order; however, he used harsh and possibly indefensible words that have been used to besmirch his reputation to this day.

It must be added that Luther's faults were, at least in part, the inevitable consequences of his many virtues. In his position he could avoid no issue; his advice and opinion were always sought, and he tried to be faithful to the Scriptures, whatever the consequences. His failure in the area of church unity must be traced to his correct and unshakeable conviction that doctrine is all important because salvation depends on it; truth must not be sacrificed for convenience. The same conviction is necessary today. His failure in the case of the peasants and in the even less excusable moral compromises over the bigamy of Philip of Hesse, his loyal supporter, can be traced to his overwhelming desire that the work of God in the Reformation should not be hindered. We, too, need such a desire, such a one-track mind, such a concern for the glory of God. We can learn almost as much from Luther's failures as from his successes.

His last days

In spite of all these difficulties the work did go on. The evangelical Protestant church grew and the gospel prospered. However, Luther's last days were full of anxiety over the future of the Reformation and of continuing hard work in the context of unremitting pain. Katie cared for him in his many afflictions: 'old, spent, worn, weary, cold and with but one eye to see with' was his self-portrait at that time. Fresh quarrels had broken out with the Swiss brethren. Nevertheless, he could now see that his work had been successful. Neither pope nor emperor could prevent the Reformation from spreading still further, although they would not give up trying. Now it was time for others to take over the reins, notably John Calvin, whose writings he admired and who, he said, could have united him and Zwingli over the Lord's Supper.

So he pressed on to the end. Wittenberg was at this time a bitter disappointment to him, with its student rioting and general immorality, so he was not sorry to leave for a time when he was called to his own birthplace of Eisleben to mediate in a dispute between two brothers. Having settled the matter he was eager to return to Wittenberg and to Katie, but it was not to be. On 18 February 1546, surrounded by friends and his sons, he commended his spirit to God. He repeated John 3:16 three times, reaffirmed his faith in Christ and in what he had taught and preached and fell asleep in Jesus.

Summary

It is impossible to sum up Luther and his work. He was not *just* one of the greatest of God's servants, just one of many in the long line. In God's purposes he was responsible for changing the whole situation of the church of Christ and ushering in the greatest work since the days of the apostles — a work that still continues.

Questions for discussion

1. *Examine Psalms 31 and 98, Isaiah 51 and 61, together with Romans 3:21; 5:17 and Philippians 3:9 to understand Luther's great discovery about God's righteousness.*

2. *What do you understand by Luther's words: 'Christ is a bloody partnership for us'? See Romans 8:17 and especially Philippians 3:10.*

3. *In what ways was Luther's contribution pivotal in the progress of the gospel in Europe and then in the whole world?*

For further reading

* R. Bainton, *Here I stand: a life of Martin Luther*, Abingdon Press, 1950.

* J. Cromarty, *A mighty fortress is our God*, Evangelical Press, 1998.

** R. T. Jones, *The great Reformation*, Bryntirion Press, 1997, pp.9-109.

** N. R. Needham, *2000 years of Christ's power*, Grace Publications, 2004, Part Three, pp.64-187.

For to me, to live is Christ and to die is gain.

— Philippians 1:21

I have written nothing out of hatred to anyone, but I have always faithfully propounded what I esteemed to be for the glory of God.

— John Calvin (1509 – 1564)

We come unto our fathers' God;
Their Rock is our salvation;
The eternal arms, their dear abode,
We make our habitation;
We bring thee, Lord, the praise they brought,
We seek thee as thy saints have sought
In every generation.

The fire divine their steps that led
Still goeth bright before us;
The heavenly shield around them spread
Is still high holden o'er us;
The grace those sinners that subdued,
The strength those weaklings that renewed,
Doth vanquish, doth restore us.

— Thomas Hornblower Gill (1819 – 1906)

6

Man of Geneva

John Calvin, the great Genevan Reformer, was in fact French, born on 7 July 1509 in a small town north of Paris called Noyon. When he came to manhood the Reformation was well under way in many European lands but was in grave danger of falling apart. The followers of Luther in Germany and Zwingli in Switzerland were some way from each other in doctrine and even further in spirit; however, both were under attack from the conservatives of Rome on the right and the Anabaptists on the left.

No one in the history of the church since the days of the apostles has been more maligned than Calvin; no one in that period deserves more to be remembered and honoured. If we owe to Luther the rediscovery of the gospel, then it is to Calvin that we owe the continuing of that glorious light as it spread across Europe. To Calvin we owe not just a few doctrines, which are usually associated with his name, but the establishment of the Protestant and Reformed faith throughout the world.

John Calvin

Preparation

Although the significance of John Calvin (1509 – 1564) was world-wide, we must begin with his early years in France, as God prepared his servant who was born and reared in the heart of enemy territory. Much of what we know of these days is deduction from the usual academic training of the day and dates are often a matter of dispute. However, there are no doubts about the presence of God's hand, moulding and shaping the young Jean Cauvin (as he was known until his early twenties) for his future work.

Calvin senior rose from quite humble origins to become a notary to the local chapter and the bishop (who was also a count), with a seat on the council and a house situated between the cathedral and the parish church. The Noyon church, still unreformed, dominated the town and its inhabitants; it was worldly, secular and superstitious. Calvin recalls,

> I remember seeing as a little boy what happened to the images in our parish church. On the feast of St Stephen (26 December) people decorated with chaplets and ribbons not only the image of the saint himself, but also those of the tyrants who stoned him. When the credulous women saw the tyrants dressed up like this, they took them for companions of the saint and burned a candle for each one. What is more, the same thing happened to St Michael's devil.

Calvin's father would naturally be proud of his second son's brilliance at school and intended him for the priesthood. At the age of twelve he technically became a clerk, received the tonsure and was allotted a third share in a local chaplaincy, a financial arrangement that would serve as a scholarship for his academic career, without any duties to burden him. For a while he lived with the family of the bishop's brother who trained him in the 'polite' life and then, probably still only twelve years old, departed for university in Paris with the children of the noble household.

The introductory 'grammar' course preceded the arts course, which was necessary preparation for theology, medicine or law. The College de la Marche was not noted for its competence, but, for that year only, one of the greatest Latin teachers taught Calvin's class! Years later Calvin dedicated a book to him, pointing out that 'For me this happy start to the study of Latin happened by the special blessing of God... I was so helped by you that whatever progress I have since made I gladly ascribe to you.' In our age we may not consider the learning of this dead language much of a blessing, but in the sixteenth century it was the language of scholarship, academic instruction and theological controversy; Calvin was to be concerned with all these fields and his Latin style was an invaluable asset.

The young student made swift progress, moving to Montaigu College for the arts course, a sort of 'educational monastery'. Noel Bedier, who led the resistance in Paris to any form of reformation however mild, effectively controlled the college. Moreover, during these three years of strict routine, which consisted of services and study with little recreation, Calvin was trained in a philosophy that denied the possibility of knowing God in truth. (Significantly the great theme of Calvin's greatest theological work was the knowledge of God.) He soon graduated as a bachelor of arts and then, combining his studies with a little teaching, became a master of arts at age sixteen or seventeen.

In 1525 or 1526 his direction was changed because his father decided that the practice of law was more lucrative than theology. So he was sent to the University of Orleans to learn law, but although there were now no moral restraints as before, there is no evidence that Calvin thought of anything but work. His disciple and successor, Theodore Beza, maintained that the Reformer's later extremely poor health dated from overwork at this stage. He was still an outstanding student and occasionally acted as a substitute lecturer.

At this time France was in religious turmoil. The beginnings of reformation, which paralleled the movement led by Luther but were by no means as clear, centred on people like the mystic Jacques Lefèvre d'Etaples and his pupil Guillaume Briconnet, Bishop of Meaux. Soon the whole of the diocese was in ferment as the friars counter-attacked. Bedier led the academic theologians of the Sorbonne University in condemning Erasmus's Greek New Testament and even the study of Greek itself. One opponent wrote, 'This language gives birth to heresies. Especially beware of the New Testament in Greek; it is a book full of thorns and prickles.'

The believer

Meanwhile Lutheran ideas came to France and were adopted by people like Guillaume (William) Farel, a pupil of Lefèvre, who began to apply them much more radically than the bishop wanted. Although the king's sister favoured moderate reform, Francis I soon began, for financial reasons, to persecute all reformers and burned some of the Lutherans. However, reformed ideas still spread.

CALVIN'S CONVERSION

We do not know exactly how Calvin came to share these evangelical views. He had many friends, some of whom were already believers, such as Melchior Wolmar and his brilliant relative Pierre Robert, usually known by his nickname, Olivetan, 'Midnight Oil'! In 1529 Calvin and his friends moved to Bourges, where the reforming influence was strong, to attend lectures of a famous Italian jurist. Here he began to learn the 'dangerous' Greek language and, through his study of the New Testament in the original and the influence of his reformed friends, was converted, probably in late 1529.

All we actually know about his conversion is to be found in an autobiographical passage in the preface to his commentary on the Psalms:

> *Out of obedience to my father's wishes I tried my best to work hard, yet God at last turned my course in another direction by the secret rein of his providence. What happened first was that by an unexpected (or sudden) conversion he tamed to teachableness a mind too stubborn for its years for I was so strongly devoted to the superstitions of the papacy that nothing less could draw me from such depths of mire. And so this mere taste of true godliness that I received set me on*

fire with such a desire to progress that I pursued the rest of my studies more coolly, although I did not give them up altogether. Before a year had slipped by, anybody who longed for a purer doctrine kept on coming to learn from me, still a beginner, a raw recruit.

The scholar

It is quite clear that Calvin was not seeking God; God tamed him, subduing the brilliant and probably arrogant young scholar to make him a humble servant of the living God. He stayed at Bourges, probably preaching in the area, until October 1530, but already his life had changed direction. This was no mere change of ideas; he had tasted 'true godliness' and was already recognized as an able teacher of the 'purer doctrine'. He began to study his Greek New Testament with renewed diligence, and his reading included Luther on the mass.

For the next two or three years he moved between Orleans, where he completed his law studies, Noyon, where his father died in 1531, and Paris. In Paris he began to add Hebrew to his linguistic accomplishments and associated with an increasing number of evangelical believers. In 1532 he published his first book, an edition of a work by the younger Seneca, which, while full of scholarship, hardly took the academic world by storm. Meanwhile, religious matters were coming to a head in the capital.

Francis I and his sister, Marguerite of Angoulême, favoured the reformist movement, if not actual Lutheranism, against which the university theologians reacted most strongly but were overruled by a commission headed by the new rector of the Sorbonne, Dr Nicolas Cop. A few days later, in November 1533, Cop had to deliver his inaugural address as rector. The address, in which his friend Calvin had more than a hand, dealt fairly harmlessly with the Beatitudes, although some may have realized that it leaned on Luther's exposition. However, owing to the state of religious feeling in Paris at that time it was condemned outright as heretical. This time the king did not intervene and Cop had to flee for his life after a last-minute warning from one of his students. Calvin also had to escape, again just in time, as his room was searched and his papers confiscated. (Reputedly, he had to slide down a rope from his bedroom window.)

Calvin was on the run for more than a year, spending some time with a friend, Louis du Tillet, but also visiting Orleans, Noyon and Paris, where he risked his life trying to recall to faith a young man whom we shall hear more of later, one Michael Servetus. (Servetus, in fact, did not keep the appointment.) During this period he broke his links with Rome by resigning his chaplaincy and, at the other extreme, began a treatise against the doctrine of soul-sleep held by some Anabaptists. Eventually, even more severe persecution arose over 'placards', notices that appeared in public places, attacking the mass in violent language. As a result 200 arrests were made and twenty people were executed, including Calvin's good friend, Etienne de la Forge, with whom he had lodged in Paris. By then Calvin had left with du Tillet, and, in spite of a servant who stole all their money and one of the horses, he arrived in Basel in January 1535. In was in this free city that was won for the Reformation that he found Bullinger, Olivetan, Cop and William Farel.

The theologian

Calvin continued his Hebrew studies in Basel and was supposed to be helping Olivetan with a new translation of the Bible into French, which was commissioned by the Waldensian Christians. More significantly he wrote and published, in March 1536, the first edition of his great *Institutes of the Christian Religion*.

The title page summed it up as 'The Basic Teaching of the Christian Religion comprising almost the whole sum of godliness and whatever it is necessary to know on the doctrine of salvation'. This was presumably the publisher's doing, as the second enlarged edition described it as 'now at last truly corresponding to its title'! Nevertheless, although this first effort had only six chapters it already bore the marks of the mind and ability that would in time set the Reformation fully on course. Calvin had two aims: first, as is evident in its dedication to Francis I of France, to present an *apologia* asserting the right of the evangelicals to be considered the true church and not a heretical sect; and second, to give instruction to men lacking peace of conscience, explaining the glory of the Christian gospel.

Of course, this was not yet the work of an established and mature theologian; he had been converted only six years! Within three years he was very critical of this first version, but he had begun his work of consolidation. Thus, he began to be known and influential, in spite of his own inclinations:

> Being of a disposition somewhat unpolished and bashful, which led me always to love the shade and retirement, I then [i.e., after his conversion] began to seek some secluded corner where I might be withdrawn from the public view, but… God so led me through different turnings and changes, that he never permitted me to rest in any place until, in spite of my natural disposition, he brought me forth to public notice.

It was the *Institutes* that caused him to be dragged into the lime-light and into the heart of the Reformation battle.

Battle in Geneva

Soon after the publication of the *Institutes* Calvin left Basel; he spent a short time in Italy, returned to France during a brief period of safety and then left for Strasbourg with his brother Antoine and his half-sister Marie. He was forced to make a detour via Geneva (1536 – 1538), where he arrived in August 1536 intending to spend just one night there. Geneva, in those days, was not a part of Switzerland but an independent and very proud republic, caught between the Swiss cantons, the Duchy of Savoy and France. To resist pressure from these surrounding powers Geneva had made an alliance with the neighbouring free city of Bern. From Bern the Reformation came to Geneva in the persons of Pierre Viret and William Farel. After a month's public disputation in June 1535 the government of Geneva suspended the mass. After many of the clergy and nuns left, but not most of the monks, and in the midst of attacks from the Duke of Savoy, in May 1536 the

city voted 'to live by the gospel'. Geneva had become by constitution an evangelical city.

The work, however, was as yet only superficial. 'When I first
came to this church', wrote Calvin twenty-eight years later, 'I found
almost nothing in it. There was preaching and that was all. They
would look out for idols, it is true, and they burned them. But
there was no reformation. Everything was in disorder.' It was to
this work of thorough reformation that God called him and which
bound him to the city for the rest of his life. Farel, in particular,
was aware of how tenuous the Reformation's hold on the city really
was, and he was most anxious that good teaching on the fundamentals of the 'new' faith should be given. So when Farel was told,
probably by du Tillet, that the renowned author of the *Institutes*
was actually within the city he acted instantly and decisively:

> Farel, who burned with an extraordinary zeal to advance the
> gospel, immediately strained every nerve to detain me. And
> after learning that my heart was set upon devoting myself to
> private studies, for which I wished to keep myself free from
> other pursuits, and finding that he gained nothing by
> entreaties, he proceeded to utter the imprecation that God
> would curse my retirement and the tranquillity of the studies
> which I sought, if I should refuse to help, when the necessity
> was so urgent. By this imprecation I was so terror-struck that
> I gave up the journey I had undertaken; but, sensible of my
> natural shyness and timidity, I would not tie myself to any
> particular office.

At first Calvin was a mere reader or lecturer in theology whose
arrival was noted only as 'the Frenchman' and whose salary began
to be paid only months later. However, by November he had
been elected as a pastor and began a full-time ministry in one of
the city churches. Almost immediately he was sent to take part in
a public disputation at Lausanne. This was being held to end the
confusion that prevailed in the district. For three days Calvin sat
in silence as Viret and Farel tried to convince the 170 Roman
priests from the Scriptures. Then, on the fourth day, when the

Reformers were accused of despising the teachings of Augustine and other early church fathers, Calvin rose to demolish the opposition. Whereas Farel could only reiterate the Reformers' dependence on Scripture alone, Calvin, entirely from memory, quoted passage after passage from the fathers in support of their position. He went on to expound positively the reformed view of the Lord's Supper. When he had finished a Franciscan friar stood up, not to answer but to confess his sin, ignorance and stubbornness and to announce his conversion to the evangelical cause. Day after day priests declared themselves for the Reformation and the moral life of the city was transformed.

Mainly, however, Calvin's work was the unaccustomed and laborious round of services and visitation. Farel, Calvin and a blind preacher named Couralt worked together to build up the church. They prepared a *Confession of Faith* and *Articles on the Organization of the Church and its Worship at Geneva*, stressing the need for godly living and church discipline, which they considered vital to the health of the Reformation in Geneva. Immediately this provoked trouble. Geneva, with its ten thousand inhabitants, was governed by a system of councils: the Little Council of twenty-five members led by four syndics, who were elected annually by the whole male assembly, and the Two Hundred, who appointed the Little Council. These councils were very jealous of their rights. Nothing could be decided apart from them and although the Two Hundred formally approved Calvin and Farel's documents, they refused to enforce them. Calvin was certainly not the dictator of Geneva as many have alleged.

Although some liked the idea of a discipline that treated high and low alike, many resisted the whole idea. The preachers were insulted and abused, and even the Lord's Supper was parodied in the taverns. In a council meeting one of the Reformers was accused of saying that he would like to drink the blood of the members! In fact Calvin tells us that when he was accused of wishing them ill he replied, 'I wish you so much ill that I would shed my blood for you.' With such misunderstandings it is hardly surprising that relations between the Reformers and the council became increasingly strained.

Matters came to a head over the so-called Bernese ceremonies. Some of the syndics were pro-Bern and demanded that the preachers conform to a request from Bern to adopt some of their ways, especially the use of unleavened bread in the Lord's Supper. Calvin and Farel regarded such things as indifferent matters; however, knowing that these things were to be discussed at an impending synod at Zurich they said that they preferred to wait for the synod in order to preserve as much uniformity as possible. When Easter came the council ordered the pastors to use unleavened bread. The pastors gave no reply, and on Easter Day there was no Lord's Supper at all!

Zurich

The enraged council banished the preachers from Geneva – Courault had to be released from prison for this – and with great relief they went immediately to Bern and then on to the synod in Zurich. There the Bernese ceremonies were agreed to and Calvin and Farel were somewhat blamed for being unduly severe and expecting too much of a people only lately rescued from Rome. Bern was asked to mediate for their return but without success; the ungodly in Geneva were glad to be rid of these troublers of their consciences. It may well be that Calvin was too demanding; he certainly humbled himself before the Lord and endeavoured to subdue his rather imperious nature. However, events proved him essentially correct in refusing to allow ungodliness in the church. He wrote to Henry Bullinger, 'We shall have no lasting church unless that ancient apostolic discipline be completely restored which in many respects is much needed among us. The generality of men are more ready to acknowledge us as preachers than as pastors.'

CHURCH DISCIPLINE

It is vital to realize that by church discipline Calvin meant much more than excommunicating offenders; he was referring to the practical outworking of the gospel doctrine in life and church order. The Genevans were prepared to be hearers but not doers of the Word. It is precisely at this point that Calvin's greatest contribution to the Reformation is seen. There had to be not merely reaction from Rome, denunciation of the mass and burning of idols but a positive understanding of the Word of God leading to a thorough and practical reign of that Word in every department of personal and church life. For this Calvin prayed and worked unceasingly. Luther had rediscovered the truth and proclaimed the principles; all this now had to be elaborated and practised consistently.

Strasbourg

Thus, in June 1538, after less than two years in Geneva, Calvin once more became a wanderer, with most of his possessions left behind. From Zurich he and Farel went to Basel. Farel was soon invited to become pastor of the church in Neuchatel, and, taking a leaf out of Farel's book by quoting Jonah to the reluctant Calvin, Martin Bucer persuaded him to go to Strasbourg (1538 – 1540). There he ministered to the church of 400 French exiles. Strasbourg was a haven for all types of religious exiles, and Calvin enjoyed his time there.

After his experiences in Geneva he examined himself before God, writing to Farel, 'Let us humble ourselves, therefore, unless we wish to strive with God when he would humble us. Meanwhile let us wait upon God.' He counselled those of his supporters remaining in Geneva to submit to the new ministers and to seek peace because 'Among Christians there ought to be so great a dislike of schism as that they may always avoid it so far as it lies in their power... It is sufficient for us if the doctrine on which the church of God is founded be recognized and maintain its place.'

Calvin lectured or preached each day, at Bucer's insistence, and twice on Sundays. Monthly communion was instituted with careful discipline to help the weak as well as exclude the careless. Congregational singing was introduced and a metrical psalter was published in 1539. One refugee described the moving practice:

Everyone sings, men and women, and it is a lovely sight. Each has a music book in his hand... For six or seven days at the beginning as I looked on this little company of exiles, I wept, not for sadness but for joy to hear them all singing so heartily, and as they sang giving thanks to God that he had led them to a place where his name is glorified. No one could imagine what joy there is in singing the praises and wonders of the Lord in the mother tongue as they are sung here.

Thus those who might have missed the outward splendour of the Roman ritual found something far better and deeper in participating in the reformed worship.

Calvin also was able to engage in private pastoral counselling, at which he excelled but which the Genevans had not permitted. But there were difficulties as well. In particular Calvin was greatly upset by the loss of close friends, of whom he had many. The blind Couralt died soon after leaving Geneva, and it was suspected that he had been poisoned. The death of Olivetan soon followed and Calvin wrote to Farel, 'Distress and wretchedness during the day seem only to prepare a lodging for more painful and excruciating thoughts of the night.' At the end of the letter he adds,

May the Lord preserve and strengthen you by his Spirit, confirm you in the enduring of all things, my most beloved brother in the Lord. Your anxiety on my account admonishes me in my turn to recommend your taking care of your health for all accounts report that you appear very much worn out.

Such references show not only the physical and mental difficulties under which these Reformers laboured but also the warm bonds that united these allegedly cold and hard men.

Calvin was still not well off, although Strasbourg, unlike Geneva, did grant him a salary without delay. He taught some students who lodged with him and even put his legal training to use. Louis du Tillet grieved him by submitting to Rome and trying to persuade (even bribe!) Calvin to recant also. An old enemy reappeared to accuse him of heresy and was believed, in part, even by Bucer. At this Calvin lost his temper and understandably reacted very bitterly, for which he grieved deeply. His health continued to be poor and his friends decided, as friends will, that he should get married. After various attempts he did eventually find a suitable wife, Idelette de Buren, whom he married in August 1540. She was the widow of a former Anabaptist whom Calvin had recalled to the evangelical faith.

He was also hard at work on two books that were published during his time in Strasbourg. The first was an expanded version of the *Institutes* already mentioned, which was three times the length of the 1536 work, but no doctrine was changed. Now, however, he was particularly concerned 'to prepare and train students in theology for the study of the divine Word, that they might have an easy access into it and keep on in it without stumbling'. By describing systematic doctrine in the *Institutes* Calvin hoped to avoid long dissertations in his projected commentaries. The first of these was on Romans, notable, as were those that followed, for competent scholarship, plain and consistent interpretation according to the ordinary sense (in contrast with medieval allegorizing) and outstanding clear and spiritual application of the Word of God to the reader.

Back to Geneva

It was not long before the Genevans began to realize what they had lost. In March 1539 two things happened. First, Geneva quarrelled with Bern and two of the syndics who had banished Calvin were themselves condemned for treason. Second, Cardinal Sadoleto, one of the ablest of the Roman hierarchy, wrote an *Open Letter* to the citizens of Geneva urging them to return to the fold. The council had to ask Calvin to reply to this, which he did – brilliantly. The supporters of Farel gained in strength and, in 1540, took power. Two of the syndics belonged to this party; the other two became involved in a brawl in which one killed the other and was then executed for his crime. Soon the two ministers who had replaced Farel and Calvin also left the city and the council commissioned Ami Perrin to bring Calvin back.

This was far easier to command than accomplish. Representatives went to Strasbourg and then followed the Reformer to Worms. In their discussion 'tears flowed faster than words' according to Calvin. To Farel he confided, 'Rather would I submit to death a hundred times than to that cross on which one had to perish daily a thousand times over.' To Viret he wrote, 'It would have been far preferable to perish once for all, than to be tormented again in that place of torture.' In fact, Viret was loaned to Geneva for six months while negotiations continued. Calvin had to be sure that it was not only he who was wanted but also the Word of God and 'godly discipline', but in the end he had to consent. In his reply to Cardinal Sadoleto he had indicated that his original call 'bound me to be faithful to it [Geneva] for ever'. So on 13 September 1541 Calvin re-entered Geneva accompanied by an escort and with a house and adequate salary awaiting him. The city register records that 'he offered himself to be always the servant of Geneva'.

Consolidation

Immediately Calvin began work to establish the Reformation in Geneva. He took up preaching at the place where he had left off to indicate 'that I had interrupted my office of preaching for a time, rather than that I had given it up entirely'. It was on his preaching that everything depended and plenty was required of him. At first he preached twice on Sundays and on alternate weekdays, but this was changed to once on Sunday and every weekday, later returning to twice on Sunday and each day in alternate weeks. He preached directly from the original Hebrew or Greek without notes. It was not, however, strictly extemporaneous preaching in the modern sense. He was well versed in the meaning of the Scriptures from his studies and commentaries and had a remarkable gift for expressing himself both lucidly and gracefully. Many of his published works were printed directly from the spoken exposition and are delightfully easy to read, even in translation. However, he took special pains over the application to his hearers lest 'I should be an arrogant upstart'. Of the preacher he wrote, 'It would be better for him to break his neck going up into the pulpit, if he does not take pains to be the first to follow God.'

Such preaching was bound to have an effect. It was especially appreciated by the French refugees and their society, the Compagnie des étrangers, employed a full-time professional scribe to record, transcribe and publish the sermons.

As well as preaching he was involved in the parish duties of weddings, baptisms and visitation of the sick. He also visited the prisoners on Saturday afternoons. His burden was increased by the low pastoral standards of his colleagues at that time. During a bad outbreak of the plague in 1542 to 1543 only one pastor would visit the affected area (Calvin was forbidden by the council because he was too valuable). Every Friday the Genevan ministers met for Bible exposition and discussion, and every four months the company of pastors over a wider area met for mutual criticism and spiritual profit. Thus the influence of Calvin was exerted by many different means.

On Thursdays the consistory met, and this was the real focus of conflict after Calvin's return to Geneva. By 20 November 1541 Calvin's *Ecclesiastical Ordinances*, aimed at establishing a 'settled government' according to the Word of God in Geneva, had been approved by the various councils and passed into law. Although church practice was thus established by law, it by no means followed that Calvin ran the city. Frequently the reverse was true: the councils tried to run the church and tell the ministers what to do. The church was ruled by the consistory, which was made up of eight pastors and twelve elders chosen from the councils. (All citizens were, by profession, members of the church.) It was here that discipline was exerted and decisions made. Although many welcomed the evangelical ministry and submitted gladly to the ministers' oversight, the majority, it would appear, were rebellious and undisciplined. The council frequently supported those who resisted the consistory's authority.

Troubles

Soon a party of 'Libertines' began to form, which consisted of several interrelated families who were accustomed to doing as they pleased. Therefore, they resented this new regime that proceeded to rebuke and discipline even them without fear or favour. The group included council members and even syndics, and the pastors had to resist attempts by the council to interfere in the church and reject demands that the sins of prominent citizens be ignored. Calvin said he 'had no less trouble when I wished to discharge my duty than heretofore'. Sometimes he attended council meetings to break up riots or prevent 'tumults' although he was not a member of the council since he was not even a citizen at this stage.

Occasionally he was the cause of the trouble through his intransigence; he acknowledged that he had been, as his friends told him, too severe and too strict. So he set out to control this fault, and, although to the end of his life he had to admit that his temper had been too uncertain and his manner too irritable, there was a great improvement. He wrote to a faithful friend,

> Even our opponents have to give me this credit and this feeling prevails to such an extent that day by day those who were once open enemies have become friends. Others I conciliate by courtesy, and I feel that I have been successful in some measure – although not everywhere and always.

He realized that the opposition would seize on such admissions of human frailty, but he despised praise and preferred his friends to tell him his faults.

More often it was his simple determination to apply the Word of God, coupled with their envy of his sheer intelligence and ability, not to mention hatred of his godliness, that provoked trouble. Although the opposition of some lessened and there was a general lull after a few years, the hard core maintained its antipathy, led by the same Ami Perrin who had called Calvin back to Geneva. He was the powerful commander of the civic guard, 'our comic Caesar' as Calvin once described him.

Calvin had other problems. Sebastian Castellio, a friend from Strasbourg days, was appointed head of the college in Geneva but caused much trouble, first over his salary, then over his translation of the New Testament into French and finally over his rejection as a pastor because of unorthodoxy. Having resigned and left Geneva, with a friendly note of recommendation from Calvin, he later returned to accuse the ministers of being immoral, persecutors and drunkards!

Other troubles were nearer home. His wife, Idelette, bore a son who lived only for a short time, and then in 1545 she became seriously ill and eventually died in 1549. Calvin wrote to Viret,

And truly mine is no common source of grief. I have been bereaved of the best companion of my life, of one, who, had it been so ordered, would not only have been the willing sharer of my indigence, but also of my death. During her life she was the faithful helper of my ministry. From her I never experienced the slightest hindrance. She was never troublesome to me throughout the whole course of her illness; she was more anxious about her children than about herself.

These children were from her first marriage and, of course, continued to live in Calvin's house. Also in the house was his brother Antoine, whose wife brought more sorrow and shame to Calvin by committing adultery with Calvin's servant, who had incidentally been stealing from his master for years. Then his stepdaughter, Judith, was also convicted of adultery. In addition to opposition outside and disloyalty within his household, Calvin was constantly ill and in pain. However, in the midst of it all he expanded the *Institutes* again and published many of his commentaries on the New Testament. In fact, he completed his series on the New Testament, excluding Revelation but including an extensive revision of Romans, in ten years.

In 1547 opposition had once more revived publicly; the Libertines controlled the councils and even had a majority of the syndics. Perrin and others attacked him publicly and incited the mob to insult him. One day he found a threatening letter in the pulpit; it turned out to be the work of a diseased and disordered mind that advocated licence in the name of liberty. The Libertines defied all church authority so that the ministers had little power, even over pastoral appointments. They tried to limit Calvin's influence by placing the power of excommunication in the hands of the council. Bolsec, a refugee physician, disputed with Calvin over predestination but was condemned by all the neighbouring churches. Eventually he became a Roman Catholic and wrote a virulent 'Life' of the Reformer which is still believed in some quarters.

In 1552 the Libertines were once again in control of the councils, syndics and judges, and Calvin wrote, 'They have never shown a more unbridled licence... The entire republic is in disorder and they are striving to uproot the established order.' Calvin's protests went unheeded and eventually he asked to be allowed to resign from his office. The council refused; they simply wanted to live as they liked in spite of him – and *to* spite him – not to make a martyr of him.

Calvin and Servetus

At this lowest point of his career came the incident that, for many, condemns Calvin utterly. Certainly by twenty-first century criteria it shows him in a very bad light but amazingly, in the providence of God, it seems to have been a turning point in the struggle. Michael Servetus, who had failed to keep his appointment with Calvin in Paris back in 1533, was a heretic, a blasphemer and a liar. For years he had attacked the truth using various pseudonyms. He practised and wrote on medicine with some success, but his theological writings were arrogant and abusive. He particularly attacked the doctrine of the trinity, which he called 'a three-headed Cerberus' and 'that triad of impossible monstrosities'. For a while he was under the unwitting protection of the Catholic Archbishop of Vienne until he was denounced to the Roman authorities. Servetus had been conducting a debate, in letters, with Calvin, who was asked to provide information against him. Calvin did this most reluctantly to confirm a friend's word. His reluctance stemmed largely from his conviction that 'his duty, as one who does not bear the sword of justice, is to convict heresies by doctrine rather than by pursuing them with the sword'.

Servetus was arrested and interrogated by the Inquisition; he lied and pretended but all in vain. Early one morning he escaped, leaving the Roman authorities to sentence him in his absence 'to be burned alive in a slow fire until his body becomes ashes'. While they burned him in effigy, Servetus had the audacity and folly to proceed to Geneva, apparently to challenge Calvin in person. The Reformer recognized and denounced him and he was arrested and put on trial by the civil authorities. The Libertines, led by Ami Perrin, now First Syndic, used the trial to harass Calvin, and Servetus who was encouraged by this became bold and insolent. Too late, however, the judges found that they had trapped themselves in a corner.

The Catholics had already condemned Servetus; all the neighbouring cities supported Calvin, calling for the death penalty, and the whole of Christendom was watching to see whether Geneva would allow this arch-heretic to escape. Eventually, in spite of Perrin's efforts to save him, they had to condemn him. Calvin had a final interview with him, trying to bring him to repentance, but in the end it was Farel who accompanied Servetus on his way to execution. In spite of the ministers' pleas for a more humane form of execution, Servetus was burned and to this day Calvin's name has been blackened because of this one event.

What was Calvin's fault? All the churches praised him for his stand for the faith and wrote to congratulate him, but from our standpoint he was at fault in believing with all his contemporaries that heresy and blasphemy should be punished by the state. Although it was in fact the civil authorities – and Calvin's enemies at that – who actually condemned and executed Servetus, there is no doubt that he agreed with the judgement. In this he was still a child of his age, not ahead of it as he was in so many other respects. It is difficult for us in our secular and materialistic society to appreciate just how the sixteenth century regarded such blasphemy against the living God. They would find it even more difficult to understand how we could have such a slack attitude towards those who seek to destroy the church of Christ.

While Calvin was involved in this matter another issue arose: the excommunication of one of his opponents. In spite of the church's decision, the Little Council demanded that this man should be allowed to attend the Lord's Supper on 3 September 1553. Calvin warned him not to attend and, fearing the worst, preached a farewell sermon on Acts 20. He was, however, too pessimistic. The original ordinances were consulted, the consistory won the debate and, although the case dragged on into 1555, the Servetus affair caused public opinion to turn in Calvin's favour.

The elections in February 1555 threw out the Perrinists and installed four pro-Calvin syndics. Seeing that they were losing ground, the Libertines made one last desperate effort to regain control. Using the alleged danger to the city implied by the presence of many French refugees, Perrin and his friends took arms, supposedly against the French, but in practice against the syndics. This was too much; the syndics resisted and Perrin had to flee from the city. He and his fellow rebels were condemned in their absence and Calvin's position was at last secure.

Peace

The last nine years of Calvin's life (1555 – 1564) saw his influence increase across Europe. Even while his position was still insecure in Geneva his name was known throughout the Christian world. By 1550 Geneva was the centre of the evangelical cause, and he was able to build on the foundations he had laid. In 1559 he opened an academy or university in Geneva, which, although it dealt with all learning, was especially aimed at training men for the ministry of the Word of God. Money was scarce in the city, but the council was adept at raising funds, partly through the sale of property forfeited by the Perrinists! There were two theological professors; one of them was Calvin who lectured three times a week on the Old Testament, apart from his preaching, pastoral work and correspondence. These lectures provided the basis for his commentaries on most of the Old Testament as they were taken down, transcribed, submitted for his approval and then published.

Not content with this, he revised the *Institutes* once more, this time with a different framework and with much new material. The eighty chapters issued in 1559 form the greatest and most influential work of Reformed theology. Here he writes as a second-generation Reformer, not innovating but consolidating, in particular integrating all the doctrines into a systematic whole: doctrine, experience and life. Although, Calvin is usually thought of today as the theologian of the sovereignty of God, where he was really following Augustine in the main, his new ideas were concerned with the person and work of the Lord Jesus Christ and the work of the Holy Spirit. Uniting all is his concern for the knowledge of God, so that the whole of life is brought into submission to God and directed to his glory.

REFUGEES IN GENEVA

One of the refugees in Geneva was the Scotsman, John Knox, who having helped the English to reform, was soon to transform his native land. He described Geneva in 1555 to 1559 as 'the most perfect school of Christ that ever was in the world since the days of the apostles. In other places I confess Christ to be truly preached, but manners and religion so sincerely reformed I have not yet seen in any other place.' (The English refugees formed their own congregation and, among other things, in 1560 published the Geneva Bible with explanatory notes — the most popular English translation until it was ousted by the Authorized Version of 1611.)

Calvin was not only concerned with building up reformed churches; he was also deeply involved in the establishing of new churches. He was responsible for sending fourteen missionaries to Brazil in 1555 with a group of Huguenot colonists. Between 1555 and 1562 over 100 men went out from Geneva to preach and pastor in other lands but mainly in Calvin's native France. The number of reformed churches in France grew from one in 1535 to over 2,000 in 1561, and many of their pastors were converted and trained in Geneva.

Many eagerly sought Calvin's advice, and his correspondence was immense, providing eleven volumes of his collected works. Until the 1550s these were all in his own handwriting lest his readers should be upset, thinking that he had not bothered to reply personally. This is the measure of the man so often regarded as cold, hard and narrow. Some letters were, in fact, lengthy theological treatises; others were unreserved, personal outpourings to old friends such as Viret and Farel; and others were wise counsel addressed to monarchs or their ministers: the Duke of Somerset, Protector during the minority of Edward VI of England; Henri of Navarre; and William Cecil, Lord Burleigh, chief minister of Elizabeth I.

He wrote also to the great Christian leaders of Europe as he had a great longing for the unity of the church. Luther, who could never agree with the followers of Ulrich Zwingli over the Lord's Supper, read Calvin's treatise on the subject and said, 'This is certainly a learned and godly man, and I might well have entrusted this controversy to him from the beginning. If my opponents had done the same, we should soon have been reconciled.' Later, however, Luther classed Calvin with the Zwinglians, and when Calvin wrote, trying to heal the breach and addressing Luther as 'the very excellent pastor of the Christian Church, Dr Martin Luther my much respected father', Melanchthon dared not show the letter to the German leader. All the same Calvin wrote to Bullinger, 'I have often said that even if he [Luther] were to call me a devil, I should still regard him as an outstanding servant of God.'

To John Knox and the English in Frankfort, exiles from Queen Mary's fury, he counselled peace and moderation, while his response to Archbishop Cranmer's proposal for a synod to promote closer union between Reformed churches is well worth reading today: 'The members of the church being severed, the body lies bleeding. So much does this concern me, that could I be of any service, I would not grudge to cross even ten seas, if need were, on account of it.'

Most moving of all are the letters written to the five prisoners of Lyons. These preachers were sent from neighbouring Lausanne in 1552 but were betrayed almost as soon as they entered France. They were arrested, imprisoned and, in spite of pleas from Calvin and others, condemned to be burned. Calvin wrote to them several times on behalf of the church in Geneva to comfort them and exhort them to faithfulness. In one he counsels them firmly but lovingly:

> Since it appears as though God would use your blood to sign his truth, there is nothing better for you than to prepare your-selves to that end; beseeching him so to subdue you to his good pleasure that nothing may hinder you from following whithersoever he shall call... It cannot be, but that you sustain hard conflicts... You know, however, in what strength you have to fight − a strength on which all who trust shall never be daunted, much less confounded.

The five died in faith, exhorting one another to have courage. In this manner Calvinists died in those days.

Last days

During these years of unceasing labours Calvin's health worsened steadily; the list of his ailments is horrendous, culminating in the tuberculosis from which he appears to have died. Frequently he had to dictate letters and lectures while lying in bed and by 1563 he often had to be carried on a chair or on horseback to fulfil his duties. After February 1564 there was no more preaching, but still he continued his correspondence. 'What!' he would say to friends who urged him to desist, 'Would you have the Lord find me idle when he comes?'

The time had come to make his will, in which he asserted, 'I have endeavoured, according to the measure of grace he has given me, to teach his Word in purity, both in my sermons and writings, and to expound faithfully the Holy Scriptures.' He had little to leave but his body: 'to wait for the day of the blessed resurrection'. The council came to see him, as did the pastors. To the latter he declared, 'I have not falsified a single passage of the Scripture nor given it a wrong interpretation to the best of my knowledge... I have written nothing out of hatred to anyone, but I have always propounded what I esteemed to be for the glory of God.'

On 27 May 1564 he died, and the city grieved. Beza his colleague and successor wrote,

> During the night and the following day, there was great lamentation in the city, for its government mourned for the prophet of the Lord; the poor flock lamented the loss of its faithful shepherd; the academy deplored its true teacher and head, and all in common wept over the departure of their father and chief comforter next to God.

The council inscribed in its minutes: 'God had imprinted on his character such a great majesty.' On 28 May he was buried in an unmarked grave according to his own instructions. A few months later no one could identify his grave for a visitor to the city.

Summary

Perhaps no man in the history of the church has been so hated as John Calvin. He knew his own faults better than his enemies, but his many friends loved him dearly. He was a man prepared, 'tamed', sustained against incredible odds and used to establish the Protestant Reformation. We are all in his debt and should be building on his foundation, directing all our energies to applying the Word of God in every part of life for the glory of God.

Nothing sums up Calvin better than a letter that he addressed to his old friend Farel three weeks before his death: 'I draw my breath with difficulty and every moment I am in expectation of breathing my last. It is enough that I live and die for Christ, who is to all his followers a gain both in life and death.'

Questions for discussion

1. How does Farel's method of persuading Calvin to stay in Geneva fit with your idea of a call to the ministry?

2. In what ways was Calvin right and wrong in the case of Servetus? What should he have done? What should and could we do today?

3. What are the popular misconceptions held about Calvin today? What were his most important strengths and virtues? Who would be more useful today: Luther or Calvin?

For further reading

* J. Calvin, *Truth for all time*, The Banner of Truth Trust, 1998.

** N. R. Needham, *2000 years of Christ's power*, Grace Publications, 2004, Part Three, pp.188-252.

** T. H. L. Parker, *John Calvin*, Lion, 1975.

* E. Stickelberger, *John Calvin*, James Clarke & Co, 1959.

F. Wendel, *Calvin*, Collins, 1963.

God soo loved the worlde that he gave his only sonne for the entent that none that believe in hym shulde perisshe: But shulde have everlastynge lyfe.

— John 3:16 (William Tyndale's translation)

Be of good comfort, Master Ridley, and play the man; we shall this day, by God's grace, light such a candle in England as I trust shall never be put out.

— Hugh Latimer (1485 – 1555)

Lo! these are they from sufferings great
Who came to realms of light;
And in the blood of Christ have washed
Those robes that shine so bright.

— Isaac Watts (1674 – 1748)

7

Reformation comes to England

The first thing to realize about the English Reformation is that it was a spiritual work of God through the Scriptures in the hands of godly men, not the result of Henry VIII's (reign 1509 – 1547) marriage problems. In God's remarkable providence Henry's quarrel with the pope shielded the Reformers, at least for a while, from Catholic rage, but the king remained a Catholic, and a most ungodly one, to the end.

Second, although the Lollards were still influential – for instance, re-issuing no less than nine Wycliffite treatises between 1530 and 1536 – and severely persecuted, the Reformation did not come from them. However, they did represent and foster a deep dissatisfaction with the church of the day. It would appear that most ordinary folk were disillusioned with the pathetic clergy (there were less than a dozen who could preach in the York diocese), the underpopulated monasteries and convents (servants outnumbered monks five to one) and the immoral lives of many of the ecclesiastical dignitaries. The Lollards and their sympathizers welcomed and assisted the Reformation when it came but lacked the power and influence needed to make any impression on the situation.

Another preparation came through the universities and the humanists. As early as 1496 John Colet had lectured at Oxford on Romans, not with Luther's insight but with a forthrightness that brought Lollard admiration and Episcopal accusations of heresy. Then came the Dutchman, Erasmus, too weak to be a Reformer but a truly great scholar whose work in producing and printing the Greek New Testament was vital for both Luther and England. Luther himself was responsible for the beginnings of real reformation in England through his books, which were smuggled into London by merchants, and through scholars and priests who visited him in Germany. In particular there was a group of Cambridge University scholars who met at the White Horse Inn to discuss the new teaching from Wittenberg. Many of the most influential Reformers of later years belonged to this group, but pride of place must go to a man who may have joined in their debates and was certainly in Cambridge at the time but whose labours were largely independent of theirs.

William Tyndale

Tutor and preacher

William Tyndale's beginnings (c. 1495 – 1536) are virtually unknown, which is fitting for one who spent much of his life in hiding. He was probably born around 1495 in the Gloucester area; he became an Oxford master of arts in 1515 but then transferred his allegiance to Cambridge. Archbishop Warham declared the university there to be 'infected with Lutheranism', and even if this most independent of men did not belong to the White Horse group he would certainly have read some of the books that were used as fuel for a great bonfire outside Great St Mary's Church in 1520.

In 1521 Tyndale moved from Cambridge to Little Sodbury Manor in the Cotswolds to become tutor to the two sons of Sir John Walsh. Here he began to translate, with a work of Erasmus, and he also preached in the local church. Before long he went further afield, walking the fifteen miles to Bristol to preach on College Green. Unlike the friars who frequented the place he was not preaching for money; also unlike them he was preaching the gospel of justification by faith, not by works. The friars were so annoyed by this attack on their source of income that they complained to the Archdeacon of Gloucester, who charged Tyndale with various kinds of heresy but allowed him to return to Little Sodbury with a stern warning.

Although he must have realized that his career and his life were in danger, Tyndale did not draw back. He continued to contend for evangelical truth, especially when there were ecclesiastical visitors at Sir John's table. Lady Walsh, rather like Luther's young emperor, assessed a divine's authority in proportion to his income, which put Tyndale at something of a disadvantage! In all other respects, however, he was infinitely superior, not only to the ignorant friars but also to the learned but Bible-ignorant church dignitaries who came to the manor.

On a memorable occasion one such visitor was so enraged by Tyndale's method of quoting the Bible as God's law that he exclaimed, 'We were better be without God's law than the pope's!' 'I defy the pope and all his laws', replied the young priest; 'if God spare my life, ere many years I will cause a boy that driveth a plough shall know more of the Scripture than thou dost.'

The translator

It would appear that he had already determined to translate the New Testament at all costs: 'because I had perceived by experience how that it was impossible to establish the lay people in any truth except the Scripture were plainly laid before their eyes in their mother tongue, that they might see the process, order and meaning of the text.' Already he had begun to prepare himself for this great work by acquiring the necessary linguistic skills. So diligent was he that in 1526 a contemporary described him as: 'an Englishman... who is so skilful in seven tongues, Hebrew, Greek, Latin, Italian, Spanish, English, French, that whichever he speaks you would think it his native tongue.'

Although it was not necessarily illegal to translate the Scriptures into English, only recently seven people had been burnt for teaching their children the Lord's Prayer, the Ten Commandments and the Apostles' Creed in English. The necessary safeguard was the authority of a bishop. So in 1523 Tyndale set off for London armed with an introduction from Sir John Walsh to seek the patronage of the scholarly Bishop of London, Cuthbert Tunstall. The political situation and the increase of Lutheran books entering the country, however, made Tunstall wary of encouraging the would-be translator. Instead, he claimed that his establishment was full and recommended him to seek patronage elsewhere in the city.

The result of this advice can hardly have been to the bishop's liking, for Tyndale soon met Humphrey Monmouth, a wealthy London cloth merchant. Monmouth belonged to the 'Christian Brethren', a group of merchants – almost a secret society – who were followers of Luther. They secretly imported Luther's books and distributed them to the descendants of the Lollards. Having become a 'Scripture-man', as the Christian Brethren were called, Monmouth heard Tyndale preaching at St Dunstan's in Fleet Street, became his friend and invited him to enter his household. There Tyndale worked zealously and diligently for six months before coming to the conclusion that he would have to leave England.

Voluntary exile

In 1524 he crossed the Channel, without asking the king's permission as he should have done, and went to Wittenberg. Monmouth continued to help by sending him money, and it is likely that this same group of godly merchants financed Tyndale's later activities.

By this time his New Testament was virtually complete and after less than a year he left Wittenberg, first for Hamburg and then Cologne, where he began to print his translation. We do not know why he left Wittenberg, but he was sufficiently independent to differ even from Luther when necessary. Although Cologne was basically a Catholic city it was nearer England and, moreover, the centre of printing in northwest Germany. There Tyndale, with both the help and hindrance of the unreliable William Roy, an ex-friar from England, began to see his work through the press. Before the printing was even half completed a fanatical Catholic discovered what was going on and persuaded the local magistrate to order both paper and type to be seized. Tyndale heard what was afoot, and he and Roy escaped just in time with armfuls of printed sheets. In the Protestant city of Worms they started again and completed the printing by the end of the year. There are some copies of Matthew 1 to 22 in existence from the Cologne edition, but the smaller Worms Testament is the real first edition. The first copies began to trickle into England in 1526 in spite of all that the authorities, who had been warned by Henry's ambassador to Spain, could do to prevent it. Monmouth and his merchant friends smuggled in the volumes with their other imports and soon the New Testament in English had spread through the cities and universities.

Bishop Tunstall was, ironically, in the forefront of those who tried to destroy the heretical book; he issued forthright instructions that all copies of the work must be seized and set an example a few days later by ceremonially burning one copy at St Paul's Cross. When he heard of this Tyndale wrote, 'In burning the New Testament they did none other thing than I looked for; no more shall they do if they burn me also, if it be God's will it shall so be. Nevertheless, in translating the New Testament I did my duty.'

In spite of all this, the original edition, pirate editions and soon, as promised, revised editions poured into the country. Many men, like Robert Barnes, Thomas Garrett and John Frith, spent and eventually gave their lives in spreading the gospel and particularly the English New Testament, so that within months many in England (even ploughboys?) were reading or listening to God's Word in their own language.

Archbishop Warham had a brilliant idea: he and his fellow bishops would buy up all the copies available. This pleased everybody; the bishops had copies to burn, the merchants made a profit and Tyndale received the capital to finance a new and revised edition!

Tyndale's New Testament

We must say a little about the translation itself. Tyndale continued to revise it to the end of his life in the interests of accuracy and clarity, but, as he wrote to John Frith who was imprisoned in the

Tower of London, 'I never altered one syllable of God's Word against my conscience.' His opponents accused him of distorting the text when he dropped such words as 'penance', 'charity', 'priest' and 'church' in favour of 'repentance', 'love', 'senior' (or 'elder') and 'congregation', but this was hardly fair. In each case Tyndale was using a word that, although certainly Protestant in content, gave the real meaning of the Greek. Here he set the Scriptures free from Catholic tradition and ecclesiastical interpretation, but far more important is the fact that he set the gospel itself before men in their own tongue. Only those who have seen the effect on converted Roman Catholics of reading the Scriptures in a modern translation can have some idea of what this must have meant.

The Authorized Version of 1611, with all those that preceded it, was heavily dependent on Tyndale's New Testament. It has been calculated that ninety per cent of the Authorized New Testament follows Tyndale's 1534 revision, and that when it varies it is usually inferior. Sometimes, as with 'charity', the Authorized Version returns to renderings that are capable of Catholic interpretation. (In fact the Authorized Version retains Tyndale's translation of 1 Corinthians 13 almost intact apart from reverting to 'charity'.)

Cardinal Wolsey and Sir Thomas More

The next years were spent in further writing and translation work, while at the same time avoiding arrest. Cardinal Wolsey had his agents scouring the Continent for Tyndale and buying up and burning all the Protestant books they could find. Tyndale and the erratic Roy parted company in 1526, the former moving on in 1527 to Marburg. There he wrote and published various controversial works, notably *The Obedience of a Christian Man*, dealing with the question of civil and ecclesiastical authority but making clear at the same time the gospel of salvation.

At this time Tyndale was also improving his Hebrew with a view to translating the Old Testament. By the beginning of 1529 he had completed the Pentateuch (the five books of Moses) and set off for Hamburg where he had friends and hoped to print the work. On the way the ship was wrecked on the coast of Holland, and he lost all his manuscripts! However, once in Hamburg the determined translator, encouraged by a new friend and disciple, Miles Coverdale, set to work again and by December the Pentateuch was once more ready for the press. If we wonder why Tyndale should choose this part of the Old Testament rather than, perhaps, the Psalms, we need only compare Exodus 20:4-5 with the view of the Catholic Sir Thomas More: 'Good folk which worship images of Christ and his saints do worship thereby Christ and his saints whom these images represent.' The new translation arrived in England in early 1530, complete with accurate but tactless anti-Catholic marginal notes.

By now Tyndale was in Antwerp, but Henry's agents failed to find him. In 1531 Stephen Vaughan came to the Continent trying to win Tyndale back into the king's service! However, in England reformers were being arrested and many burnt, and Tyndale wisely refused to be enticed back home, although he did arrange three secret meetings with Vaughan. At these he stressed his loyalty to the king and also, according to Vaughan, promised to return and submit if the king would 'grant only a bare text of the Scriptures to be put forth among his people, be it of the translation of what person soever shall please his majesty'.

SIR THOMAS MORE

About this time Sir Thomas More, the author of Utopia *and widely praised in our own times as a tolerant and liberal humanist scholar, had taken Wolsey's place as Lord Chancellor. He was not a priest, but in order to write against Tyndale he was given permission to read heretical books. This supposedly tolerant Catholic would rather a priest live with a woman than commit the sin of clerical marriage, rather have Muslims than heretics (that is, Protestants) and, although he claimed to deal gently with Protestants, expressed the desire that 'there should have been more burned by a great many than there have been within this seven years past'. In fact, during the last two years of his chancellorship at least ten Protestants went to the stake.*

From time to time Tyndale was encouraged by the companion-ship of friends and fellow labourers like John Frith. However, Frith ventured back to England where he was arrested and burnt. During his imprisonment he was comforted by a letter from Tyndale. Other friends were less helpful, notably George Joye, who later impudently took it on himself to issue a revision of the great translator's 1534 New Testament. Tyndale's enemies were also active and soon a group of citizens from Antwerp began to make trouble for all Protestants but especially for the heretical teacher from England. Although Tyndale was not arrested at this time, the noose was evidently tightening slowly.

In 1534 he took refuge in the English house of the Merchant Adventurers, which was regarded as virtually part of England, almost like an embassy today. These men, who played such an important part in getting his New Testament into England, provided him with an income. As well as studying and writing, Tyndale made a point of visiting English refugees in the town and helping them from his meagre resources. This was typical of his character for although his writing could be very sharp, after the manner of the time, in private he was known as a most gentle man. Even Sir Thomas More was compelled to describe him as 'a man of sober and honest living… [who] looked and preached holily'.

The chaplain at the house was John Rogers. He was at first no friend of reform, but this soon changed and by 1535 he had become Tyndale's friend and helper. The translator was now busy on a revision of his New Testament, which was published in 1534 and sent to England. It was this edition in the language of the people that provided the basis of the Authorized Version of the New Testament and that transformed England.

Betrayal, imprisonment and execution

In 1535 an Englishman named Henry Phillips registered as a student in the University of Louvain, about thirty miles from Antwerp. He was soon welcomed into the home of Thomas Poyntz (a relative of Lady Walsh of Little Sodbury, with whom Tyndale lodged) because of his obvious Lutheran sympathies. In fact Phillips was a spy sent from England to capture Tyndale. In spite of his scheming

Phillips failed to turn the merchants against Tyndale so he changed his tactics. He obtained help directly from the imperial court in Brussels and returned to Antwerp while Poyntz, who had his suspicions, was away. Having persuaded the unworldly Tyndale to lend him £2 on the pretext of having lost his purse, he enticed him out of the safety of the house and had him arrested by the officers of the emperor.

Very soon Tyndale was imprisoned in one of the foul dungeons of the Castle of Vilvorde near Brussels. When Poyntz returned home he immediately stirred up protests both on the Continent and in England, but Phillips, alarmed at Poyntz's progress, had him arrested too. Although Poyntz eventually escaped he had to leave the Low Countries altogether and his business was ruined for the sake of Tyndale and the gospel. Meanwhile Tyndale stayed in his cell, using what opportunities he had to continue his work.

We have a letter written by Tyndale to the governor of his prison requesting, with dignity, a few essentials to help him in his study: some warmer clothes, a lamp in the evenings, and especially, 'that he will kindly permit me to have the Hebrew Bible, Hebrew grammar and Hebrew dictionary, that I may pass my time in that study'. He desires the salvation of the governor's soul and submits to the will of God. Many generations of Christians have been reminded of the words of the apostle Paul, written from prison to Timothy: 'When you come, bring the cloak that I left with Carpus at Troas, and my scrolls, especially the parchments' (2 Tim. 4:13).

It took many months to prepare the charges against Tyndale and to interrogate him in an attempt to convince or convict him, but by 1536 all was ready for the trial to begin. He was charged with, among other things, denying purgatory and maintaining that faith alone justifies. In August 1536, sixteen months after his arrest, he was inevitably condemned. Since he had been a priest there had to be a ceremonial casting out of the church before he could be handed over to the secular authorities for execution. Attempts to force him to recant went on for two months, but in October the day arrived and Tyndale was strangled and then burnt. Before he was put to death Tyndale uttered one last prayer: '*Lord, open the King of England's eyes.*'

In the year 1536 there were two English Bibles in circulation, both dedicated to Henry and hoping for the king's blessing: the Matthew Bible, prepared by Tyndale's friend from Antwerp, John Rogers, and the other prepared by Miles Coverdale. Both contained Tyndale's New Testament and used his Pentateuch and other parts of the Old Testament. A printer in Southwark gained Cromwell's support against the bishops who wanted both Bibles banned. Apparently the king asked the bishops if there were any heresies in Coverdale's Bible, which tactfully did not have Tyndale's name anywhere on the title page! When they assured him that there were none he is said to have replied, 'If there be no heresies, then in God's name let it go abroad among our people.' Eventually Cromwell licensed both Bibles and in 1538 sent a circular letter, which seems to have been generally observed, to all the bishops urging them to exhort the lay people to read the Bible and to fix a date by which every local church must be provided with a copy for public reading. The Lord had done more than Tyndale had asked for because his translation was not only available but also effective, by the work of the Spirit, in transforming the land.

The English Reformation

Thomas Cranmer

Almost eighteen years after Tyndale's martyrdom, four men shared a cell in the Tower of London. The story of how these Reformers came to be there illustrates the changing fortunes of the Reformation and charts the work of God in England. Thomas Cranmer (1489 – 1556) was the Archbishop of Canterbury, Nicholas Ridley was Bishop of London, Hugh Latimer had been Bishop of Worcester and John Bradford was an authorized preacher of King Edward VI. Now, with Mary newly on the throne, their lives were in serious danger.

In spite of the liberation of the Word of God in England by Henry VIII, the king had not become a Protestant. Although he had renounced the pope's authority because of the divorce question, he was still Catholic in his beliefs, which he set forth at great length. On one occasion he personally acted as judge, dressed all in white, at the trial of a Protestant heretic, John Lambert. In 1539 he issued the Six Articles on which a severe persecution was based, and in 1543 an act was passed limiting Bible reading to the 'safe' upper classes. He objected strongly to the Bible's being 'disputed, rhymed, sung and jangled in every ale-house and tavern' and forbade it to be read by 'women, artificers, apprentices, journeymen, serving men under the degree of yeoman, husbandmen and labourers'. This makes his earlier permission all the more remarkable and, moreover, gives us proof that the Bible was being read – and believed – by such people. Two days after the execution of his faithful servant, Thomas Cromwell, Henry showed his colours very clearly by executing three Protestants by burning as heretics and three Catholics by hanging as traitors.

Nevertheless the Reformation continued to spread under the protection of Henry's newly appointed Archbishop of Canterbury. Thomas Cranmer's life shows the weaknesses as well as the strengths of the Reformers, yet God used him quite amazingly to further his purposes. A Cambridge graduate and Fellow of Jesus College, Cranmer lived in comparative obscurity until 1533. He may have attended the meetings at the White Horse Inn in 1521 and certainly gained, a few years later, a reputation as a university examiner for demanding thorough biblical knowledge from ordinands. He attracted Henry's attention through his opinions on the king's divorce and, as a friend of the Boleyn family, was clearly seen as a useful tool to be used against the pope. He had been married and widowed before becoming a priest but had then married again, this time to the niece of a Lutheran divine on the Continent, Andreas Osiander. The king had such a hatred of clerical marriage that Cranmer's wife had to be kept very much in the background, to such an extent that it was rumoured that Cranmer took her around in a chest!

Nevertheless, such was his political usefulness that in 1533 Henry appointed him as his archbishop and protected him from all his enemies, even taunting them with his obvious affection for this most useful servant. On one occasion he took Cranmer for a trip in his barge and on the way told him that he now knew who the greatest heretic in Kent was. Cranmer, as Archbishop of

Canterbury, in Kent, must have been alarmed, but then Henry put him in charge of the enquiry against himself. Later, when various members of the council tried to get rid of Cranmer, Henry's simple but effective request was: 'I pray you, use not my friends so.'

The archbishop was able to prevent some of the worst excesses of the Six Articles. However, he had to send his wife back to the Continent and is often condemned, probably with justice, for acquiescing in far too much because of his subservience to his royal master. We must not judge Cranmer by the standards of the Continental Reformers, whose views were far more advanced, or of his own later beliefs. At this time he was no more than a 'half-Protestant' and his ideas on the Lord's Supper were still Catholic. As well as encouraging the publication of Coverdale's revision of the Matthew Bible, known as the Great Bible, and even writing a preface for its second edition, Cranmer had plans for an English language prayer book, and in 1544 published a litany in English as a first step. Since 1538 he had also been rethinking his doctrine of the mass.

Nicholas Ridley

At this point we must look at Nicholas Ridley (1505 – 1555), a much more shadowy figure but very important in terms of doctrine. Cranmer had a good mind but it would appear that Ridley was the real 'brains' behind the next stage of the Reformation. One enemy said of the three most prominent Reformers of this era: 'Latimer leaneth unto Cranmer, Cranmer leaneth unto Ridley, and Ridley leaneth unto the singularity of his own wit.' A Northumbrian by birth, he was yet another Cambridge graduate and probably attended the White Horse Inn meetings. In 1537 he became Cranmer's chaplain and was appointed vicar of Herne in Kent by his patron. There he studied and from 1538 began to alter his views on that most significant of doctrines, the Lord's Supper. When on trial later, Cranmer acknowledged that it was Ridley who had convinced him of the Protestant doctrine and that they had given up their belief in the Catholic teaching of transubstantiation in 1545.

Ridley became chaplain to Henry and, in 1547, Bishop of Rochester. In this year Henry died, and although the king had not changed his views, the Word of God had spread so extensively in the land that, with the accession of the Protestant-trained boy king, Edward VI, the way was open for even greater progress. Under the protectorates of Somerset and Northumberland, Cranmer and Ridley continued to rewrite the official documents of the church. Cranmer himself wrote four or five of the *Book of Homilies*, in which the doctrine of justification by faith is taught with reasonable clarity. He then showed both his command of the English language and his gift for compromise in the production of the first English prayer book. Making use of old and new materials he produced a masterpiece of devotional English in which transubstantiation was denied. Typically, however, the denial was not clearly articulated and one of his chief conservative opponents, Bishop Gardiner, agreed to use it as expressing the Catholic doctrine of the mass.

John Hooper

Cranmer's genius for survival kept him safe even when Northumberland replaced Somerset as protector for the young king, and he continued the Reformation in his own way. Many scholars from the Continent were welcomed to England, such as Peter Martyr; Martin Bucer, who became Regius Professor at Cambridge; John à Lasco, who established a truly reformed Puritan-style church in London; and even John Knox, who influenced the Reformation in England long before he made his mark in Scotland. Evangelical bishops were appointed to many dioceses, including John Hooper (died 1555), the most forward-looking from our point of view but a menace in the eyes of Cranmer and Ridley who could see their cause being ruined if Hooper's 'pernickety' conscience was allowed free rein.

However, Hooper was also a most effective and hard-working diocesan bishop who achieved a large measure of reformation among the unpromising clergy of his area. After examining 311 clergy he found that 168 could not repeat the Ten Commandments, 39 did not know where to find the Lord's Prayer in the Bible and 34 could not even name its author!

Hugh Latimer

Another such bishop was Hugh Latimer (1485 – 1555). He was a popular and powerful preacher who epitomized the spiritual, grass-roots Reformation as well as being a stirring example of zeal and faith. He was born in Leicestershire in 1485, the son of a yeoman farmer, who, having no land of his own, had to make sacrifices to provide the young Hugh with a good education. He went to Cambridge University at the age of fourteen and became a fellow of Clare Hall in 1509. He shared in all the superstitions of Rome, believing that a friar's cowl would deliver him from the fear of death. He was as he said in a sermon, 'as obstinate a papist as any was in England' and in another, 'All the papists think themselves to be saved by the law, and I myself was of that dangerous, perilous and damnable opinion till I was thirty years of age.'

It was in 1524 that all this changed. One of his contemporaries was Thomas (Little) Bilney. When Erasmus's Latin version of his Greek New Testament first arrived in Cambridge, Bilney obtained a copy and was charmed by the elegance of the Latin style. Soon he became entranced by the content and was converted. While reading 1 Timothy 1:15 he said, 'Immediately, I seemed unto myself inwardly to feel a marvellous comfort and quietness, insomuch as my bruised bones leaped for joy.' Bilney naturally associated with the White Horse Inn group and also began to pray for the pope's latest champion, Hugh Latimer. Having graduated, Latimer had to preach before the whole university and chose to attack the continental Reformer Melanchthon.

Shortly afterwards Bilney went to see him. 'For the love of God, be pleased to hear my confession', pleaded Bilney. Probably thinking that his oration had reconverted the heretic, Latimer readily agreed, only to have Bilney pour out the history of his spiritual pilgrimage and his new-found faith. 'I learned more by his confession than before in many years', recalled Latimer. 'From that time forward I began to smell the Word of God, and forsook the school doctors and such fooleries.'

As Bishop Ryle says, 'Hugh Latimer was not a man to do anything by halves.' Without delay he began to study the Scriptures, to accompany Bilney in visiting the prisons and, most important of all, to preach the gospel in the university with plain but striking eloquence. The Bishop of Ely heard of this and did not approve. He banned him from preaching and had him appear before the much-feared Cardinal Wolsey. He demanded a sermon against the 'errors of Luther', but Latimer wisely replied that this was beyond his power as he was not allowed to read the works of the great heretic.

Back in Cambridge Latimer continued his preaching ministry from 1527 to 1529. The church was crowded with students and local people who delighted in his homely and often witty style. It was not that he flattered his hearers; indeed he was noted for rebuking sins and for leaving 'pricks or stings in the heart of his hearers'. His originality is seen in a series of sermons he preached on *The Card*, in which he used the university custom of spending Christmas playing cards to point to Christ.

There were many complaints about his plain speaking, but he also gained the favour of King Henry and was frequently invited to preach at court over the next two years. The king's physician, Dr Butts, had taken a great liking to him, but it had also become known that Latimer's views on the divorce issue were favourable to the king, as were Cranmer's. In 1531 this royal favour led to his becoming rector of West Kington in Wiltshire, and he immediately took up his work there. This was not regarded as essential as Latimer's bishop, the Italian Cardinal Campeggio, had been in England only once, and that was in connection with the divorce. Latimer, however, was a preacher and pastor, not a politician.

In spite of this, controversy followed him to Wiltshire. Matters were not helped by garbled reports of an admittedly bold sermon on the text, 'All that ever came before me were thieves and robbers', provoked by the Bishop of London's cruel persecution of Protestants. Again he was invited to preach in London and did so with equal boldness but without the bishop's permission. This time Bishop Stokesley put him on trial and Latimer must have wondered if he was to share the fate of the unstable but godly 'Little' Bilney, who had recently found his 'Jerusalem' when he was burnt as a heretic at the Lollard's Pit outside Norwich.

It was not for heresy, but on account of his attack on the abuses of the church that Latimer was tried, for he had not as yet advanced very far in reformed doctrine. Nevertheless he showed considerable skill when examined by Stokesley and the other bishops. After several days he noticed that the furniture in the room had been moved around. The fire was out and a cloth had been draped across the fireplace. As he listened he could hear the squeak of pen on paper, and when one of the bishops asked him to speak up because he was hard of hearing Latimer realized that his words were being recorded in an effort to ensnare him. After six weeks he appeared before Convocation. Three times he refused to retract his statements and the archbishop promptly excommunicated him but this raised the awkward question of what to do with one of the king's chaplains! After some negotiation and persuasion they modified their demands and Latimer met them halfway. This was the lowest point of his career as he had to apologize to Stokesley and plead humbly for his release from excommunication. Never again would Latimer compromise on the advice of friends.

Soon the situation changed in Latimer's favour when Cranmer succeeded Warham as archbishop. When he was in trouble again for preaching in Bristol without a licence and Thomas Cromwell ordered an enquiry, it was Cranmer who gave Latimer a licence to preach anywhere in the province of Canterbury, which included Bristol. With the favour of archbishop and king, Latimer no longer had to fear Stokesley, and in 1534 Cranmer persuaded Henry to invite Latimer to preach at court in the Chapel Royal, whose dean had been a member of the Convocation that condemned him as a heretic! From this time Latimer appears to have been secure in the favour of the king and his new queen, Anne Boleyn. So in August 1535 Latimer, the 'heretic', was appointed Bishop of Worcester.

During his four years as bishop, Latimer worked hard to reform his diocese, which was probably in the same state as Hooper's a few years later. He supported attempts to reform the monasteries but not to rob them; Latimer, ever the pastor, wanted some of them kept for study and prayer for the benefit of the church. He spent some of his time in the House of Lords, but his usual place was in the pulpit. He was often asked to preach at court where Queen Anne loved to hear him and even accepted his private rebukes. Henry had already tired of her in favour of Jane Seymour, and Latimer even dared to rebuke the king. Apparently it was the custom for each bishop to present the king with a New Year's gift. Latimer chose to give his monarch a New Testament together with a napkin bearing the inscription, in Latin: 'Fornicators and adulterers God will judge' (Heb. 13:4). Amazingly Latimer was preserved, but Anne soon fell to the executioner's sword, her dying testimony bearing witness to the reality of her faith at last.

Latimer continued to preach boldly against clerical abuses, even before Convocation, but further moves towards reformation were thwarted by the 'conservative' bishops. The king himself was aware of the increasing Protestantism and drew up 'Ten Articles' for all the bishops to sign. Latimer signed with the rest, thus showing how slowly the Reformers were changing their ideas in submission to Scripture. In 1539 the 'Ten' were succeeded by 'Six', the so-called 'Whip with six strings', which put everything back to square one as Catholic. As soon as these became law Latimer resigned his bishopric, declaring himself 'rid of a heavy burden'. He much preferred preaching to administration.

Henry, of course, was not pleased; bishops should submit like everybody else. Latimer was put under house arrest in London and, as he said in a later sermon, 'looked every day to be called to execution'. The danger eventually passed but Latimer spent the rest of Henry's reign in some anxiety and public silence. In God's providence perhaps this gave him a much-needed opportunity to study the Scriptures and become clearer on the doctrines of the Reformation. Latimer's uneasy peace ended in 1546 when Henry had him arrested. The king's health and temper had deteriorated seriously and he became more severe against the Reformers. In May Latimer refused to submit and was sent to the Tower but not for long.

The 'boy king'

In January 1547 Henry died and was succeeded by the boy king, Edward VI (reign 1547 – 1553). Henry's death released Latimer from prison and although he refused the offer of his old diocese of Worcester, he was now able to play his full part in the Reformation of the land by his popular preaching. As well as preaching the gospel truths of the Reformation, he became the conscience of the nation. His preaching was always practical, and he attacked the sins of the day without mercy. He was chief spokesman of the 'Commonwealth Men', a Protestant group that opposed covetous landlords and favoured the common man. In 1548 he preached his famous 'Sermon on the Plough', which gives a good idea of his homespun but highly effective style. He criticized 'unpreaching prelates, lording loiterers and idle ministers' and then went on:

> And now I would ask a strange question: who is the most diligentest bishop and prelate in all England, that passeth all the rest in doing his office? I can tell, for I know him who it is... It is the devil. He is the most diligent preacher of all the others; he is never out of his diocese; he is never from his cure; ye shall never find him unoccupied... When the devil is resident and hath his plough going, there away with books, and up with candles; away with Bibles, and up with beads; away with the light of the gospel, and up with the light of candles... There never was such a preacher in England as he is.

Latimer was licensed to preach anywhere in the country and did so but was often found in London, staying at Lambeth with Cranmer and preaching before the godly young king. By 1548 Latimer also had come to agree with the continental Reformers over the Lord's Supper and had abandoned his belief in transubstantiation, but his strong point was still preaching. He proclaimed the gospel and defied Rome but also denounced Protestant nominalism and ungodliness. From 1551 he ceased to be the king's chaplain and preached mainly out of London. In that same year six itinerant preachers were appointed to cover neglected areas of the country; one of them was John Bradford, the fourth member of the quartet in the Tower.

John Bradford

John Bradford (c. 1510 – 1555) was born and brought up near Manchester but later entered royal service under Sir John Harrington. In 1547 he became a law student and was converted through a fellow student, Thomas Sampson. Soon, however, he gave up the study of law to concentrate on the Scriptures to prepare himself for the preaching of the gospel. In London he heard Latimer preach on restitution, hardly a popular subject with the courtiers, and was deeply convicted not on his own account but because he had kept silent about Sir John Harrington's defrauding of the king. He consulted Latimer and, in accordance with his advice, wrote to Harrington and insisted that he make restitution, which was duly done. Such was the effect of Latimer's preaching. It was also on Latimer's advice that Bradford went to Cambridge and there prepared himself most effectively for the ministry.

Bradford was noted for his godliness and his humility. When he saw anyone drunk or heard them swearing he would say, 'Lord, I have a drunken head; Lord, I have a swearing heart'. The familiar story is told that when seeing men taken out for execution he would exclaim, 'There, but for the grace of God, goes John Bradford.'

As one of Edward's six itinerant preachers Bradford had a notable ministry in his home area of south Lancashire and Cheshire for a brief two years. He also preached before the king in London, and one sermon that 'spared not the proudest' brought praise from none other than John Knox, himself no timid preacher. However, soon time ran out for Bradford, Latimer, Cranmer, Ridley and many other Reformers.

'Bloody Mary'

In July 1553 the sickly young king died at the age of sixteen and was succeeded by the ardently Catholic Queen Mary I (reign 1553 – 1558). Through the influence of the English Scriptures and a multitude of reformed preachers the gospel had spread, the clergy had been reformed and worship had been purified. The number of godly men over the next five years who were prepared to confirm their faith and seal their testimony to the truth of the Protestant gospel by their death confirms the reality of this spiritual work. On 6 February 1555 the fires of Smithfield began with the martyrdom of John Rogers, the Bible translator. During Mary's reign no less than 288 Protestants were burnt at the stake and over 800 others left the country in time to save their lives.

Prisoners in the Tower

Soon after Mary's accession Cranmer, Ridley, Latimer and Bradford were arrested and sent to the Tower. Initially they were kept apart and could only encourage one another by writing letters via their servants, but the failure of Sir Thomas Wyatt's rebellion in 1554 meant that the Tower became overcrowded with prisoners and the four were herded together in one cell. For two months they spent their time reading, studying the Scriptures and praying together. There they hammered out in clearer detail the biblical teaching on the Lord's Supper, which they knew would be the crucial issue when they came to trial. Then they were separated again; Cranmer, Ridley and Latimer were taken to Oxford for public disputations. There they were examined and imprisoned separately and, after show trials, duly declared heretics and condemned to death, but it was sixteen months before their time came.

Meanwhile England had returned to the Roman fold, and it was Bradford, in London, who died first. On 1 July 1555 he was taken to be burnt at Smithfield, watched and supported by a crowd so immense that the authorities became very anxious. Bradford and his fellow sufferer, a young man named Leaf, had their prayers cut short. After a last warning to England to repent and beware of idolatry Bradford encouraged his companion: 'Be of good comfort, brother, for we shall have a merry supper with the Lord this night.' And so they were burnt.

Latimer and Ridley's turn came on 16 October 1555. They had been kept apart since their trial and greeted each other with joy: 'Be of good heart, brother', said Ridley, 'for God will either assuage the fury of the flames or else strengthen us to abide it.' Then the two men were burnt as Latimer's memorable words rang out: 'Be of good comfort, Master Ridley, and play the man; we shall this day, by God's grace, light such a candle in England as I trust shall never be put out.' And so it has proved.

It was not until 21 March 1556 that Cranmer followed them to the fire. Initially he too stood firm in his denial of Roman errors and was condemned to be burnt. Then his courage, which had often seemed suspect, failed and he signed a paper denying the reformed doctrines that he had come to hold. In their moment of triumph the devil and his servants went too far. They decided to burn him in spite of his retraction, which they had printed together with a further one he was to make before his execution. However, on the day of his execution Cranmer received grace to return to his earlier profession. While fastened to the stake, instead of a recantation he uttered a denunciation of the pope as Antichrist and repeated his Protestant views against the mass. Then, as the fire rose he held his guilty right hand, which had signed the recantation, in the fire until death came.

Mary died in 1558, and when Elizabeth began her long reign the Reformation, though not complete by any means, was secure. The Scriptures, the gospel of salvation by faith alone, reformed doctrine and godly living had come to England. They had been tried in the fire and not found wanting.

Questions for discussion

1. *What do Tyndale's words about the ploughboy have to teach us about Bible translation, versions and preaching today?*

2. *How would you answer Roman Catholic claims that the Reformation was just a device to secure Henry VIII's divorce? How important was the role of rulers in the Reformation, both in Germany and in England? Does this in any way depreciate the work?*

3. *What is the difference between the weakness of a Peter and the treachery of a Judas? What help does this give in understanding Archbishop Cranmer?*

For further reading

** D. Daniell, *William Tyndale: a biography*, Yale University Press, 1994.

* J. M. D'Aubigné, *The Reformation in England*, The Banner of Truth Trust, 1962.

** A. G. Dickens, *The English Reformation*, Fontana, 1974.

* B. H. Edwards, *God's outlaw*, Evangelical Press, 1976.

M. L. Loane, *Masters of the English Reformation*, Church Bookroom Press, 1954.

** N. R. Needham, *2000 years of Christ's power*, Grace Publications, 2004, Part Three, pp.375-403.

* D. C. Wood, *Such a candle*, Evangelical Press, 1980.

If the trumpet does not sound a clear call, who will get ready for battle?
— 1 Corinthians 14:8

A certain reverential fear of my God who called me, and was pleased of his grace to make me a steward of divine mysteries, to whom I knew I must render an account, when I shall appear before his tribunal, of the manner in which I have discharged the embassy which he hath committed to me — had such a powerful effect as to make me utter so intrepidly whatever the Lord put into my mouth, without any respect of persons.
— John Knox (c. 1515 – 1572)

Fear him, ye saints, and you will then
*   Have nothing else to fear;*
Make you his service your delight,
*   Your wants shall be his care.*
— Nahum Tate (1625 – 1715) and Nicholas Brady (1659 – 1726)

8

A trumpet in Scotland

The condition of Scotland was every bit as bad as that of England before the Reformation reached its shores: ignorance, irreverence, greed and immorality ruled both land and church. One bishop who rebuked a subordinate for preaching every Sunday gave thanks 'that I never knew what the Old and New Testament was', declaring that he would stick to his breviary and book of ceremonies. While priests who married were sometimes condemned to death, David Beaton, the Archbishop of St Andrews and Primate of Scotland, a so-called celibate priest, fathered at least eleven sons and three daughters.

As in England the situation was not entirely black. The Lollards greatly influenced the west of Scotland, both directly and via Bohemia. They prepared the way for the real Reformation, not least by urging that the people should be given the Bible in their own language. In spite of severe punishment and even martyrdom this 'heresy' persisted into the sixteenth century. It was then that students began to bring back from the Continent the ideas and books of both John Hus and Martin Luther, in spite of acts of Parliament forbidding the importing of such 'filth and vice'.

In 1582 'Master Patrick' Hamilton was burnt at the stake as a heretic; he had learned the true gospel at Marburg and returned to Scotland in 1527 to preach it, even at the risk of his life. About twenty others were put to death for their faith, including George Wishart. Wishart was born about 1513 and taught at Montrose Academy. For teaching his pupils to read the Greek New Testament he was charged with heresy. He fled to England, where he was befriended by Latimer, and then to the Continent but soon came back to his native land. On his return Wishart introduced the method of lecturing on a passage of Scripture, often preaching in the open air. He moved around the country and was often in great danger, both from assassins and from the plague (he insisted on preaching in Dundee where it had broken out). In 1546 he was betrayed, tried and executed, after praying for his enemies and pardoning his executioner, who had been moved to ask for his forgiveness.

During these preaching tours Wishart spent five weeks in Lothian; he had a constant companion who carried a two-handed sword to defend the preacher. This self-appointed bodyguard wanted to accompany Wishart from Haddington on the night of his arrest, but the preacher told him to return to his pupils, saying, 'One is sufficient for a sacrifice.' This man, one of many who were stirred by Wishart's preaching and martyrdom, was John Knox.

John Knox

The minister

The murder of Cardinal Beaton also occurred in 1546, and that event aroused further opposition to those of reformed views. Many took shelter in St Andrews Castle and these soon included John Knox (1514 – 1572), who took his pupils there for their safety. By this time, Knox, a native of Haddington, was probably in his early thirties, a graduate of St Andrews University and an ordained priest. He seems to have become a Protestant by 1543, but we know nothing of his conversion except that when asking on his deathbed for John 17 to be read to him, he described the chapter as 'where I cast my first anchor'.

At first Knox concentrated on teaching the three boys, but he also read a catechism on which he examined them publicly and lectured on John's Gospel in the Castle chapel. When John Rough was preaching in the castle and encountered opposition from a certain Dean Annand, he asked for help from Knox, who provided him with written arguments. As a consequence the leaders in the castle urged him to work with Rough as a spiritual leader, but he refused saying, 'that he could not run where God had not called him'. So they arranged for Rough to preach a sermon on the election of ministers, after which he issued a public call on behalf of the congregation for Knox to accept the office of minister!

This put Knox in a most difficult position and his immediate response was to burst into tears and withdraw. In effect he was being asked to take up Wishart's mantle, with all that it implied. A few days later he found himself compelled to challenge Annand, which he did by preaching against him from Daniel 7:24-25. The reaction of his hearers to this sermon convinced him that God had, in fact, called him to this ministry, and he took up the position with characteristic determination. Some said that whereas others 'lopped off the branches of papistry', Knox had struck 'at the roots to destroy the whole'. Other declared, 'Master George [Wishart] spake never so plainly, and yet he was burnt; even so will he be.' They were wrong, but they had rightly discerned that Knox's clarity and resoluteness would bring him into many dangers.

Exile

Rough and Knox continued preaching with great success among both the garrison and the townsfolk until Rough left for England. However, it was not long before the national authorities, with their Roman sympathies, enlisted French support to end the siege of St Andrews. The occupants were taken prisoner and Knox, along with others who were not gentry, was sent as a slave to a French galley, the *Notre Dame*. He endured great hardships chained to an oar with hardened criminals as companions for nineteen months and made at least two trips to Scotland in this fashion. On one trip he saw in the distance the steeple of St Andrews Church where he had first preached and expressed this conviction: 'How weak that ever I now appear... I shall not depart this life, till that my tongue shall glorify his godly name in that same place.'

Those in charge tried to compel the prisoners to conform to Roman Catholicism, but Knox led them in resisting by putting on hoods or hats when forced to attend mass and suffering 'torments' and 'sobs of my heart' in return.

On one occasion an attempt was made to compel the Protestants to kiss an image of the Virgin Mary. Knox refused and when the statue was placed in his hands he threw it into the river saying, 'Let our Lady now save herself; she is light enough, let her learn to swim.' No further attempts were made!

In England

In March 1549, perhaps through the intervention of friends or the now-Protestant English authorities, Knox was set free. He went to England where Archbishop Cranmer, under the godly Edward VI, was busy reforming the Church of England. Here he rejoined his former friends but now as their leader. His time in the galleys had undoubtedly strengthened him spiritually as well as clarified his ideas; he emerged with a strong sense of God's calling to destroy Romanism. England at this time was deeply divided between those who supported Cranmer and those who resisted all Protestant innovations. So when Knox was appointed as minister of the gospel in Berwick, on the border with Scotland, he went to an area that was strongly Catholic under the Bishop of Durham, Cuthbert Tunstall, and where there were many soldiers who had only recently been fighting the Scottish 'vermin'.

Here for the first time Knox had to work as an ordinary pastor of the flock and had time to recover from the physical effects of the galleys and also to study both the Scriptures and the commentaries of men like Calvin. Thus he developed his Reformation theology and learned to express it in 'the blowing of my Master's trumpet', as he described his preaching. He also had an important and comforting pastoral ministry, reassuring the many Protestants that they were accepted of God without the Roman ceremonies. One of these troubled souls was Elizabeth Bowes, wife of the Captain of Norham Castle and mother of Marjory, later to be Knox's wife.

In 1551 he was moved to Newcastle, a far more important sphere, where he became involved in public affairs and was appointed as one of the king's chaplains. In 1552 he was taken to London by the new effective ruler, the Duke of Northumberland.

THE BLACK RUBRIC

In London Knox found a very different and difficult situation, with a radical group led by John Hooper trying to push Cranmer and Ridley along more speedily. Taking Hooper's side in a debate over the new Prayer Book, Knox was largely instrumental in securing from Cranmer the statement that kneeling at the Lord's Supper was not worship of the elements but simply reverence. This statement was printed and pasted in already printed copies of the Prayer Book and has been known by its opponents ever since as the Black Rubric.

Northumberland's support decreased when the Reformer refused the bishopric of Rochester because he did not wish to become too involved in this unsatisfactory situation, but the noble still defended him when some ardent Catholics in Newcastle took exception to his preaching.

In 1553 Knox was removed to London but not before he had the joy of welcoming his brother from Scotland, now a Protestant, and also of becoming betrothed to Marjory Bowes, then about nineteen years old. For a while he preached in the neighbourhood of Amersham, but when Edward died and Mary took England back into the Catholic fold Knox's friends insisted that he escape the ensuing persecution and leave the country. This he did in January 1554, grieving over the state of the land and aware of much opposition from Marjory's family to his proposed marriage.

In Geneva

From Dieppe he visited Geneva where he consulted Calvin, Viret and Bullinger, mainly about female rulers and the question of rebellion. Later he returned to Geneva to study but, under pressure from Calvin, accepted an invitation to become minister to a congregation of English exiles in Frankfurt. After many 'troubles', especially in debates with those who supported the Prayer Book and wanted a church with 'an English face', Knox was rejected and expelled. In spite of misrepresentations from the Anglicans at Frankfurt, Calvin expressed his opinion: 'Master Knox was neither godly nor brotherly dealt withall.' It may be that this unhappy experience finally convinced Knox that he could do nothing more for the English church and that he should devote his attention, in due course, to reforming the church in Scotland.

Knox stayed in Geneva from 1555 to 1559. Opposition to Calvin had at last collapsed and there were many groups of refugees there. Knox concentrated on his studies in what he called, '*the most perfect school of Christ that ever was in the earth since the days of the apostles*'.

He left to spend a year in Scotland where he found that Mary of Lorraine, the Queen Mother, was ruling the country with French support. This alliance with her French relatives irritated the Scottish nobility, arousing opposition, but, more important, the Reformation was spreading. To his surprise Knox found the masses of ordinary people 'night and day sobbing and groaning for the bread of life'. A preaching tour was followed by private consultations that had a great influence on many of the leaders. After losing one debate with Knox about the lawfulness of Protestants attending mass, Maitland admitted, 'I see perfectly that our shifts [excuses] will serve nothing before God, seeing that they stand in so small stead before man.'

Thousands under the influence of Lollard teaching and Wishart's testimony were ready to defend the Protestant cause, and the nobles began to realize that they must stand firm for the gospel. Knox was summoned to appear before the bishops in Edinburgh, but when he arrived, supported by the nobility, the bishops, like the prophets of the grove faced by Elijah, thought better of it and failed to appear.

'Privy kirks' had been formed, which now began to take shape like the congregations in Geneva. Although Knox encouraged these moves, much of it had taken place during his absence from Scotland; there was a genuine work of the Spirit in progress.

During this period Knox visited northern England and was married to Marjory Bowes, who then preceded him to Dieppe with her mother. On his return to Geneva Knox found that the English refugees had established a reformed church to which he ministered for the next two years. This group prepared the Geneva Version of the Bible that was so popular with the Puritans. They also returned to England after the accession of Elizabeth in 1558 to continue the struggle to reform the Church of England.

During this period also, Knox clarified his views on the subject of rebellion, which were so influential in the following decades, and published his *First Blast of the Trumpet against the Monstrous Regiment of Women*. This book – 'against the unnatural rule of women' – was aimed primarily at Mary Tudor of England and Mary of Lorraine, the Queen Mother in Scotland, but Elizabeth, not unnaturally, took great exception to it in due course.

It was to Scotland that Knox's thoughts increasingly turned, so when most of the English exiles returned after Elizabeth's accession he decided to return to his own land. He had, in fact, made an earlier attempt at the end of 1557, but the Lords of the Congregation who had invited him decided that the time was not opportune and he got no further than Dieppe. While he was there over the winter he preached with such great power and success that the few converts meeting in secret were transformed into a congregation of nearly 800 taking communion in public! When he came back to Dieppe in 1559 he hoped to return through England, but Elizabeth refused him permission so he sailed directly to Scotland.

Back in Scotland

Since his abortive attempt to return in 1557 the situation had changed considerably. Knox's written rebuke to the nobles for favouring the proposed marriage of the child queen, Mary, to Francis, the Dauphin of France, had convicted them and stirred them to enter into a covenant to promote a true reformation in the land. The response of Mary of Lorraine to this was surprisingly mild, but the Catholic clergy reacted violently by arresting, trying and burning at the stake for heresy an aged priest, a deed that roused the Protestants to new fervour. A St Giles's Day procession resulted in the image of St Giles being stolen, 'drowned' and burned and a substitute image being smashed on the road. As soon, however, as Mary was safely married to Francis, now co-sovereign, the Queen Regent took steps to crush the Protestants. She ordered all the Protestant preachers to appear before her on 10 May 1559.

On 2 May Knox landed at Leith and was immediately accepted as leader, even by the proud nobles, the Lords of the Congregation. Their response to Mary's command had been to gather in force at Perth, though without armour, ready to march in support of the preachers. Knox joined them there and when the preachers who refused to obey the regent were outlawed, feelings ran high. Knox, whose outlawing in 1556 had been renewed, preached against the mass as idolatry and what he called 'the rascal multitude' ran amok and destroyed not only images but also churches and monasteries. Mary naturally regarded these gatherings of soldiers as rebellion, but they asserted that they were only concerned with the reforming of religion, although they did also want to rid Scotland of the French. She determined to attack the few Protestants at Perth, but they were reinforced to such an extent that she had to negotiate a treaty with them. This she broke almost immediately, causing even more of the nobility to desert her cause.

The Congregation, originally only a religious organization, was now a political force. After entering into a solemn covenant they set out for St Andrews where Knox preached in the cathedral in spite of threats from the archbishop. Within a few days the majority of the citizens, who a week earlier had shown no enthusiasm for reformation, joined the Protestant movement, followed shortly by many of the Catholic clergy. Such was the power of Knox in the pulpit.

The Queen Regent played for time; while Knox was looking for help from England she secured the aid of the French since Mary, Queen of Scots, was now also Queen of France as the wife of Francis II. French soldiers, together with a papal legate and learned 'doctors' to deal with the heresy, arrived in Scotland. The Lords of the Congregation deposed the regent, ostensibly on the grounds of her unconstitutional government, and besieged her and the French forces in Leith. In fact, the Scots were outnumbered and after several defeats morale began to suffer and desertions began. It was at this time that Knox's faith and exhortation proved vital. Preaching in Stirling he asserted,

> I no more doubt that this our dolour, confusion and fear shall be turned into joy, honour and boldness, than that I doubt that God gave victory to the Israelites over the Benjamites... For as it is the eternal truth of God, so shall it once prevail, however for a time it be impugned.

This sermon stirred the Protestants to greater heroism and proved to be a turning point in the Reformation. (This is truly a message for today also!) Knox's voice, wrote the English ambassador of another such sermon, 'is able in one hour to put more life in us than four hundred trumpets continually blustering in our ears'.

After one French victory the Regent Mary sneered, 'Where is now John Knox's God? My God is now stronger than his!' However, it was the arrival of an English fleet that settled the issue. Elizabeth, understandably doubtful of Knox and real Protestantism, had eventually decided where her own interests lay. After much wearisome fighting and negotiating and the death of the Queen Regent, apparently penitent and trusting in the death of Christ, a peace treaty was settled in June 1560. Parliament assembled with greater numbers than ever before, and in due course the Protestant ministers were instructed to draw up a confession of faith for the nation. Knox and a few others presented this within a few days, and it was approved with little opposition, marking the beginning of a new era in Scotland's history. Parliament confirmed what the people had already adopted. Queen Mary, in Paris, refused to ratify these measures, but they were put into effect all the same, and on her return to Scotland in 1561 she agreed not to upset this settlement.

Next, the church established in law had to be established in practice, with a constitution and administration. This was done in the *Book of Discipline*. It provided for ministers, of whom there were only twelve at this time, and superintendents, who were not bishops but ordinary ministers charged with extending and establishing the church throughout the land. As well as ecclesiastical discipline, the right administration of the sacraments, education and poor relief were dealt with. Knox drew on his experience from the Continent and was largely, but not entirely, responsible for this work. It is, perhaps, important to note a comment by the ardently Catholic Bishop of Ross on these proceedings: 'Yet the clemency of the heretic [i.e. Protestant] nobles must not be left unmentioned, since at that time they exiled few Catholics on the score of religion, imprisoned fewer, and put none to death.'

Knox now turned to his primary work as a preacher and pastor, ministering at St Giles in Edinburgh where he remained for nearly the rest of his life. Soon, however, the clouds began to gather once more. Tragedy struck with the death of his wife at the end of 1560, leaving him with sons aged two and three. Then in December the nobles refused to accept the *Book of Discipline*, especially the financial provisions for the ministry, which would have prevented them from profiting from the Reformation as they had hoped. Also in December Francis II of France died, which encouraged Catholics with the hope of Mary returning to Scotland. When she arrived at Leith in 1561 it was inevitable that there would be a confrontation with Knox. He had good reason to fear that if she and her French supporters gained control it would not be long before others shared the fate of George Wishart and the more recent French Protestant martyrs.

Mary, Queen of Scots

Modern romantic opinion has always sided with the beautiful young queen by accusing the Reformer of bullying intolerance in his dealings with her. In fact he only appeared before her at her command and it was she who constantly tried to humiliate him. She wanted not merely to celebrate mass privately but to impose her own French version of absolute monarchy on the nation. Whereas most of the politicians were falling over each other in their attempts to gain the queen's favour, Knox realized what her real aim was and continually 'thundered out of the pulpit' against the mass. So within three weeks of her arrival Knox was summoned to appear before the queen.

She accused him of writing against her in his *First Blast of the Trumpet*, and, although denying any rebellion on his part, he did assert that persecuting rulers might lawfully be resisted. She declared her intention of defending 'the Kirk of Rome, for, I think, it is the true Kirk of God', but Knox described it as 'that Roman harlot'.

When the queen tried to appeal to her conscience, Knox replied that 'Conscience requires knowledge and I fear that right knowledge ye have none.' When she tried to refer to the matter of the difficulty of scriptural interpretation, saying, 'Whom shall I believe and who shall be judge?', he answered without hesitation, 'Ye shall believe God, that plainly speaketh in his Word; and farther than the Word teacheth you, ye shall neither believe the one nor the other.' Mary's reaction was to shed tears of frustration that a monarch should be opposed in this way. Knox left with the conviction that she was possessed of 'a proud mind, a crafty wit and an indurate heart against God and his truth'.

As Mary toured the country encouraging the Catholics and celebrating mass wherever she went, Knox declared from the pulpit of St Giles that 'One mass was more fearful unto him than if ten thousand armed enemies were landed in any part of the realm of purpose to suppress the whole religion.' In fact mass began to be celebrated publicly and Mary denied the right of the General Assembly to meet. Nevertheless, as the lairds and burgesses were supporting the ministers, some financial provision was made for the church in spite of the nobles who favoured Mary. The ministers and superintendents were about their work, and the gospel was increasingly being proclaimed. But the battle was far from over.

Mary versus Knox

In cunning and unscrupulous ways Mary continued the fight. While professing to allow her Protestant subjects liberty, even knighting some of them and imprisoning some Catholics who had celebrated mass (although they were released almost immediately), she carried on negotiations with her French Catholic relatives and even with the pope. To her credit she resisted the urgings of the pope to 'follow the example of Queen Mary of England, now departed in Christ' by burning Protestants. Nevertheless she schemed so successfully that Parliament failed to ratify the *Book of Discipline*. Once again it was Knox who saw beneath the veneer to detect the devoted and ardent Roman Catholic.

On at least three further occasions he was summoned before the queen where she attempted to browbeat him. In reply he was always courteous but much firmer than she liked or was accustomed to. When Mary held a ball at Holyrood Palace after hearing of the murder of Protestants in France, he assumed that the two events were connected and preached against balls in general. When he appeared before Mary to answer for this, he maintained that he had spoken only in general, but when she asked him to reserve his criticisms for her private hearing he insisted that his was a public ministry. He left her angry presence saying to those who marvelled at his courage, 'I have looked in the faces of many angry men, and yet have not been afraid above measure.' Another interview at Lochleven apparently ended amicably, although Knox had taken the opportunity to warn Mary that if she expected obedience from her subjects she must provide them with 'protection and defence against evildoers'.

On hearing of the negotiations for her marriage to the Catholic heir of Philip II of Spain, Knox inevitably preached against it and equally inevitably was summoned to the royal presence at Holyrood. She complained bitterly that her marriage was nothing to do with him and, in any case, who did he think he was in the commonwealth? This produced his famous answer: 'A subject born within the same, madam. And albeit I am neither earl, lord nor baron within it, yet has God made me how abject that ever I am in your eyes a profitable member within the same.' Mary burst into tears when he repeated his warning against the marriage, and his attempts to comfort her only made matters worse; he was dismissed.

Finally, towards the end of 1563 Knox was summoned before the council and charged with treason for obeying the assembly's instructions to watch for injustice. He had no supporters there and was urged to confess and ask for mercy. Mary thought that she was about to gain the revenge she had sworn at Holyrood to achieve. She laughed and told the sycophants around her, 'Yon man made me greet [cry]... I will see if I can gar him greet [make him cry].' However, she failed to crush the Reformer, and the council acquitted him. Knox himself recorded, 'That night was neither dancing nor fiddling in the court, for Madam was disappointed of her purpose, which was to have had John Knox in her will by vote of the nobility.'

Marriages and conspiracies

Nevertheless, Knox was now completely alienated from the nobles as Mary's rule became more and more dictatorial. He was not entirely alone: the General Assembly gave him loyal support and he had married again in 1563.

JOHN WELSH

Knox's second wife, Margaret, was over thirty years younger, but Mary's indignation at the union was not on account of this of this but because Margaret was of royal blood, and, therefore, John Knox was now distantly related by marriage to the queen herself!

Margaret bore three daughters to Knox, one of whom married the famous and godly John Welsh. In 1621 Knox's daughter entered into a disputation with James VI (James I of England) on his behalf. On discovering whose daughter she was the king exclaimed, 'Knox and Welsh! The devil never made such a match as that', to which she replied that they had, indeed, never asked the devil for his advice. The king also expressed his relief that only Knox's daughters were alive because, 'If they had been three lads, I had never enjoyed my three kingdoms in peace.'

Mary's marriages dominate the rest of the story, which led to the final official establishment of the reformed church in Scotland. While constantly plotting to strengthen the Catholic cause and overthrow Knox and his friends, Mary allowed herself to be governed by her emotions and this proved fatal to her. She was busily engaged in scheming with Philip II of Spain, who would literally do anything to prosper his church and was appointing more and more Catholic officials. Early in 1565 Henry, Lord Darnley, son of the Earl of Lennox, returned to Scotland. To Mary he seemed to be the ideal husband. Not only was he a Catholic, but he was also next after herself in line for the English throne.

Knox rallied support against such a marriage with an 'infidel', but others, led by the Earl of Moray, went further and rebelled. Mary and Darnley were married in July and spent much of their 'honeymoon' chasing Moray and his fellow rebels around the countryside until they eventually escaped into England. Incidentally, the modern sentimentalized picture of poor Mary being bullied by a fierce Knox does not square very well with the contemporary record of the queen taking part personally in this chase, 'in a steel cap with pistols at her saddlebow'. Knox continued preaching against Mary and Darnley's rule. On one occasion the king, as Darnley considered himself even though Mary refused to give him the 'crown matrimonial', was present and took exception to Knox's words. Knox was banned from preaching while the queen was in Edinburgh, but the city council backed Knox and he continued his ministry.

Mary carried on scheming, encouraged by her new Italian secretary, David Riccio. Darnley became very jealous of him and plotted with certain disaffected lords to murder Riccio. This they did in Mary's presence, leaving Darnley's dagger in his back. Mary succeeded in separating Darnley from the rest and all the conspirators betrayed each other. Mary continued to allow Catholic ecclesiastics into the country and encouraged them to celebrate mass, but Darnley was now in disgrace. He was not in attendance in June when Mary gave birth to a son, James, nor was he there in December when the infant heir to the throne was baptized with full Catholic ceremonial. Arrangements for this occasion were in the hands of the 'Protestant' and unscrupulous Earl of Bothwell, with whom Mary was now infatuated.

At this time Knox had left Edinburgh, very depressed. All his predictions of Mary's insincerity and determination to restore

Catholicism were coming true and he felt like Elijah under the juniper tree, wishing that he might die. He said he was, 'taking goodnight at the world and at all the fasherie [trouble] of the same'. The General Assembly of 1566 gave him permission to spend six months in the north of England visiting his sons and members of his former congregations. Thus he was not present when Darnley was murdered and his house blown up. Mary and Bothwell were both suspected of the murder, but Bothwell was put in charge of his own trial and, not unnaturally, acquitted. Soon Bothwell gained a divorce from his wife of only sixteen months and married Mary. By prearrangement, he carried her off to Dunbar Castle where they went through a Protestant ceremony.

All this was more than anyone would stand for, lords or people, Catholic or Protestant, and in July 1567 Mary was forced into a humiliating abdication in favour of the young prince. The Earl of Moray was brought back as regent. Knox, who had returned only in June, preached at the young king's coronation as James VI and then, with the support of the General Assembly, demanded the death penalty for Mary for murder and adultery. Parliament, meeting in December, condemned Bothwell, imprisoned Mary and ratified arrangements to establish the reformed church on a legal and financial basis.

Apparent triumph

At this point of apparent success and triumph, when Knox again looked forward to devoting himself to spiritual matters in church extension and pastoral care, fresh troubles arose. Mary escaped from prison, was defeated in battle and then fled to England where she lived for nineteen years, a thorn in the side of both Elizabeth and Scotland. There were constant attempts to restore her to the throne, especially after the assassination of the godly Moray in 1570. At his funeral Knox preached with such fervour that 3,000 were moved to tears. The Hamiltons, Maitland of Lethington and even Knox's former companion in the galleys, Kirkcaldy of Grange, fought against the king's party. The Catholic Lennox became regent and Kirkcaldy virtually controlled the whole of Edinburgh from the castle.

Knox was again in despair, longing only to die; he signed a letter to a friend in England: 'John Knox, with one foot in the grave'. He was weakened by a stroke, threats of violence and attacks on his integrity and eventually had to yield to his friends' pleas that he should leave Edinburgh. For over a year he was in exile in St Andrews. The Archbishop of St Andrews, a Hamilton, confessed to the murder of Moray and had been executed, so Knox was able to preach on Daniel in the parish church.

James Melville, one of the next generation of reformed leaders, went as a student to hear Knox preach. He described how Knox, after a quiet beginning showing his age and weakness, would then become 'so active and vigorous that he was like to ding the pulpit in blads [knock it to pieces] and then fly out of it'. He began to take notes but found that when Knox came to apply the Word, 'he made me so to grew [shudder] and tremble that I could not hold a pen to write'. Melville also tells how Knox would visit St Leonard's College and sit outside advising the students and exhorting them to 'stand by the good cause'.

During this year some of the queen's supporters killed the regent, and the Earl of Mar took over, with the Earl of Morton as the real power in the land. There were moves to appoint bishops and archbishops again, mainly so that their noble patrons could lay their hands on the income of the offices. Knox preached against the whole idea at the induction of a new Archbishop of St Andrews and then refused to take part in the induction itself. He continually denounced the greed and ungodliness of both parties for neither side had any real interest in the gospel, but he still supported the party of the child king.

Last days in Edinburgh

In 1572 Knox was recalled to Edinburgh, insisting on his right to preach as he liked in St Giles and to denounce those whom he regarded as immoral or enemies of the Reformation. To those who objected to this he later replied from his deathbed:

God knows that my mind was always free from hatred to the persons of those against whom I denounced the heavy judgements of God. In the mean time, I cannot deny but that I felt the greatest abhorrence of the sin in which they indulged; still, however, keeping this as one thing in view, that if it were possible I might gain them to the Lord.

This was his attitude also when from that deathbed he spoke solemn words to Morton, soon to become regent, and sent his new ministerial colleague, John Lawson, to plead with Kirkcaldy of Grange to repent. While waiting for execution and remembering Knox's warnings, Kirkcaldy called him a 'true servant of God' and was comforted to be told that Knox believed that God would have mercy on him. Similarly dying in shame, Morton lamented that he had not taken more notice of Knox's words.

Knox arrived back in Edinburgh at the end of August 1572, just before news of the terrible St Bartholomew's Eve massacre arrived in the capital. This treacherous and barbaric murder of 20,000 French Protestants by the Catholic supporters of Charles IX horrified both England and France and was partly responsible for the downfall, after Knox's death, of the queen's party. Morton now kept the land at peace, ruling ruthlessly and efficiently. Figurehead bishops were appointed so that the nobles could make money, but the General Assembly kept control of the church. Great progress had been made from the twelve gospel preachers of 1560 to 500 reformed ministers in 1573, with another 500 parishes served by exhorters and readers. The horizon was not without clouds, but at least the church could busy itself with preaching the gospel and caring for the flock. All this, however, takes us beyond Knox's lifetime.

St Giles was now too large for the frail old man's voice so he had to preach in the Tolbooth instead. He did visit St Giles once more to preach at John Lawson's induction, after which a great crowd of people accompanied him back to his home. Two days later he was taken seriously ill and did not leave the house again, although on the Friday he got up, thinking it was Sunday, and intending to preach.

Visitors thronged his bedroom – the office bearers of St Giles, ministers and ordinary folk – but his mind, according to his servant Richard Bannatyne, was always on the state of the church in Scotland, and for this he prayed. On Monday, 24 November 1572, he asked his wife to read from 1 Corinthians 15 and then from John 17 'where I cast my first anchor' and died before the end of the day. The lords and members of Parliament accompanied him to his burial place, headed by the new regent, the Earl of Morton, who pronounced his epitaph: *'Here lies one who neither feared nor flattered any flesh.'*

The one whom 'God has made both the first planter and the chief waterer of his kirk amongst us' was gone, but the Reformation, being of God, continued.

Questions for discussion

1. *How was Knox prepared, in the providence of God, for his work as a Reformer in Scotland? Why is it significant that he was unable to return to Scotland until 1559?*

2. *Was Knox right and wise to oppose Mary, Queen of Scots, publicly? Is it true, as he asserted, that 'persecuting rulers might be lawfully resisted'?*

3. *If Knox feared 'one mass' more than 'ten thousand armed enemies', what should our attitude be? What enemies does the evangelical church face today that Knox did not have to deal with? What can we learn from his example?*

For further reading

** N. R. Needham, *2000 years of Christ's power*, Grace Publications, 2004, Part Three, pp.404-426.

** W. S. Reid, *Trumpeter of God*, Baker, 1982.

A. M. Renwick, *The story of the Scottish Reformation*, Inter-Varsity Fellowship, 1960.

* E. Whitley, *Plain Mr. Knox*, Scottish Reformation Society, 1972.

Go, my people, enter your rooms
and shut the doors behind you;
hide yourselves for a little while
until his wrath has passed by.

— Isaiah 26:20

I have followed holiness; I have taught the truth; I have been most in
the main things.

— Donald Cargill (c. 1619 – 1681)

I've wrestled on towards heaven,
'Gainst storm and wind and tide;
Now, like a weary traveller
That leans upon his guide,
Amid the shades of evening,
While sinks life's lingering sand,
I hail the glory dawning
From Immanuel's land.

— Anne Ross Cousin (1824 – 1906), based on words by Samuel Rutherford
(c. 1600 – 1661)

9

For Christ and the Covenant

Robert Bruce

During the year that Knox spent in St Andrews, from July 1571, one of the students at the university was Robert Bruce (1554 – 1631). His father was descended from the king, Robert the Bruce, and he was also of royal blood on his mother's side, a devout and bigoted Catholic. Robert, born around 1554, began his studies in 1568, graduated in 1571 and became a master of arts in the following year; from then on he was usually known as Master Robert Bruce. There is no evidence that Bruce actually heard Knox preach, but James Melville, whose impressions of the Reformer's preaching we have seen already, was his great friend and colleague in later days. Bruce took over the leadership of the reformed cause in Scotland from James's uncle, Andrew Melville.

After leaving the university Bruce began to practise law but soon turned from the path his father had planned for him to enter the ministry. He records, 'I was first called by grace before I obeyed my calling to the ministry. He made me first a Christian before he made me a minister. I resisted long my calling to the ministry; ten years at least I never leaped on horseback nor alighted, but with a justly accusing conscience.' His conscience was finally healed on 31 August 1581 when he lay wakeful in his home at Airth Castle. After a terrible conflict with the accusations of Satan he wrote,

> I confessed, restored God to his glory, and craved God's mercy for the merits of Christ: yea, appealed sore to his mercy, purchased to me by the blood, death and passion of Christ. This court of justice, holden upon my soul, turned of the bottomless mercy of God into a court of mercy to me: for that same night, ere the day dawned or ever the sun rose, he restrained these furies and these outcries of my justly accusing conscience, and enabled me to rise in the morning.

Significantly, Bruce became a most skilful physician of troubled consciences.

Bruce confided to James Melville that he would rather 'go through a fire of brimstone half a mile long' than return to his burdensome resistance to God's call, but entering the ministry proved difficult in practice. His father agreed to his change of direction, but his mother refused her consent until he gave up all claim on the family estate. This he did: 'I did willingly, cast my clothes from me, my vain and glorious apparel, sent my horse to the fair and emptied my hands of all.' In 1583 he was back in St Andrews as a student of theology under Andrew Melville as principal and James Melville as professor of Hebrew. These men brought light and learning to the church in Scotland that amazed their contemporaries, and Bruce made great progress in his studies. 'So it pleased God', wrote James Melville, 'to begin to train up and mould that most notable preacher for the time of restitution of his decayed and captive Jerusalem.'

The times were certainly 'decayed'. The country was ravaged by the plague and both James and Andrew Melville were forced to leave the country because James VI tried to reintroduce episcopacy and reassert the royal supremacy over the church. Bruce, who had stood with the Melvilles against the king, also withdrew for a time. Soon a reaction set in and the Melvilles and Bruce were able to return to St Andrews, where Andrew and Bruce preached in the college chapel while the king's archbishop, who had been excommunicated by the assembly, preached to a smaller number in the parish church.

In the following year, 1587, Andrew Melville took Bruce to the assembly in Edinburgh where he was given a call to the pulpit of Knox's old church of St Giles. Typically, Bruce was in an agony of indecision having also received a call to St Andrews where he would have preferred to go: 'for I had no taste for preaching before the Court, for well I knew that the Court and I would never agree'. However, he went to St Giles but refused ordination because he found within him 'such a mountain of iniquity dividing between his Majesty's comfortable presence and me, that I thought it was not his Majesty's pleasure that I should take the full burden upon me till the impediment were removed'. This Majesty's name was not James; James and Bruce never did agree after the early days.

Bruce never was formally ordained with the laying on of hands, but his brethren overcame his scruples at the Lord's Supper. Bruce was present while a fellow minister served several tables before leaving the church. The elders then called on Bruce to carry on the work. This he did, accepting it as ordination and afterwards refused to submit to any ceremony that would invalidate all his earlier ministerial acts. In later years this was to bring him much trouble.

The man of prayer

For the next thirteen years Robert Bruce ministered in St Giles, exercising his considerable pastoral gifts as well as preaching with great power. One hearer testified, 'He made always an earthquake upon his hearers and rarely preached but to a weeping auditory.' He was usually quite brief and his great ambition was to 'make it clear'. Much of the secret of his power must have lain in his private spiritual life.

One who knew him well wrote, 'Mr Bruce was a great wrestler who had more than ordinary familiarity with his Master. He was very short in prayer when others were present, but every sentence was like a strong bolt shot up to heaven. I have heard him say that he wearied when others were long in prayer, but, being alone, he spent much time in wrestling and prayer.'

Shortly before his death Bruce was praying in his home with some who had come to tell him about the troubles of the church. As he prayed they were all unusually affected, as were others who were elsewhere in the house. One who was present said, 'Oh! What a strange man is this, for he knocked down the Spirit of God upon us all.' This referred to Bruce's habit of knocking on the table with his fingers when growing earnest in prayer.

In the early days of his ministry in Edinburgh Bruce was very much in the king's favour; in fact, when James spent six months out of the country bringing back his bride, the preacher shared with the council in ruling the land and its peace was largely attributed to his efficiency. James was very pleased and rewarded him with a pension; Bruce anointed the new queen and preached at the coronation. The king had a special 'royal box', a gallery in St Giles, and often heard Bruce preach. This, however, was not always to his liking as the preacher never minced his words.

On one occasion the king, as was his notorious custom, began talking to his courtiers during the sermon. After pausing twice Bruce turned to the royal gallery and said, 'It is said to have been an expression of the wisest of kings, "When the lion roars, all the beasts of the field are quiet"; the Lion of the tribe of Judah is now roaring in the voice of his gospel, and it becomes all the petty kings of the earth to be silent.'

The King

These Reformers were utterly resolute in their stand for the rights of their King. Andrew Melville once informed James, 'There are two kings in Scotland: the one, King James, the other Jesus Christ, of whose kingdom James is but a subject and a member.'

When the king followed the deceitful methods of his mother, Mary, Queen of Scots, and tried to bring back various Catholic lords, the church, led by Bruce, opposed him. James took the opportunity afforded by a riot in the streets of Edinburgh to harass the ministers. Bruce and others fled to England for safety and were only allowed back to their pulpits eight months later. The king appointed ecclesiastical commissioners with quasi-episcopal powers to run the church and further conflict ensued over Bruce's lack of formal ordination. Bruce won this particular battle, but relations with the king grew worse and he dishonestly withdrew the pension he had granted Bruce years before.

In 1600 'the matter of Gowrie' occurred, the death of the young Earl of Gowrie and his brother allegedly during an attempt to murder the king. Many doubted the king's version of the affair, but it was Bruce, with his 'pernickety' conscience, who refused to say publicly that he was 'fully persuaded' of the king's innocence. To the amazement of the Earl of Mar, Bruce maintained that he could not use these words even about the articles of his faith. Bruce's answer to the earl's protest may give us all cause to think. He said he was not, 'fully' persuaded, 'not, my lord, as I should be; if you and I both were fully persuaded that there were a hell, we would do otherwise than we do!'

Exile in Inverness

James was determined to keep Bruce out of the pulpit of St Giles and in 1605 he was exiled to Inverness. In spite of the king's ban he preached there for the next eight years, but only a few seem to have responded to his ministry at this stage. James persisted in his attempts to restore episcopacy in his northern kingdom – he was now also James I of England – and both Melvilles and John Welsh of Ayr died in exile as a result of his efforts. In 1613 Bruce was allowed to return to his estate at Kinnaird. Many came to see him there and he preached in the church that he had restored at nearby Larbert. He had many trials, such as, ill health, the loss of his wife and harassment from the rulers, but the Lord was with him and in the dark lonely nights he could cry out, 'I am the happiest man that ever was born, happy that ever I served God.'

Many young men came to sit at his feet, but in 1622, after a necessary but ill-advised visit to Edinburgh, he was once more banished to the north. 'We will have no more popish pilgrimages to Kinnaird', said James. However, before setting out on horseback for Inverness Bruce appeared to be in a kind of trance for fifteen minutes. When asked what he had been doing he replied, 'I was receiving my commission from my Master to go to Inverness, and he gave it me himself, before I set my foot in the stirrup, and thither I go to sow a seed in Inverness that shall not be rooted out for many ages.'

And so it proved. During the next two years Bruce resumed his preaching in and around Inverness, and the warring Highland clans came with their chiefs to hear, believe and be reconciled with God and each other. One man is said to have offered Bruce two cows, 'if you'll agree me and God'. When the Covenanters came to the north a few years later they found their chief support in the area covered by Bruce's ministry.

Bruce was allowed south for his daughter's marriage in 1624, and with James's death in 1625 he was permitted to stay at Kinnaird until the end of his life. Although he still, rather pathetically, regarded himself as the true minister of St Giles he preached only at Larbert and in the surrounding area. Nevertheless, the people came to him, including many of those who would be leaders in the next period. One of these was John Livingstone, who wrote of Bruce, 'No man in his time spake with such evidence and power of the Spirit; no man had so many seals of conversion; yea, many of his hearers thought no man since the apostles spoke with such power.'

KIRK O'SHOTTS

John Livingstone (1603 – 1672) played a humbling, but leading, part in one of the great events of these days in preparation for the Covenanting period ahead. This was on the communion season at Shotts. In return for his help when her carriage broke down, the Marchioness of Hamilton provided a new manse for the minister of the Kirk o'Shotts (i.e. Church of Shotts). He then agreed to her request that certain notable ministers be invited to take part in the communion services in June 1630. These included Bruce himself, Robert Blair, David Dickson and the young John Livingstone. The services were full of power and awe, and because the people refused to go home, an extra thanksgiving service was arranged for the Monday morning. When the expected preacher was taken ill, it was not Bruce to whom they turned but Livingstone.

Overawed by the prospect of preaching in such company he wandered out into the fields early in the morning and seriously contemplated running away! He remained and preached on Ezekiel 36:25-26, using the churchyard because of the great numbers present. He enjoyed much liberty, 'the like of which I never had before in public in my life'. Towards the end of his sermon rain began to fall and the preacher exhorted the people to flee from God's wrath. 'What a mercy it is that the Lord sifts that rain through these heavens on us, and does not rain down fire and brimstone as he did on Sodom!' The power of the Spirit was showered down on them and nearly 500 people traced their conversion to that day. This area proved to be a stronghold of the faith in the terrible years that lay ahead.

Bruce's death

After the removal of Andrew Melville, Bruce's influence was crucial, but in 1631 the end came. While breakfasting with his daughter he realized that the Lord was calling him to his rest. He asked his daughter to read from the Scriptures: 'Cast me up the eighth of Romans.' He repeated the last two verses, asking her to place his finger on those words, and then took his farewell: 'God be with you my children. I have breakfasted with you and shall sup with my Lord Jesus this night. I die believing in these words.' His life was over, but his influence was far from finished.

Alexander Henderson

Charles I and Archbishop Laud

The next stage in the battle was the attempt by Charles I (reign 1625 – 1649) to impose his ecclesiastical will on Scotland. When this began God had his champion ready, 'a man truly excellent and divine, famous for all sorts of virtue, but chiefly for piety, learning and prudence'. These three qualities enabled Alexander Henderson (1583 – 1646) to guide the church of Scotland through the stormy seas of the next few years, from 1637 to his death in 1646. We know little of his earlier years before he came into the limelight, but they were clearly an excellent preparation for his vital role in the church's struggle.

Henderson was born in 1583, studied at St Andrews University and for eight years taught there. His only link with the Melvilles seems to have been to support those who opposed them, and for this he was rewarded with the quiet country parish of Leuchars in 1614. The people of the parish were opposed to the bishops and, therefore, hostile to the new minister. On the day of his induction they nailed up the doors of the church and the ordination party had to climb ignominiously in through a window and perform the ceremony in an empty building. The next two years must have been bleak ones for the unwanted minister. In 1615 or 1616 the hand of God intervened.

The great Robert Bruce came to preach at nearby Forgan, and Henderson – out of curiosity or something more – went to hear him, creeping unnoticed into the darkest corner of the church under the gallery. He was greatly surprised and convicted by Bruce's choice of text: 'Verily, verily, I say unto you, he that entereth not by the door into the sheepfold, but climbeth up some other way, the same is a thief and a robber.' He was then converted by the sermon that followed.

Immediately he declared his support for the evangelical party, who were opposing the king's policies, and soon became known for his wisdom and courage, although he made no significant entry on the national stage. Instead he devoted his efforts to continuing as a shepherd, where he had begun as a hireling. One convert from those days told him, 'I love you, sir, because I think you are a man in whom I see much of the image of Christ.'

Meanwhile Charles supported William Laud, first as a bishop and then from 1633 as Archbishop of Canterbury, in his attempts to impose episcopacy and a Roman liturgy on the church in Scotland.

Matters came to a head in 1637 when the new Prayer Book was to be read in St Giles in Edinburgh. The ordinary folk of the city attended, uninvited, and when the dean began to read from 'Laud's

Book' a poor local stallkeeper, Jenny Geddes, threw her stool at his head, crying, 'Will ye dare read that book in my lug [ear]?'

Henderson and many others resisted the archbishop and his liturgy, and it was soon obvious that a crisis was approaching. The godly Samuel Rutherford, famous even today for his spiritual letters, had been banished from his charge at Anwoth and wrote to Henderson from his place of exile:

> As for your cause, my reverend and dearest brother, ye are the talk of the north and south… God hath called you to Christ's side and the wind is now in Christ's face in this land, and seeing ye are with him, ye cannot expect the lee-side or the sunny side of the brae… Let us pray for one another.

In spite of the royal command, opposition to the imposition of 'the Book' had spread, and Henderson's 'cause' was his courageous public refusal to use it in his church. In fact the Privy Council in London vindicated his refusal, but the king was not deterred from pressing on with his plans.

Henderson and the National Covenant

As the struggle continued it was Henderson who suggested the idea of a National Covenant, and who was charged with drafting it. Then on 28 February 1638 a fast was proclaimed and the nobles of Scotland assembled at Greyfriars Church to hear the terms of the Covenant and then sign it. The signing lasted from four in the afternoon until eight in the evening. The next day the people of Edinburgh signed also and copies were dispatched to every part of the land. Virtually the whole nation united behind the solemn vow, 'to resist these contrary errors and corruptions, according to our vocation, and to the utmost of that power that God hath put in our hands all the days of our life'.

This Covenant was based on a previous one known as the 'King's Confession', initiated by James VI in 1581, which gave force to their contention that no 'diminution of the king's greatness and authority' was intended. The whole point was of course, religious, and great stress was laid on 'godliness, soberness and righteousness'. This was a great national and spiritual movement as we can see from the words of John Livingstone: 'I may truly say that in all my lifetime, excepting at the Kirk of Shotts, I never saw such motions from the Spirit of God… I have seen more than a thousand persons all at once lifting up their hands, and the tears falling down from their eyes.'

Henderson sent a copy to London, but the king refused to read the 'damnable' Covenant and sent it back. The church, however, followed her declaration of intent with actions. With Henderson as moderator at the next General Assembly the members carried out the 'Second Reformation', removing the king's bishops and Laud's liturgy. Henderson's leadership and wise guidance were crucial in the public proceedings and his spirituality was most evident, not least in the time spent with his friends in prayer. When the king's commissioner tried to prevent these decisions by dissolving the assembly Henderson courageously responded, 'In the name of the Lord Jesus Christ, the only Head and Monarch of his church, from a consciousness of our duty to God and his truth, this kingdom, this assembly and her freedom, we profess with heavy and loyal hearts, we cannot dissolve this assembly.'

The king's reaction was not unexpected; he made preparations to invade Scotland. An army assembled to resist him under a banner that read, 'For Christ's Crown and Covenant', with Henderson, Gillespie, Livingstone and others as chaplains. In the face of this army Charles had to agree to a free assembly and a free parliament in Scotland but again refused to accept their decisions. Meanwhile events were moving in England also and in 1642 the Civil War began. The English parliamentary army found itself in difficulties and appealed to the Scots for help. As a result of this the two nations entered into a 'Solemn League and Covenant', providing for military assistance but also pledging themselves to work towards ecclesiastical uniformity as 'most agreeable to the Word of God' and 'by the example of the best reformed churches'.

This noble aim was never achieved largely because the Scots and the English were not really agreed as to their aims. Robert Baillie, one of the Scottish Commissioners to the great Westminster Assembly from 1643 to 1647 wrote, 'The English were for a civil league; we for a religious covenant.' The assembly is justly famed for its magnificent *Confession* and the *Shorter* and *Larger Catechisms* that were prepared by a most godly and learned gathering of divines, but it was never able to accomplish the kind of uniformity envisaged by the Solemn League and Covenant. Differences between Presbyterians and Independents, mutual suspicion and, finally, the rise and success of Oliver Cromwell and his Model Army prevented agreement and eventually the two nations even adopted a different attitude to Charles.

The king sought the protection of his Scottish subjects, and Henderson performed his last service for his country and church by going to Newcastle in 1646 where he tried, unsuccessfully, to persuade Charles to accept the Solemn League and Covenant. The king respected and listened to Henderson but would not move from his insistence on episcopacy, regarding it as essential to his royal authority. In the midst of these negotiations Henderson's health failed and in August he returned to his native land. 'I am near the end of my race', he told a friend, 'and there was never a schoolboy more desirous to have the play than I am to have leave of this world.' Eight days later he died, disappointed in his great desire for unity in the lands but certain to hear his Master's 'Well done'.

The Covenanters

When Charles paid for his treachery and obstinacy in 1649 the two countries became even more estranged. Indeed, after the Scots crowned Charles II at Scone in 1651 Cromwell invaded Scotland, defeated the Scots and forced Charles to flee to the Continent. During the next years Cromwell ruled Scotland but the church had a large measure of freedom and great progress was made before the Restoration of Charles II in 1660. A contemporary Scottish historian tells us:

> At the king's return every parish had its minister, every village its school, every family almost had a Bible, yea, in most of the country, all the children of age could read the Scriptures… In many places the Spirit seemed to be poured out with the Word… by the multitude of sincere converts.

God was preparing for the dreadful days that were to follow.

'No bishop, no king'

Although Charles II had promised the Scots, at his coronation in 1651, to support Presbyterianism and the Covenant, he conveniently forgot all this once supreme power was in his hands. He was determined to rule both country and church, regarding his grandfather's dictum, 'No bishop, no king', as the height of wisdom. Moreover, Charles said, 'Presbyterianism is no religion for a gentleman!' (By 'Presbyterianism' he meant not just a particular form of church government, although that is included, but genuine evangelical faith and godliness.) Both the National Covenant and the Solemn League and Covenant were declared unlawful. Bishops and archbishops were appointed, not to shepherd the flock but to become weapons for dealing with the king's enemies in the Church of Scotland.

Samuel Rutherford

James Guthrie, the Covenanting preacher and author of the spiritual classic, *The Christian's great interest*, was soon executed but Samuel Rutherford (c. 1600 – 1661), the writer of many Christ-filled letters, escaped the hangman. Rutherford had written many theological works, but *Lex Rex* (Law is King), which completely destroys any idea of the divine right of kings that Charles so loved, could not be forgiven. Copies of the book were ordered to be burnt by the hangman in Edinburgh and at St Andrews where Rutherford was a professor. Rutherford himself was put out of the ministry and dismissed from his post in the university. He was commanded to appear before Parliament in London on a charge of treason, but he was too ill to make the journey and gave his reply to the messengers: 'Tell them that I have a summons already from a superior Judge and judicatory, and I behove to answer my first summons; and, ere your day arrives, I will be where few kings and great folk come.' The council's response to this was to turn him out of his rooms in the university, provoking the courageous rebuke from Lord Burleigh: 'Ye have voted that honest man out of the college, but ye cannot vote him out of heaven.' Soon Rutherford saw his King 'in Emmanuel's land'.

The field preachers

Two years later came the Great Ejection of 1662 when 400 ministers in Scotland were deprived of their positions. For the next twenty-five years the Covenanters were persecuted without mercy by the bishops and their willing servants, Graham of Claverhouse, Grierson of Lag, 'bloody' Dalziel and the dragoons.

These were confused and confusing times; the Covenanters were not always united nor were they always wise or their actions always justifiable. Nevertheless, the story of their testimony and sufferings for 'Christ's Crown and Covenant', for the Word of God and the gospel of Jesus Christ should stir every one of their present-day successors in any land.

Banished from pulpit and manse the ministers became field preachers. Although some were able to continue to shepherd their own flocks in secret others were driven far and wide but still preached and counselled the people of God.

A FIELD PREACHER

John Welsh of Irongray, the great-grandson of John Knox, was known to 'ride three days and two nights without sleep, and preach upon a mountain at midnight on one of the nights'. On one occasion he was pressed so closely that he had to take shelter in a home that was, in fact, unsympathetic to the Covenanting cause. His host did not recognize him and complained about the difficulty of capturing this man Welsh! Welsh described his business as 'apprehending rebels' and promised that the next day he would take him to where Welsh was to preach. The two men went to the appointed place where a great congregation had assembled and, giving his host the one chair, Welsh proceeded to preach on sin and salvation. That one special hearer's response was, 'You told me yesterday that you were sent to apprehend rebels and I, a rebellious sinner, have been apprehended this day.'

The people gathered in thousands to hear the gospel, to listen to the lectures (i.e. biblical expositions) and to have their children baptized. They even managed to hold communion in the open air. John Blackader records one such occasion when over 3,000 took communion:

> There was a rich effusion of the Spirit shed abroad in many; their souls breathed in a diviner element, and burned upwards as with the fire of a pure and holy devotion. The ministers were visibly assisted to speak home to the consciences of the hearers; they who witnessed declared, they carried more like ambassadors from the court of heaven than men cast in earthly mould.

Such were the 'rebels' and 'criminals' whom the king's soldiers harassed, attacked and murdered.

The killing time

The accepted number of those who suffered either death or 'the utmost hardship and privation' in these years, especially the 'Killing Time' from 1684 to 1688, is 18,000. Of these, 2,500 were banished to inhospitable places, 200 were drowned in a shipwreck, 360 were formally executed, well over 1,000 were killed in the fields, 3,000 were imprisoned and another 7,000 went into 'voluntary' exile. Many more must have died from accidents or exhaustion as the dragoons harried the people of the Covenant over the moors, bogs and mountains. It is amazing that anyone could justify these cruelties in the name of Christ, either then or since, but many who share the persecutors' hatred of evangelical religion have attempted it.

The words of a twenty-six-year-old minister, Hugh McKail, epitomized the spirit in which the martyrs died; crippled by torture he struggled up the ladder to the gallows and said, 'Every step of this ladder is a degree nearer heaven.' Then he took his farewell:

> Farewell father and mother! Farewell friends and relations! Farewell the world and all delights! Farewell meat and drink! Farewell sun, moon and stars! Welcome God and Father.

Welcome sweet Lord Jesus, the Mediator of the new covenant. Welcome Spirit of grace, God of all consolation. Welcome glory. Welcome eternal life. Welcome death.

Fifteen years later sixty-two-year-old Donald Cargill was able to confess after nineteen years as a field preacher, 'I have followed holiness; I have taught the truth; I have been most in the main things.' Then he asserted, 'I go up this ladder with less fear, confusion, or perturbation of mind, than ever I entered a pulpit to preach.' Drums were beaten constantly in an attempt to drown his voice, but he was able to declare,

> Now I am near to the possession of my crown, which shall be sure; for I bless the Lord that he hath brought me here, and makes me triumph over devils and men and sin; they shall wound me no more. I forgive all men the wrongs they have done me; and I pray the Lord to forgive the elect the wrongs they have done against him.

In this manner he and many others took their farewell of 'reading and preaching, praying and believing, wanderings, reproaches, sufferings'.

John Brown of Priesthill

We could consider a host of others, such as Alexander Peden, Richard Cameron and James Renwick, but the martyrs were not all preachers by any means. Of the others none was more outstanding than John Brown of Priesthill. He was not a minister; he would have loved to be one, but a speech impediment prevented this. Instead he gathered young people around his isolated croft to instruct them in the Word of God. While working on the hillside in 1685 he was surprised by the greedy and cruel Graham of Claverhouse who immediately 'sentenced' him to die. Back at his home, watched by his wife, John Brown asked and was granted permission to pray. Claverhouse soon interrupted him harshly: 'I gave you time to pray, not preach.' Brown, still on his knees, turned around to answer and his stammer left him. 'Sir,' he replied, 'you know neither the nature of preaching nor praying if you call this preaching!' When he had finished praying, chiefly for 'poor Scotland', he said farewell to his wife and children and prepared to die.

However, the hardened soldiers refused to shoot, and the enraged Claverhouse had to murder him himself. Then he taunted the widow: 'What do you think of your husband now?' to which she responded: 'I ever thought muckle [much] of him, but never so muckle as I do this day.' When the persecutor threatened to kill her too she answered again, 'If you were permitted, I doubt not but that your cruelty would go that length. But how will ye answer for this day's work?' The nature of the opposition to the Covenanters is clear from his reply: 'To man I can be answerable and as for God, I will take him into my own hands.'

The two Margarets

As the martyrs were not all ministers, so they were not all men. In 1685 the Wigtown Martyrs also died: the two Margarets. For refusing to take 'the oath of abjuration' they were sentenced to be drowned, a deed so black that the opponents of the Covenant have tried desperately, but ineffectually, to deny the historicity of the account ever since. Margaret Lachlison, aged seventy, was tied to a stake below the high-water mark in the Solway Firth, further out than her eighteen-year-old companion, Margaret Wilson, in the hope that the younger woman would be intimidated into yielding as she saw the incoming tide cover the first victim. As the older woman was covered, young Margaret was asked what she thought. Her reply was 'What do I see but Christ wrestling there?' As the tide came in further she read from Romans 8, repeating the last few verses: 'Who shall separate us from the love of Christ?… in all these things we are more than conquerors through him that loved us.' She turned down a last opportunity to save herself by taking the oath saying, 'I will not. I am one of Christ's children; let me go.' So they tied her to the stake once more where she continued to sing her psalm of praise (Ps. 25:7) until the waters ended her life:

> My sins and faults of youth
>   Do thou, O Lord, forget;

> After thy mercy think on me
> And for thy goodness great.

We could fill many pages with the record of the martyrs of the Covenant – men, women and children, for the last to die for his faith, George Boyd, was only sixteen when he was shot in the summer of 1688 – but these will suffice. James II succeeded to the throne in 1685, and, as an avowed Catholic, continued and intensified the persecution until he was deposed in the 'Great Revolution' of 1688. Once again peace and liberty of conscience came to the blood-stained hills of Scotland. It is noteworthy that the persecuted saints of Eastern Europe show great interest in the Covenanters of 300 years ago. Both groups call to our minds the words of Samuel Rutherford: 'They are not worthy of Jesus, who will not take a blow for their Master.'

Questions for discussion

1. *What do you understand by 'conscience'? What light can we gain from Knox's reply to Mary, Queen of Scots, and from Robert Bruce's experience?*

2. *What evidence does this chapter provide of the providence of God in action? How does this apply to both individuals (i.e. Alexander Henderson) and the church (i.e. at the Kirk o'Shotts)?*

3. *In what ways might you disagree with the actions of the Covenanters and, more importantly, what benefits can you gain from their example? How do the 'Crown-rights of the Redeemer' apply today?*

For further reading

M. Grant, *The lion of the covenant: the story of Richard Cameron*, Evangelical Press, 1997.

M. Grant, *No king but Christ: the story of Donald Cargill*, Evangelical Press, 1988.

* D. C. MacNicol, *Robert Bruce*, The Banner of Truth Trust, 1961.

* J. Purves, *Fair sunshine*, The Banner of Truth Trust, 1968.

* S. Rutherford, *Letters of Samuel Rutherford,* ed. A. Bonar, abridged, The Banner of Truth Trust, 1973.

** A. Smellie, *Men of the covenant*, Andrew Melrose, 1911.

Watch your life and doctrine closely. Persevere in them, because if you do, you will save both yourself and your hearers.
— 1 Timothy 4:16

The Lord hath more truth and life yet to break forth out of his holy Word.
— John Robinson (c. 1576 – 1625)

Who would true valour see,
 Let him come hither;
One here will constant be,
 Come wind, come weather;
There's no discouragement
 Shall make him once relent
His first avowed intent
 To be a pilgrim.
— John Bunyan (1628 – 1688)

10

The Puritans

It is easier to say who the Puritans were than what they were. Definitions vary tremendously, yet the essence of sixteenth- and seventeenth-century English Puritanism is reasonably clear. When Elizabeth I came to the throne the Reformation was secure but not complete; it was the Puritans' aim to make it complete. There were many at that time who shared the Puritans' views on the great doctrines of salvation and the practice of personal religion but were content with the amount of reformation that had been achieved. The Puritans, on the other hand, wanted the church to conform exactly to the biblical pattern and to be purged or purified of all the Roman and idolatrous practices that remained in the Church of England and that were enshrined in the Prayer Book.

As early as 1550 John Hooper, Bishop of Gloucester, had earned the disapproval of Calvin and annoyed Cranmer and Ridley by refusing to wear the usual vestments. Said Hooper, 'Let the primitive church be restored, which never yet had nor shall have any match

or like. Let all the movements and tokens of idolatry and super-
stition be removed and the true religion of God be set in their
place.' Hooper was referring to 'candles, vestments, crosses, altars'
and the like. Led by the Presbyterian Thomas Cartwright this attitude
soon developed into a full-scale movement to reform the practice
and government of the Church of England from within.

Others went further. Robert Browne led the way with his
Reformation Without Tarrying for Anie (that is, the civil rulers)
and separated from the national church. Although he returned
later after enduring many trials, he was succeeded by many
separatists who modified his position but followed him in
giving up hope of purifying the Church of England. In this
respect they were not strictly Puritans. However, they were
looking for a pure church, in their own way, and shared the
Puritan concern for spiritual and personal religion, for practical
holiness, for communion with God and for the salvation of
souls. In fact, although the Puritan movement sometimes
appeared to be making progress, it never overcame the fears of
the central government, especially the monarch, or the preju-
dices of the people sufficiently to achieve the reforms that they
desired. Gradually, therefore, they began to concentrate on
preaching and caring for the flock, whether within or without
the established church and, by so doing, changed the face of
both church and nation far more radically than all their ecclesiastical and political planning could have done. Both Elizabeth I
and James I believed in the latter's dictum: 'No bishop, no king',
and made every effort to put down Puritanism. The Word of
God, however, was not bound and Puritan preachers and
hearers multiplied.

William Perkins of Cambridge

Among the many great men at the end of the sixteenth century
we may single out William Perkins of Cambridge (1558 – 1602).
He experienced a dramatic conversion when he heard a woman
threatening her child with 'drunken Perkins' and subsequently
entered the ministry. His preaching and writings influenced not
only Cambridge and the rest of England but also Europe and,

through his disciple William Ames, the new world of America. Cambridge was the source of much Puritanism, especially through Emmanuel College, which was founded in 1585 by Sir Walter Mildmay. The queen accused him of erecting 'a Puritan foundation', to which he wisely replied, 'No Madam, far be it from me to countenance anything contrary to your established laws; but I have set an acorn, which, when it becomes an oak, God alone knows what will be the fruit thereof.' Scores of Puritan preachers came from the college and stirred the minds and hearts of the nation. When they were not allowed to preach they wrote books, many of which have been republished in recent years and have demonstrated that their power remains.

The popular modern picture of Puritans as purely negative, joyless, pleasure-denying, narrow-minded hypocrites may have some basis in a few extremists, but the real Puritan was warm as well as orthodox, joyful as well as solemn and truly godly as well as strict. In short, their religion has never been surpassed and rarely, if ever, equalled. On the one hand we read of Richard Rogers who when told, 'Mr Rogers, I like you and your company well, only you are too precise', replied, 'Oh, sir, I serve a precise God.' On the other we hear of men saying of John Rogers of Dedham, 'Let us go to Dedham to fetch fire.' Names such as Richard Sibbes, Thomas Brooks, Thomas Manton, Thomas Goodwin, John Owen and a host of others will be found in treasured second-hand volumes or twentieth-century reprints on many ministers' shelves today. They still promote gospel truth, purity of practice, God-fearing holiness, humble devotion and a longing for the manifest working of God in the land.

The Pilgrim Fathers

From Scrooby to Leyden

At the beginning of the seventeenth century one area 'leavened' with Puritanism was the border of Lincolnshire and Nottinghamshire. There a separatist church emerged, first at Gainsborough and then at Scrooby, led by William Brewster as elder and soon joined by John Robinson as teacher. Soon persecution forced them to emigrate to Holland, following and followed by many others, as James pursued his intention towards those who refused to conform: 'to harry them out of the land'. After much difficulty the Scrooby church arrived in Amsterdam in 1608, but finding many unedifying quarrels there they moved on to Leyden. Under the wise leadership of John Robinson they lived there in peace and godliness for a dozen years, with the membership growing to 300. After much prayer, fasting and deliberation they decided to move again, this time to America. The problems involved in securing a licence, patents and the financial support of a group of backers, the 'Adventurers', were enormous. They were subject to much deception, anxiety and hardship before they even set sail for the New World.

William Bradford, who was an elder of the church and later the governor of the settlement in New England, wrote of their departure from Leyden: 'So they left that goodly and pleasant city, which had been their resting-place near twelve years. But they knew they were *pilgrims*, and looked not much on those things, but lifted up their eyes to the heavens, their dearest country, and quieted their spirits.' Therefore, they have become known as the Pilgrim Fathers. They left so that they might worship and serve God according to their conscience and the Word of God and bring up their children in the fear of the Lord without the fear of men. For this they risked danger and death and encountered and conquered many hardships.

John Robinson

For various reasons not all were able to leave at this time; John Robinson remained to care for the flock because he was their pastor. He was to have followed later, as many did, but as it turned out he never went, dying in Leyden in 1625. He was noted not only for his theological ability, serving at the famous Synod of Dort, but also for his peaceable spirit.

An eyewitness records that he told the departing members of the congregation that 'If God should reveal anything to us by any other instrument of his, to be as ready to receive it, as we were to receive any truth by his ministry; for he was very confident the Lord had more truth and light yet to break forth out of his holy Word.' Although this saying has been perverted in recent years into a denial of doctrinal certainty and a justification of all sorts of teaching apart from the Word, it breathes in reality the air of genuine Puritanism, in submission not to the dictates of man but to the Word of God.

The Mayflower

Only thirty-five from Leyden set sail for Southampton in the *Speedwell* to be joined by sixty-seven from separatist churches in the London area. At Southampton they embarked in the famous *Mayflower* as well as the *Speedwell*, the former being much smaller than they had anticipated. Conditions became even more overcrowded when the *Speedwell*, after turning back twice for repairs first to Dartmouth and then to Plymouth, proved completely unseaworthy, and all the pilgrims eventually crammed into the *Mayflower*. They finally sailed from Plymouth on 6 September 1620 and after a horrific voyage sighted Cape Cod on 9 November. As well as the inevitable sickness their troubles included violent storms, lack of privacy and exercise and even persecution by one of the sailors who then died in the mid-Atlantic. Then they discovered that the main beam was cracked. After much prayer by the pilgrims they discovered a large iron screw that had been brought on board, which the captain used to make a collar to hold the beam secure. In the midst of all this one servant died and a baby, to be named Oceanus, was born.

Their landfall should have been much further south but all attempts to reach their proper destination failed. After electing John Carver as governor they investigated the shore and found traces of Indians and even some Indian corn buried in a large ship's kettle! After thirteen days they succeeded in reassembling a small boat that had been dismantled for the voyage and began to search the coastline. With much difficulty and after various adventures with very unfriendly Indians, they sailed the *Mayflower* to the opposite side of the bay on 9 December. The next day was the sabbath so they rested, but on the Monday they at last began to disembark and settle at Plymouth. Their troubles, however, were far from over. Before they had even managed to build a 'Common House' to shelter themselves and their goods while they worked on their own dwellings, William Bradford's wife was accidentally drowned and several fires hindered the work. All through the early months of 1621 fever raged in the settlement so that before the end of March exactly half of the 102 settlers had died as well as half of the *Mayflower*'s crew. Only remarkable faith could have enabled them to survive that year as they did. In the providence of God friendly Indians showed them how to plant and care for Indian corn because their own seeds proved useless. One of these Indians, called Squanto, had been kidnapped by an unscrupulous English captain and taken to Europe where he had learned some English and was thus especially helpful to the pilgrims. He was able to warn them about the less friendly inhabitants of the land and to introduce them to the local paramount Indian chief Massasoit, who proved to be a steadfast friend during the early years.

In November 1621 a further thirty-five settlers arrived from England but without the promised supplies (from the Adventurers) or even food for themselves. The pilgrims took them in and soon they shared in the first harvest (the origin of Thanksgiving Day kept annually in America). The next year proved to be, if anything, even harder, and by May 1622 rationing had been imposed. Matters were not improved by the arrival of fifty more settlers of a different kind: ungodly men, drunkards and liars. The pilgrims helped them, in spite of their attitude and ingratitude, but they moved on to form their own settlement at Wessagusset. There they antagonized the Indians by stealing from them and in the end had to be rescued and supplied by the Plymouth pilgrims in the person of Captain Miles Standish. (One modern American author has managed to turn this story completely around, accusing the pilgrims of attacking the Indians and describing Standish as their 'chief cut-throat'. This is an interesting example of much modern treatment of the Puritans in general.)

John Eliot and the Indians

After all these trials, plus a six-week drought in 1623 that ended suddenly during a day of prayer, the settlement began to prosper. In 1630 the last of the members of the church in Leyden arrived, 292 having made the journey altogether, and in spite of many deaths the population reached 300. From this and another Puritan settlement in Massachusetts Bay, New England Puritanism may be said to have grown. It was to the Bay Colony that a young minister came in 1631. His name was John Eliot, and after preaching for some months in Boston he was called to be pastor of the Congregational Church at nearby Roxbury. There he stayed for the rest of his life becoming the first real missionary to the Indians. He ministered to them in many different ways, but always the gospel of salvation was in the forefront. He began preaching to them after spending two years studying their language, and after a couple of months several expressed their desire to receive the gospel. For the next forty-four years, until his death in 1690, Eliot laboured among the Indians. He organized the converts in 'praying towns', pleading their cause before the government and the Christian public. By 1660 there were about 1,100 'yielding obedience to the gospel', and twenty-four had been trained as evangelists. He also translated the Scriptures into the Algonquin language, and by 1663 the whole Bible was available, together with a complete set of metrical psalms! This was the first Bible printed in any language in North America.

By 1675 the number of 'praying' Indians had reached 3,500, but, sadly, in that year Massasoit's son and successor, Philip, declared war on the 'white man' and in the course of this conflict much of Eliot's work was destroyed. After Eliot's death the Indians of Massachusetts were virtually wiped out and soon no one remained who could read his translation. Eliot kept up his links with England, particularly with Richard Baxter who was one of the greatest, though by no means the most consistent, of the English Puritans. It is through the life of this man that we shall pursue the development of Puritanism in the 'homeland'.

Puritanism in England

Richard Baxter

His early years

Richard Baxter (1615 – 1691) was born near Shrewsbury on 12 November 1615, but his story really begins with his father's conversion when the boy was nearly ten. Until then Richard had lived with his mother in his grandfather's house, probably because of his father's wayward life. 'It pleased God', writes Baxter, 'to instruct and change my father' and that 'by the bare reading of the Scriptures in private, without either preaching or godly company, or any other books but the Bible'. The boy's education had been in the hands of the local clergy who were both idle and ignorant, but now his father taught him to love the Bible. He also introduced him to good books by such Puritan notables as Richard Sibbes (*The Bruised Reed*) and William Perkins, although, strangely, his first conviction came from an abridgement of a Jesuit work! Baxter senior was 'reviled commonly by the name of Puritan, Precisian and Hypocrite', but his son was always grateful for his help.

These books awakened him to a concern for his salvation, but he could not put a date to his conversion: 'God breaketh not all men's hearts alike.' A few of the local clergy gave him help, especially one, a namesake but no relation, who was less learned than the rest: 'but yet did profit me more than most, because he would never in prayer or conference speak of God or the life to come, but with such marvellous seriousness and reverence as if he had seen the majesty and glory which he talked of'. So when Baxter began to study in earnest it was in divinity that he specialized. The young man's health was far from good. Indeed, he was so constantly ill that 'the face of death and nearness of eternity' kept him serious in his studies and careful in his living.

During this time, largely through meeting some godly nonconformists like the noted Walter Cradock, Baxter became concerned for 'discipline', that is, the effective rule of Christ in his church. Nevertheless he determined to enter the ministry of the national church led by 'a thirsty desire of men's conversion and salvation', a desire that was never to leave him. He was ordained deacon by the Bishop of Worcester in December 1638 but continued his studies while teaching in Dudley for nine months. During this time he also preached to 'great congregations'. When he later visited Dudley from Kidderminster he observed, 'The poor nailers and labourers would not only crowd the church as full as ever I saw any in London, but also hang upon the windows and the leads without.'

During this time also he read further in the works of the Puritans, William Ames and Anthony Burgess, which strengthened his doubts about some of the ceremonies in the Book of Common Prayer. In 1639 he went to Bridgnorth as assistant curate. There his scruples increased and nearly got him into trouble with the ecclesiastical authorities. He was there for nearly two years, but his labours were 'not so successful as they proved afterwards in other places'. Baxter regarded the people as being gospel-hardened and determined never again to minister to such a congregation. Certainly Kidderminster, where he moved in April 1641, fulfilled his requirements!

Baxter of Kidderminster

By now the situation in England had changed. The so-called 'Long Parliament' had removed Archbishop Laud and others from power, freed Puritan prisoners and begun to reform the clergy. As a result of these moves the vicar of Kidderminster, although allowed to stay, had to forfeit one-third of his stipend to pay for a preacher instead of a curate. The committee of trustees apparently knew Baxter already and chose him for this position. So began a ministry most memorable for evangelism and pastoral care, although strangely this position was technically free from that. Nevertheless Baxter confesses, 'I can truly say that a fervent desire of winning souls to God was my motive.' This was in spite of bodily weakness and, more important, a period of doubting 'the certain truth of the sacred Scriptures, and also the life to come and immortality of the soul' and even Christianity itself. He writes,

I was fain to dig to the very foundations and seriously to examine the reasons of Christianity and to give a hearing to all that could be laid against it, that so my faith might be indeed my own. And at last I found that nothing is so firmly believed as that which hath been sometime doubted of.

Soon his preaching began to have an effect. 'God touched the hearts of young men and girls with a love of goodness and delightful obedience to the truth.' In some cases these 'jewels' led parents and grandparents to faith also. Not all, however, were pleased with his dogmatic preaching of sin and the new birth and even fewer liked his insistence on holiness of life and discipline in the church. The conforming clergy opposed him; slanders were spread about him and he was even taken to court. The 'rabble' attacked him as a 'Roundhead', and he had to withdraw from Kidderminster to Gloucester.

The Civil War

With the onset of the Civil War (1642 – 1647) he was unable to return and eventually was away for five years. At first he lived and studied quietly in Coventry but then travelled around the country as a chaplain to the parliamentary army. Although Baxter was always a moderate in politics, both national and ecclesiastical, he was convinced that no Puritan could remain neutral. The truly 'religious' from Kidderminster 'fell in with the Parliament' whereas 'almost all the drunkards went into the king's army'. While still at Coventry, Baxter preached twice a week in the town. On one occasion he is said to have persuaded a magistrate, who wanted to arrest him, to accompany him to a village where he was going to preach by telling him he was a 'man-catcher'! As he prayed, the magistrate was reduced to tears.

From 1645 to 1647 he was chaplain to Colonel Whalley's regiment in the New Model Army. Baxter never got on with Cromwell; mutual suspicion dated from Baxter's refusal to become chaplain to the original 'Ironsides'. Later Baxter suspected Cromwell of favouring the extremists – the 'sectaries', as Baxter called the Levellers, Diggers and other separatist groups. He often debated with them and on one occasion, at Amersham, he seems to have routed them completely, partly by refusing to leave the scene before his opponents so that they could not claim that he had been defeated. In spite of one bout of ill health he accompanied the regiment around the country, preaching to the living and praying with the dying, although he hated the life with its discomfort, crudities and dangers. Eventually he collapsed, and it was while recuperating that he began his first book.

The Saints' Everlasting Rest was completed only after his return to Kidderminster. It was described by a fellow Puritan as 'a book for which multitudes will have cause to bless God for ever' and a more recent writer has said that it will 'endure as long as men require a star of hope in a world of tears and trouble'.

Kidderminster transformed

Having largely recovered, Baxter was called back to Kidderminster (1647 – 1662) in June 1647 by a letter bearing 265 names, including, to his delight, forty-five 'souldiers'. He refused to go as vicar because he doubted the legality of the other man's deposition and therefore its morality but consented to return as lecturer, leaving the vicarage for the ex-vicar. In spite of much drunkenness and immorality there was an open door for the preaching of the gospel. Not only had most of his old opponents been killed fighting on the king's side, but he writes that under Cromwell, 'Godliness had countenance and reputation also, as well as liberty.' Somewhat reluctantly he had later to admit, 'God gave me, even under a usurper whom I opposed, more liberty and advantage to preach his gospel with success, which I cannot have under a king to whom I have sworn and performed true subjection and obedience.' Moreover, after the sufferings of the war many were ready to listen seriously, and even the open sinners were so extreme that they gave sin a bad name!

BAXTER THE PREACHER

His main asset was himself — eloquent in preaching and living. He preached from a manuscript for an hour. 'Words must be used and weighed; but the main work is heart work', he wrote, and here he excelled. Samuel Wesley heard him preach in his last years with 'a strange fire and pathos'. His sermons were a combination of cutting and piercing words and a gentle and loving spirit. His mixture of clarity and force of the awareness of God and generosity of life had a tremendous effect on the whole town.

'He talked', wrote the Puritan Edmund Calamy, 'in the pulpit with great freedom about another world, like one who had been there, and was come as a sort of express from thence to make a report concerning it.' His constant ill health and pain made him aware of the shortness of the time. He says, 'As a dying man my soul was the more easily brought to seriousness' and so:

> I preach'd, as never sure to preach again
> And as a dying man to dying men.

Although his tender heart reacted against the whole idea of hell, he found the doctrine in the Bible and so preached it. 'Do you think there is one merry heart in hell?' he asked his people.

From about 1653 onwards he began his renowned system of catechizing. With the help of his assistants he devoted two days a week to examining his charges on the Catechism, helping them to understand it. He then:

> Next enquired modestly into the state of their souls, and lastly endeavoured to set all home to the convincing, awakening and resolving of their hearts according to their several conditions... though the first time, they came with fear and backwardness, after that they longed for their time to come again. Few families went from me without some tears, or seemingly serious promises for a godly life.

His view of the importance of this work led him to what is, perhaps, something of an overstatement in isolation: 'It is but the least part of a minister's work, which is done in the pulpit.'

By these means a remarkable work was done in a population of about 4,000, of whom 1,600 were of communicant age:

> The congregation was usually full... Our private meetings also were full. On the Lord's Day there was no disorder to be seen in the streets, but you might hear a hundred families singing psalms and repeating sermons, as you passed through the streets. In a word, when I came thither first, there was about one family in a street that worshipped God and called on his name and when I came away there were some streets where there was not past one family in the side of a street that did not do so; and that did not by professing serious godliness give us hopes of their sincerity... We had 600 that were communicants, of whom there was not twelve that I have not good hopes of, as to their sincerity.

Baxter's concern for souls extended beyond England. He suggested the establishing of a college to train ministers to 'undertake the conversion of some of the vast nations of infidels... with the plain and pure gospel'. It is not surprising, therefore, that he had a great respect for John Eliot and his work among the Indians of New England. Eliot wrote to thank Baxter for *The Saints' Everlasting Rest*, to which Baxter replied, 'That anything of mine should be useful to you is a matter of thankfulness to God; but it is as his and not as mine', adding, 'I know no work in all the world that I think more highly and honourably of than yours.'

The Reformed Pastor

Another of Baxter's great concerns was unity among Christians. In 1653 he established the Worcester Association of Ministers, which was joined by seventy-two men in the first three years. Every month they met to discuss doctrine and discipline. Many other county associations were formed, but to his sorrow no wider unity emerged. Most of these men acknowledged no party, observing Baxter's exhortation to concentrate on 'Christ and the great fundamentals. Unite in those with men of holiness and righteousness. Prosecute that union affectionately and unweariedly, and keep your eye upon that glory where we shall be one.'

One of his greatest works was born out of these meetings when he was prevailed on to put into print an address on catechizing, which illness had prevented him from delivering. This book was *Gildas Salvianus*, better known to us by its subtitle, *The Reformed Pastor*. More works followed, especially on the subject of conversion; the most famous, *A Call to the Unconverted*, sold 20,000 copies in the first year and Baxter learned of whole households converted through reading it. These years after 1654 were among his most fruitful, but unknown to him his ministry was drawing to an end.

The Great Ejection

Moves were afoot to bring back the monarchy with the restoration of Charles II. At first Baxter played a prominent part in this for he had always been a monarchist, although he realized that it would also mean the restoration of episcopacy and the deposition of Puritanism. 'We all look to be silenced, and some or many of us imprisoned or banished', he wrote. And so it proved in spite of the king's promises. The vicar of Kidderminster resumed his position, and Baxter went from being offered a bishopric, which he refused, to being silenced altogether when the Act of Uniformity was passed in May 1662. This required 'unfeigned consent and assent' to everything in the Prayer Book, and those who could not conform were to be ejected on 24 August 1662, significantly the ninetieth anniversary of the St Bartholomew's Day massacre of Protestants in France. This was just a month before the ministers would normally have received their tithes, their annual income. Baxter preached his farewell sermon well before the due date saying, 'I would let all ministers in England understand in time whether I intended to conform or not.' This is a fair indication of his reputation and influence. In the end nearly 2,000 men, the cream of the ministry including all the Puritan leaders, left the Church of England; thus nonconformity was born. 'I lay in tears in deepest sorrow', wrote Baxter.

A Puritan love story

In his deep distress Baxter had a great consolation; seventeen days after his ejection the forty-seven-year-old bachelor married a twenty-six-year-old bride, Margaret Charlton from Kidderminster. The record of their courtship, marriage and life together is a genuine love story that kills forever the notion of Puritans as cold and unfeeling religious fanatics. She had moved to Kidderminster with her widowed mother in 1657, and after hearing Baxter preach and having a serious illness she made her personal covenant with the Lord in April 1660. Correspondence followed when Baxter left for London, and Baxter gradually accepted that the time had come for him to be married.

In spite of unkind gossip and the disparity in their ages the marriage proved happy and successful. Not only did Margaret look after all practical matters, in which her husband was utterly incompetent, but she also gave helpful advice on many of the problems about which he was consulted. She even dared to criticize his writing! From the Great Ejection of 1662 to his death in 1691 Baxter's life was a mixture of persecution and intermittent ministry, preaching when he could and writing when he was silenced. During the time of persecuting legislation – the Conventicle Act and the Five Mile Act – and various Declarations of Indulgence, Margaret supported him, finding houses in which they could live and halls in which he could preach. She was never so encouraging, he records, as when he was in prison. Her charm and 'winning conversation' provided a restraint on Baxter's over-sharp manner and drew many to godliness. When she died in 1681 he wrote a memoir, *The Breviate of the Life of Margaret Baxter*, a moving tribute to one whom, in his letters, he always called 'Dearest Heart'.

Last days

After a 'trial' before the notorious Judge Jeffreys he spent more time in prison but survived to see the revolution of 1688 and to resume preaching. He continued writing to the end of his life, producing 130 works as well as a voluminous correspondence. He wrote quickly and without revision (and too much, according to his wife!), anxious rather to see the truth in print than to be known for a refined style. In his last illness he was able to say to a friend, '*I was but a pen in God's hand and what praise is due to a pen?*'

This last illness came in 1691. Gradually the old man, worn out by life-long sickness and more recent persecution, became confined to his home, his room and then to his bed. Shortly before his death he told a visiting minister, 'I have pain; there is no arguing against sense; but I have peace, I have peace!' Two days later he told a friend, 'Oh, I thank him, I thank him! The Lord teach you to die.' This, above all, was a lesson he had learned for himself and taught so many others. In her personal covenant thirty years earlier Margaret had written words that Baxter turned into poetry and which, with a slight change, have found their way into our hymn books as:

> Lord, it belongs not to my care
>> Whether I die or live.
> To love and serve thee is my share
>> And this thy grace must give.

In this spirit he had lived and in this spirit he died. This was a Puritan indeed.

John Bunyan

Grace Abounding to the Chief of Sinners

One book, *The Pilgrim's Progress*, has made John Bunyan (1628 – 1688) one of the most widely known of all Englishmen, but few who have heard of the writer realize that he was first and foremost a Puritan pastor and preacher. While Baxter was ministering in Kidderminster, Bunyan was going through a deep and traumatic experience of conversion. This equipped him not only to chart Christian's progress from the City of Destruction to the Celestial City but also to preach the gospel in a way that touched the heart, an ability for which Dr John Owen, the great Puritan theologian, said he would willingly have exchanged his massive learning.

Bunyan was born in 1628 at Elstow, near Bedford, of humble parents who nevertheless owned their own house and were able to send him to school. There he at least learned to read and write, although he wasted and almost lost his ability during the sinful early years before his conversion. He has often been accused of exaggeration in his description of his sinful youth, but Bunyan had come to see what sin is in the eyes of a holy God. 'I had but few equals', he records in his spiritual autobiography *Grace Abounding to the Chief of Sinners*, 'especially considering my years, which were tender, being few, both for cursing, swearing, lying and blaspheming the holy name of God.' Early terrors of hell soon passed and he grew up a stranger to the grace of God, although he mentions several instances of God's preserving care, most notably during his military service in the Civil War. He served in the Parliamentary Army, probably for two years. On one occasion he was ordered with others to go and besiege a certain town. Another soldier asked to go in his place and was shot and killed while on sentry duty.

After this period he followed in his father's footsteps as a travelling tinker and soon got married. Although we do not know the name of his first wife we do know that 'her father was counted godly' and that she brought with her two religious books, which they used to read and discuss together. Bunyan even began to attend church with her, not with real conviction but with 'some desire to religion'. Then all this changed.

One Sunday in 1650 the parson preached on the topic of the sabbath, and Bunyan began to feel guilty because he, with many others, was in the habit of spending most of that day in games and dancing, encouraged by James I's *Book of Sports*. Putting this out of his mind he went out to play tip-cat on the village green. Then he records, 'A voice did suddenly dart from heaven into my soul, which said, "Wilt thou leave thy sins and go to heaven, or have thy sins and go to hell?"' At this he was terribly convicted but concluded that as there was no hope for him, he might as well be hanged for a sheep as for a lamb and resumed his sinful life with greater 'greediness of mind'. Then, once again he was rebuked, this time by an ungodly woman, and he began to reform.

Soon, he writes, 'I thought I pleased God as well as any man in England.' However, after a year of this self-righteousness he happened by 'the good providence of God' to hear some poor women discussing the things of God: 'about a new birth, the work of God on their hearts'. From this time he began to search for faith and conversion. He went from text to text, always increasing in awareness of his sinfulness and fearing that the day of grace was past.

About this time he met 'holy Mr Gifford', the pastor of the Congregational Church in Bedford. Under Gifford's careful, step-by-step teaching, both in preaching and in the pastor's home, Bunyan progressed towards an assurance of salvation. Then another, and greater, storm broke on him. He was assailed by temptations to 'sell' Christ, and at last believed that he had done so and thus committed the unpardonable sin.

For two years he believed that he was eternally lost, but then, at his lowest point, he thought he heard his bitter cries echoed with the words, 'This sin is not unto death' and began to hope. Gradually various texts had 'their visage changed; for they looked not so grimly on me as before' and eventually he realized that his righteousness before God was Christ himself (1 Cor. 1:30). Soon he was admitted to membership in the little church, number nineteen on their list, and began to grow in grace. There were still dark times but also experiences of great light. Of one such time he says, 'Christ was a precious Christ to my soul that night; I could scarce lie in my bed for joy and peace and triumph, through Christ.'

Preacher in chains

Bunyan's experience is not, as some have thought, a model for all, but his record in *Grace Abounding* is a salutary corrective to much modern superficiality and a great encouragement to those who have to undergo similar darkness. It also meant that he was eminently suited to minister to his fellow believers, and this he soon began to do: 'I preached what I felt, what I smartingly did feel… I went myself in chains to preach to them in chains and carried that fire in my own conscience that I persuaded them to beware of.'

After Gifford's death in 1655 Bunyan preached with increasing acceptance for five years while still working at his trade. Gifford, in his last letter to his flock, had exhorted them to a spirit of toler-ance and this Bunyan observed. The church was Congregational in name, Baptist in practice, but accorded fellowship to anyone who was 'discovered to be a visible saint by the Word, the Christian who walketh according to his light with God'. 'I own water-baptism to be God's ordinance', wrote Bunyan himself, 'but I make no idol of it.'

The Restoration of the monarchy

In 1658 the newspaper that announced Bunyan's first book (another followed in 1659) also carried the death notice of the Protector, Oliver Cromwell. In 1660 the Restoration of the monarchy was followed by an order from the Bedfordshire magistrates for the restoration of the Prayer Book in public worship. In November Bunyan went to preach in a farmhouse about thirteen miles from Bedford. He was warned that a local magistrate, Francis Wingate, had issued a warrant for his arrest if he should preach but refused to cancel the service. Soon after he began to preach a constable appeared and Bunyan was arrested, taken to Wingate's house and, the next day, committed to prison until the Quarter Sessions, two months later. Bunyan's first wife had died in 1655, and he and his second wife, Elizabeth, had moved into Bedford. At this time Elizabeth went into premature labour and the baby died.

At the hearing in January 1661 Bunyan appeared before five magistrates, presided over by Sir John Kelynge. He was given an opportunity to argue his case, since Kelynge had no fear of defeat. To those who wanted the prisoner silenced he replied, 'No! No! Never fear him; we are better established than so; he can do no harm. We know the Common Prayer Book hath been ever since the apostles' times and is lawful to be used in the church.' When pressed Bunyan admitted, 'We have had many meetings together, both to pray to God and to exhort one another, and we had the sweet, comforting presence of the Lord among us for our encouragement.'

Twelve years in prison

He was imprisoned for a further three months, with the distinct possibility of transportation or even execution before him. He feared what he was bringing on his wife and family and also that he might dishonour the Lord by his fear of death. Nevertheless he came to the conclusion that it was his duty to hold fast, whatever might come: 'Come heaven, come hell, Lord Jesus, if thou wilt catch me, do; if not, I will venture for thy name.' In the event he stayed in prison for twelve years in spite of an amnesty and in spite of his wife's courageous efforts to petition the House of Lords and the judges. The prison was crowded and unpleasant, but occasionally he was allowed out to visit his family. At other times they went to him, his blind daughter bringing him soup in a jug. The Bedford saints cared for his family with loving charity, although later on he made shoelaces to sell for their support.

Occasionally he preached to the Bedford meeting and once even in London! He and two other ministers preached in the prison and Bunyan spent much of his plentiful 'leisure' in reading and writing. He read Foxe's *Book of Martyrs*, wrote tracts and, between 1660 and 1666, had nine books published. Among these was *Grace Abounding*, which has moved the hearts of generations since. It is simple and unadorned:

God did not play in convincing of me, the devil did not play in tempting of me, neither did I play when I sunk as into a bottomless pit, when pangs of hell caught hold upon me: wherefore I may not play in my relating of them, but be plain and simple, and lay down the thing as it was.

While Bunyan was in prison great changes took place. The Great Ejection was followed by persecution of the ministers and their flocks. The Bedford congregation, which, like many others, had been meeting in the parish church, was now forced to meet in secret. In 1670 the house where nearly thirty of the congregation were gathered was raided and two leaders arrested and fined. Then in 1671 the church chose the still-imprisoned Bunyan as pastor, and when he was released in 1672, in the company of many others, he began his ministry, both in Bedford and more widely.

The Pilgrim's Progress

In 1675 he was again imprisoned for a year, this time in the old town jail on the bridge. It was probably here that he wrote the first part of *The Pilgrim's Progress*, which was published in 1678. Written 'in the similitude of a dream', it is full of Puritan theology and practice. This is not the place to retell the story of Christian's pilgrimage; in fact it is far better that people should read it for themselves. In any case, much of the book has already become familiar to us; its language influenced religious and even secular vocabulary almost as much as the Authorized Version. Who has not heard of sin as 'a great burden on his back' or the 'Wicket Gate' and the 'Slough of Despond'?

Every Christian can accompany the pilgrim as he 'ran... till he came to a place somewhat ascending, and upon that place stood a cross, and a little below, in the bottom, a sepulchre. So I saw in my dream', continues Bunyan, 'that just as Christian came up with the cross, his burden loosed from off his shoulder, and fell from off his back, and began to tumble, and so continued to do, till it came to the mouth of the sepulchre, where it fell in, and I saw it no more.' And we can rejoice with him: 'Then Christian gave three leaps for joy, and went on singing.'

People should read for themselves about the characters Christian meets along the way: Talkative, Legalist, Pliable, Faithful, Hopeful, Mr By-Ends of Fair Speech, who is always 'most zealous when religion goes in her silver slippers', and many more. Is there still anything more helpful to a believer than the story of how Christian and Hopeful stray into the hands of Giant Despair and are imprisoned in Doubting Castle? Is there anything more solemn than the final warning? Ignorant, crossing the river with the aid of the ferryman, Vain-Hope, is refused entry to the Celestial City because he lacks a certificate and is taken, bound, to a door in the side of the hill. 'Then I saw', concludes Bunyan, 'that there was a way to hell, even from the gates of heaven, as well as from the City of Destruction. So I awoke, and behold it was a dream.'

Part One had become very popular, passing through eleven English editions in ten years, apart from editions in Dutch, French and German, and it was 1684 before Bunyan published Part Two. This account of how Christiana, with the children, follows her husband is gentler in pace and mood but surprisingly does not fall flat. The final triumphant crossing of the river is perhaps best of all, a glorious testimony to the aims and achievements of Puritanism in pastoral practice. Even Mr Despondency goes to the brink of the river with the words: 'Farewell night, welcome day', while his daughter, Much-afraid, goes through the river singing. Mr Valiant-for-Truth 'called for his friends and told them, "I am going to my Father's and though with great difficulty I am got hither, yet now I do not repent me of all the trouble I have been at to arrive where I am." … So he passed over and all the trumpets sounded for him on the other side.'

'Bishop Bunyan'

The church to which Bunyan ministered after 1672 (later known as the Bunyan Meeting) met in a barn, and he preached there until his death. He became known as 'Bishop Bunyan' because he organized the churches of the district, from Bedford to the outskirts of London; he applied for licences for twenty-five other preachers and thirty buildings. His visits to London continued and his preaching was greatly appreciated by the ordinary people as well as by John Owen. In fact the Lord Mayor presented him with a silver-mounted walking stick! Charles Doe, who later published some of Bunyan's books, writes of his preaching in London,

> If there were but one day's notice given, there would be more people come together to hear him preach than the meeting-house would hold. I have seen to hear him preach by my computation about twelve hundred at a morning lecture by seven o'clock on a working day in the dark winter-time.

He published six new books in his last year and left sixteen manuscripts when he died. The end of his earthly pilgrimage came in London in 1688. He journeyed there after riding to Reading to try to patch up a quarrel. He was taken ill quite suddenly, recovered sufficiently to preach and then relapsed and died on 31 August. The description of a preacher given in *The Pilgrim's Progress* is said to be based on John Gifford but in fact fits any true Puritan pastor, especially Bunyan himself:

Christian saw the picture of a very grave person hung up against the wall; and this was the fashion of it. It had eyes lifted up to heaven, the best of books in his hand, the law of truth was written upon his lips, the world was behind his back. It stood as if it pleaded with men and a crown of gold did hang over his head.

Questions for discussion

1. How do you understand John Robinson's assertion that 'the Lord [hath] more truth and light yet to break forth out of his holy Word'? What are the merits and dangers of this saying?

2. Consider the conversions of Baxter and Bunyan in the light of Baxter's saying that, 'God breaketh not all men's hearts alike'. Is it essential, nevertheless, to have one's heart broken?

3. What did Baxter mean by saying, 'It is but the least part of a minister's work which is done in the pulpit'? How is our situation different from his? Can we still learn from his example and from The Reformed Pastor?

For further reading

R. Baxter, *The Reformed Pastor*, The Banner of Truth Trust, 1979.

* J. Bunyan, *Grace Abounding to the Chief of Sinners*, Evangelical Press, 2000.

* J. Bunyan, *The Pilgrim's Progress*, The Banner of Truth Trust, 1977.

** E. Hulse, *Who are the Puritans?*, Evangelical Press, 2000.

D. M. Lloyd-Jones, *The Puritans: their origins and successors*, The Banner of Truth Trust, 1987.

** J. I. Packer, *Among God's giants*, Kingsway, 1991.

I will pour out my Spirit on all people.

— Joel 2:28

The dispensation of grace we are now under is certainly such as neither we nor our fathers have seen; and in some circumstances so wonderful that I believe there has not been the like since the extraordinary pouring out of the Spirit immediately after our Lord's ascension. The apostolic times seem to have returned upon us.

— William Cooper (1693 – 1743), from his preface to *The distinguishing marks of a work of the Spirit of God* by Jonathan Edwards, 1741

See how great a flame aspires,
 Kindled by a spark of grace!
Jesus' love the nations fires,
 Sets the kingdoms on a blaze;
Fire to bring on earth he came;
 Kindled in some hearts it is;
Oh, that all might catch the flame,
 All partake the glorious bliss!

— Charles Wesley (1707 – 1788)

11

The Great Awakening

One of the best reasons for studying the history of revivals is the encouragement it brings to those who are living in a time of spiritual decline. In the light of this it is important to realize just how low the religious state had become before God moved and worked in mighty power. England in the early eighteenth century is a prime example of this. Amazingly, after the great days of the Reformation followed by the Puritans the prospect in the land was one of almost unrelieved bleakness. True, there was, as always, a faithful remnant; Isaac Watts, Philip Doddridge and others kept the flame of the gospel burning, but even their witness had weakened and their orthodoxy, while by no means dead, lacked real power.

THE STATE OF THE CHURCH

Nonconformists, in general, had drifted into unorthodoxy (Unitarianism or Socianism) or hyper-Calvinism, while the

Church of England, having banished most of the evangelicals from her ranks in 1662, was more deistic than Christian. The famous lawyer William Blackstone went to hear all the well-known preachers in London and reported that he heard nothing that was more Christian than the Roman orator Cicero! Bishop Ryle tells us that 'Natural theology, without a single distinctive doctrine of Christianity, cold morality, or barren unorthodoxy, formed the staple teaching both in church and chapel.' Bishop Butler, living at the time, wrote, 'It has come to be taken for granted that Christianity is no longer a subject of enquiry, but that it is now at length discovered to be fictitious', or in twenty-first-century terms, a fable.

Ignorance, drunkenness and immorality prevailed in the country at large as the inevitable consequences of the lack of gospel in the pulpit and godliness in the church. The king, at the instigation of the good Countess of Huntingdon, rebuked the Archbishop of Canterbury for holding balls and revelries in his palace, and the nobility in general spent its days in selfish pleasure, while disease, poverty and misery dominated the life of the despised lower classes. There were some attempts to stop the decline: books on apologetics, efforts at education, medical treatment and prison reform, the 'reformation of manners' (that is, morals) and, more important in the light of subsequent events, the establishing of many religious societies. These met regularly, with ecclesiastical approval, to study the Bible, pray and relieve the poor. All these well-meant remedies had little effect on the disease, and it was only when the Lord in his mercy raised up and empowered his servants in revival that the situation changed. And when it did change, it did so most remarkably!

George Whitefield

The Holy Club

George Whitefield (1714 – 1770) began life in December 1714 at the Bell Inn in Gloucester, which was kept by his parents. As he grew up he became very interested in reading romances and acting in plays, but he also showed great seriousness of mind. His father died when George was two and his mother's second marriage was unsuccessful. However, her ambition for George to go to Oxford University was eventually fulfilled when he entered as a servitor, the lowest rank of student serving other students in return for free tuition. He intended this as a preparation for entering the ministry and had already made a start by reading the classics and studying his Greek New Testament.

When he arrived in Oxford in 1732 he was soon invited, and tempted, to join in the riotous living that was the rule in the university. Instead, he became more religious, and, after being invited to breakfast with Charles Wesley, he was introduced to the other members of the Holy Club. They were also known as 'Methodists' because they lived their lives by method. Although many of them were the same people who later bore that nickname, they were at this time still unconverted, trying rather to save their souls by ascetic self-discipline, fasting and praying, devoting themselves to the sacraments and to charitable good works. These men were both scholarly and devout and such men as Benjamin Ingham, James Hervey and, of course, John Wesley were to be greatly used in the evangelical awakening. However, although the Holy Club, like the religious societies, may have prepared the way, the revival began only when George Whitefield was converted, at the age of twenty, in the notable year of 1735.

The Life of God in the Soul of Man

Whitefield's experiences with the Holy Club left him deeply dissatisfied, especially after reading Henry Scougal's book, *The Life of God in the Soul of Man*. From this he learned 'that a man may go to church, say his prayers, receive the sacrament and yet not be a Christian'. Reading on he received more light 'and from that moment, but not till then, did I know that I must become a new creature'. His search for new life occupied some months and involved terrible experiences as he increased his ascetic practices. For instance, Whitefield said he, 'continued in silent prayer under one of the trees for near two hours, sometimes lying flat on my face, sometimes kneeling upon my knees'. The other members of the Holy Club became impatient with him and so did his tutors as his work inevitably suffered.

Lent in 1735 naturally provided the stimulus for yet more mortification of the flesh but all to no avail. Then, although he does not tell us exactly how, he received mercy:

> After having undergone innumerable buffetings of Satan, and many months of inexpressible trials by night and day under the spirit of bondage, God was pleased at length to remove the heavy load, to enable me to lay hold on his dear Son by a living faith, and, by giving me the spirit of adoption, to seal me, even as I hope, unto the day of everlasting redemption. But oh! with what joy – joy unspeakable – even joy that was full of and big with glory, was my soul filled, when the weight of sin went off, and an abiding sense of the pardoning love of God, and a full assurance of faith broke in upon my disconsolate soul! Surely it was the day of my espousals – a day to be had in everlasting remembrance.

He later tells us that he knew the exact place: 'Whenever I go to Oxford I cannot help running to that place where Jesus Christ first revealed himself to me and gave me the new birth.'

Whitefield was so worn out by his spiritual struggles that he had to spend some time recovering in Gloucester. There he continued his devotions and even made restitution of certain objects that he had stolen as a boy. In spite of minute self-examination, the keynote of his life was joy – joy in studying the Word of God, joy in praying, joy in reading Matthew Henry's *Commentary* and joy in meeting together with some young people who already had been awakened under his influence. With these seven or eight 'disciples' he began a religious society, the first of many, and also began to visit the sick and imprisoned. All the time he was studying diligently and becoming clearer in his understanding of the gospel of justification 'by faith only'.

The whole nation 'in an uproar'

Soon after Whitefield's twenty-first birthday the bishop, at the instigation of some who knew the young man, offered to break his own rule and ordain him without waiting until he was twenty-three.

Several gifts of money enabled Whitefield to return to Oxford to complete his studies and there, in the absence of the two Wesleys in Georgia, America, he took over the leadership of the Holy Club. Although he now shrank from entering the ministry, success in his public examinations encouraged him, and in January 1736 he was ordained in Gloucester by Bishop Benson, and the following Sunday he preached his first sermon.

'Some few mocked', he records, 'but most for the present seemed struck and I have since heard that a complaint has been made to the bishop that I drove fifteen mad the first sermon.' The bishop, it appears, merely expressed the wish 'that the madness might not be forgotten before the next Sunday'! So began the public ministry of England's greatest evangelist.

After returning to Oxford and graduating Whitefield accepted pressing invitations to substitute for ministers, first in the Tower of London and then for a country rector. During this time, in response to a letter from John Wesley requesting assistance, he determined to become a missionary in Georgia. Although he intended to leave immediately he was delayed for nearly a year waiting for General Oglethorpe, the Governor of Georgia, with whom he was to sail. Consequently he was invited to preach for the religious societies in London. These services, many at 6 A.M., drew great crowds and for four months he preached up to nine times a week with tremendous effect: 'The sight of the congregation was awful. One might, as it were, walk upon the people's heads and thousands went away from the largest churches for want of room. They were all attention and heard like people hearing for eternity.' No doubt there were factors, such as the preacher's youth, that contributed to this amazing success but later events confirmed that the real explanation was the hand of God by his Holy Spirit.

Soon opposition arose to the content of his sermons, particularly his insistence on the new birth. There was dislike also for his association with 'many of the serious Dissenters'. He was labelled a fanatic, and parish clergy began to refuse him their pulpits. This did not prevent many from being convicted and apparently converted, so that he had to spend many hours 'in giving advice to awakened souls', whom he passed on to the religious societies.

When Whitefield eventually left for Georgia in January 1738, in Charles Wesley's words, 'the whole nation' was 'in an uproar'.

Whitefield in Georgia

During the voyage Whitefield carried on his work and by the time they arrived in Georgia many of the crew and soldiers on board, including both captains, had been converted. The situation in America was difficult in various ways, not least in that John Wesley had been expelled from the colony five months earlier! Whitefield's actions and attitude were very different from those of the still unconverted Wesley, and he was kindly received, especially as he brought with him gifts of food and medicine. He visited every part of the colony but soon decided to return to England to raise money for the building of an orphan house, a project that was to burden him for the rest of his life. The return voyage was stormy and dangerous, but Whitefield arrived safely in November 1738 only to find that other storms awaited him. During his absence there had been significant developments: a pamphlet war had been set off by the publication of Whitefield's rather immature journals and some of his sermons; the religious societies had grown in life and vigour, but the Moravians had influenced many with their 'blood and wounds' theology; and the fanatical 'French Prophets', mainly women, were trying to lead many astray. However, on the positive side we must reckon the conversion of the Wesley brothers.

John Wesley

John Wesley (1703 – 1791) returned from Georgia some time after his brother, but just before Whitefield left, with the conviction 'that I who went to America to convert others, was never myself converted to God'. Storms on the voyage back had brought him to see that 'I have a fair summer religion. I can talk well; nay, and believe myself, while no danger is near: but let death look me in the face and my spirit is troubled.' He and Charles looked for help from some of the Moravians whom they had met in Georgia and began to search for faith. The preface to Luther's *Commentary on Galatians* proved of great help to Charles and on Whit Sunday

John 'received the surprising news that my brother has found rest to his soul'. Luther was also of use to John himself. The following Wednesday, 24 May, he:

> ...went very unwillingly to a society in Aldersgate Street, where one was reading Luther's preface to the *Epistle to the Romans*. About a quarter before nine, while he was describing the change which God works in the heart through faith in Christ, I felt my heart strangely warmed. I felt I did trust in Christ, Christ alone, for salvation: and an assurance was given me, that he had taken away my sins, even mine, and saved me from the law of sin and death.

On his return from America Whitefield expected to take up preaching where he had left off, but he found that opposition to his ministry in London had increased. Although some pulpits were now closed to him others were available for the preaching of the gospel, and he also spent much time with the religious societies, especially the Moravian Fetter Lane Society. These were days and nights of fellowship, rejoicing and prayer. Whitefield and the Wesleys preached to huge congregations, and it became clear that God was doing a great work and about to do a greater. Further evidence of this appeared as Whitefield learned of what was happening in other parts of Britain.

Revival in Wales

Howell Harris and Daniel Rowland

A letter to Whitefield from Howell Harris described the situation in Wales:

> Oh, how ravishing it is to hear of such demonstrations of the divine love and favour to London! And to make your joy greater still, I have some good news to send you from Wales. There is a great revival in Cardiganshire through Mr Rowland, a church minister, who has been much owned and blessed in Carmarthenshire also.

Howell Harris (1714 – 1773) and Daniel Rowland (c. 1711 – 1790) were converted in 1735, the same year as Whitefield, and began to preach the same gospel with the same power, but their early independence is sound evidence that this work was of God, not man.

Harris, who was also born in the same year as Whitefield, received a good education and became a teacher at the age of seventeen. Although his life was devoted to pleasure he had some desire for a better life and used 'at the same time to behave like a hypocrite'. He enjoyed mocking the godly nonconformists of the district, but, sadly, they 'were very ready to debate with me concerning outward things, but no one told me that I was on the way to hell'. At the age of twenty-one conviction came when he heard the local vicar declare, 'If you are not fit to come to the Lord's Table, you are not fit to live, not fit to die.' His immediate response, as is so often the case, was to turn to religious duties and moral reformation, even asking forgiveness from his enemies. He did not find peace by this route, but he attended church on Whit Sunday all the same. There he was attacked by the devil:

> Satan roared dreadfully within me, so that I could almost have shouted out, 'There is no God'... But immediately before the sacrament, the One who is stronger came in... At the table, Christ bleeding on the cross was kept before my eyes constantly and strength was given me to believe that I was receiving pardon on account of that blood. I lost my burden: I went home leaping for joy; and I said to a neighbour who was sad, 'Why are you sad? I know my sins have been forgiven.' ... Oh, blessed day! Would that I might remember it gratefully evermore!

Around the same time Daniel Rowland, already a curate and a married man, was awakened and converted. He was born around 1711 in Llangeitho, where his father was rector, and educated locally but thoroughly. His brother, John, took over as rector and Daniel became his curate; neither of them knew anything of the gospel and each was notorious for ungodly living in his own way. During the winter of 1734 to 1735 Daniel was present when Griffith Jones, the evangelical clergyman and herald of the revival in Wales, preached in a churchyard, probably at Llangeitho itself. Jones noticed Daniel, especially his restlessness and rebellious expression, and pointing to him said, 'Oh! for a word to reach your heart, young man!' Rowland listened intently to the rest of the sermon and was a changed man and a changed preacher from that day.

So within a few days in 1735 these three men found peace with God and began to preach with power. None of them was very clear about the principles of the gospel at this stage; at the beginning there was more stress on the thunderings of the law, the necessity for repentance and the new birth than on the cleansing of the blood of Christ. Light on the brighter aspects of the biblical message came as the evangelists devoted themselves to study. Rowland, in particular, studied so hard that Harris heard he was losing both 'hair and sleep' by it. The effect of this early 'defect' appears to have been a depth of conviction and humbling that is not common in our more enlightened days. This, in turn, produced an equivalent depth of devotion and love to God when peace of conscience was eventually gained. The moral and decent as well as outcast sinners were brought down and remarkable conversions resulted.

Harris, neither trained nor ordained, began to 'read' with his neighbours and the sick of the surrounding villages, and as he did crowds gathered to listen. From this began a tremendous ministry that roused the whole district. 'Oh, the beginning was small, indeed!' he writes, but 'Behold, what a great bonfire came from a little spark.' He spent a short time at Oxford University, but 'The Lord brought me again from there… I soon tired of the place and I longed for my freedom, which I soon obtained.' He did not want to be called a preacher, but 'I thought I ought to go and exhort those with whom I had formerly sinned.' When he applied for Anglican orders in 1736 he was refused on the grounds of his exhorting, so he carried on with his unofficial work. He would read a short Bible passage, the Lord's Prayer, the Creed or a chapter from a book and then speak as he felt he must for two or three hours without preparation. He would go to the local fairs where he denounced 'the swearers and cursers, the gentry, the carnal clergy and everybody' without fear or favour.

This he continued for two years in spite of considerable opposition and many afflictions, both physical and financial, strengthened by unusual communion with God. Opposition near home simply meant that his work spread further afield. He was encouraged by some of the nonconformists and especially by the evangelical clergymen such as Griffith Jones of Llandowror. For a time he returned to teaching, exhorting in school and after school, often getting home about midnight. During this time he 'led some hundreds of ignorant people to a knowledge of their duties, and what it means to be a Christian', and these converts he encouraged to form religious societies; by 1739 there were nearly thirty of these.

Rowland was also preaching with fire, earning the nickname of 'the angry clergyman', and the whole neighbourhood was stirred. Crowds came to Llangeitho to hear him and he also went outside his own parish to preach. One notable convert was a local squire who made a point one Sunday of returning from his usual hunt to attend Rowland's service. He stood up in his pew opposite the preacher in order to put him off, but as Rowland spoke of the wrath of God he was terrified, convicted and his heart broken. Soon he sat down and wept in a corner of the pew until the sermon ended, then he went to Rowland, confessed his sin and invited him to dinner; this was a Zacchaeus indeed.

Another remarkable demonstration of God's power came while Rowland was reading part of the Anglican Litany, with its reference to Christ's 'agony and bloody sweat'. What has been described as 'a sudden amazing power' took hold of the reader and was then communicated to all the people standing in the church so that many fell to the ground.

Rowland and Harris met for the first time in 1737 when Rowland was preaching thirty miles from home. Harris travelled fifteen miles 'to hear him, in Defynnog church... where, on hearing the uncommon gifts given him and the amazing power and authority by which he spoke and the effects it had on the people, I was made indeed thankful, and my heart burst with love to God and to him'. Harris later described Rowland on this occasion as 'surrounded with glory in the pulpit'. The two soon met again and began to labour together in the gospel. Others, both ordained clergymen and 'laymen', quickly joined them. Multitudes gathered to hear them; thousands were converted and societies formed. Increasingly they preached the 'whole counsel of God', and the work of reformation, as well as revival, became established more firmly.

Open-air preaching

Whitefield in Bristol

Opposition from clergy or sheer numbers often drove the two men into the open air, and soon Whitefield was to follow their example. In 1739 he went to Bristol hoping to preach there and raise funds for the orphanage in Georgia, but the churches were closed to him. Instead he preached to the societies, which had resulted from his earlier work there, and visited the prisons. One Saturday afternoon he made his way to the district of Kingswood where thousands of miners and their families lived in poverty and degradation. In many ways it was a 'no-go' area and the inhabitants had been known to terrorize Bristol itself. Whitefield pitied them as 'sheep having no shepherd' and decided to follow not only Harris but also his Master, who 'had a mountain for his pulpit and the heavens for his sounding-board', by preaching in the open air. He spoke to over 200 from a place used earlier by a man named Morgan, then announced that he would come again the following Wednesday and returned to Bristol having 'broken the ice'.

In spite of a ban by the chancellor of the diocese Whitefield carried on preaching in and around Bristol, including to a congregation of 2,000 at Kingswood on the Wednesday. He also went to consult with Griffith Jones of Llandowror, who was, providentially, at Bath at this time: 'His words came with power and the account he gave me of the many obstructions he had met with in his ministry convinced me that I was but a young soldier, just entering the field. Good God, prepare me manfully to fight whatsoever battles thou hast appointed for me.' This was necessary counsel and a prophetic word indeed!

He went back to Kingswood the following Sunday and gives this description of a remarkable day in his journal:

At a moderate computation there were about ten thousand to hear me. The trees and hedges were full. All was hush when I began; the sun shone bright, and God enabled me to preach for an hour with great power, and so loudly that all, I am told, could hear. Mr B_____n spoke right. The fire is kindled in the country; and I know all the devils in hell shall not be able to quench it.

Elsewhere he describes the effects of this sermon:

Having no righteousness of their own to renounce, they were glad to hear of a Jesus who was a friend of publicans, and came not to call the righteous, but sinners to repentance. The first discovery of their being affected was to see the white gutters made by their tears which plentifully fell down their black cheeks, as they came out of their coal pits. Hundreds and hundreds of them were soon brought under deep convictions, which, as the event proved, happily ended in a sound and thorough conversion. The change was visible to all, though numbers chose to impute it to anything rather than the finger of God.

Soon after this Whitefield visited Cardiff to meet Howell Harris, whom he asked immediately, 'Do you know your sins are forgiven?' This was a meeting of great significance for the unity of the evangelical movement and led, four years later, to the formation of the Welsh Calvinistic Methodists. Someone was needed to lead the work in Bristol and Whitefield persuaded John Wesley to do this. Wesley was amazed at the huge congregations there and in his own words, 'submitted to be more vile' by preaching in the open air, an astonishing step for one so keen on ecclesiastical propriety! In his journal he wrote,

I could scarce reconcile myself at first to this strange way of preaching in the fields, of which he [Whitefield] set me an example on Sunday; having been all my life (till very lately) so tenacious of every point relating to decency and order, that I should have thought the saving of souls almost a sin if it had not been done in a church.

In fact, contrary to Charles' fears that this journey to Bristol might 'prove fatal to him', it opened the way to his life's work of preaching the gospel in the hedges, highways and byways of Britain.

America

Whitefield and the doctrines of grace

Whitefield was thus freed to return to America after eight months in England, during which he had preached, according to his own figures, to nearly two million people and religion, 'which had long been skulking in corners and was almost laughed out of the world', had now begun 'to appear abroad and show herself openly at noonday'. The voyage gave Whitefield time to read and meditate and to examine himself. As a result he came to a new and deeper understanding first of his own sinfulness and then of the grace of God. In this second discovery he was helped by correspondence and books but declared that he had learned the doctrines, not from John Calvin, but from the Bible and Jesus Christ. This growth in understanding prepared him for his association with the ministers in America, who would have agreed wholeheartedly with his open commitment to the doctrines of grace: 'I am more and more convinced that they are the truths of God; they agree with the written Word and the experience of the saints in all ages.' Again he writes, 'Election, free grace, justification… I intend to exalt and contend for more and more, not with carnal weapons, but with the sword of the Spirit, the Word of God! No sword like that!'

When Whitefield arrived back in America at the end of October 1739 his new reputation had preceded him and he was awaited with great expectancy. As soon as he began to preach in Philadelphia crowds went to hear him. He also began to make the acquaintance of some of the foremost evangelical ministers who were leading the fight against the deadness and formality that had overtaken the churches of America. Even before Whitefield's arrival this reforming zeal had produced divisions in the Presbyterian,

Congregational and Baptist denominations between those who were content with confessional orthodoxy and morality and those who looked for conviction, repentance and conversion. Nothing highlights this division more than the prevailing opinion that as long as a minister did not deny the gospel he did not have to be converted!

Whitefield and the Tennents

William Tennent, the venerable Presbyterian minister who visited Whitefield within a week of his arrival, led the fight with his four sons whom he had trained himself at the so-called Log College. Of these sons the most notable was Gilbert, who had ministered at New Brunswick since 1726. For the first six months he saw no converts, but while seriously ill he pleaded with God for just six months more, 'that I might stand on the stage of the world, as it were, and plead more faithfully for his cause and take more earnest pains for the salvation of souls'. The result of this prayer and his subsequent restoration was 'the conviction and conversion of a considerable number of persons, at various times and in different places in that part of the country'. The Tennents were noted for their searching preaching and scathing denunciation of sin (and of unconverted ministers) and there were some who, though sympathetic to their beliefs, regarded their methods as rather extreme. Some of them also had some success. For instance, Jonathan Dickinson records that all was dead, 'till some time in August 1739, (the summer before Mr Whitefield came first into these parts) when there was a remarkable revival at Newark especially among the rising generation'. Such men, true descendants of the Puritans, thought in terms of revival and were ready to support Whitefield and reap the full harvest that was shortly to begin.

All was not easy for Whitefield, however. The clergy of the Church of England, only lately having come to this area, opposed him bitterly, attacking him and his teachings publicly. Whitefield, it must be said, was not entirely free from blame, making some ill-advised statements and rather rash attacks on the clergy. Nevertheless, he showed himself willing to learn and admit his faults, and the Lord's blessing continued on his labours. He alternated preaching tours with working on the establishment of his orphanage, a venture that proved to be a lifelong burden to him. His relations with the trustees were never happy, and as they put difficulties in his way he began to wish that he had never taken up the task. On the other hand his preaching was very successful; great crowds attended everywhere he went and many were converted. One who did not yield to the preacher's oratory, which he greatly admired, was the famous publisher, inventor and writer, Benjamin Franklin. It was Franklin who gave as his considered opinion that Whitefield could be heard by 'more than thirty thousand' and, more important, described the effects of his ministry in Philadelphia:

> It was wonderful to see the change soon made in the manners of our inhabitants. From being thoughtless or indifferent about religion, it seem'd as if all the world were growing religious, so that one could not walk through the town in an evening without hearing psalms sung in different families of every street.

In the autumn of 1740 Whitefield visited New England, where the expectancy was, if anything, even greater. The Church of England clergy again rejected him, being particularly angry that Whitefield associated with 'that Tennent and his brethren' and that he referred to them as 'faithful ministers of Jesus Christ'. The rest of the people welcomed him enthusiastically, filling the church buildings and overflowing into the open air. This was all the more remarkable because the fervour of the early Puritan settlers had long gone. In Cotton Mather's words, 'There is a general and an horrible decay of Christianity among the professors of it.' After Whitefield's visit all was changed. One minister wrote to Isaac Watts in England, 'Our lectures flourish, our sabbaths are joyous, our churches increase and our ministers have new life and spirit in their work.'

Jonathan Edwards

One place, however, had proved an exception to the general decline and there the young preacher went next. This place was Northampton, where the Congregational minister was Jonathan

Edwards (1703 – 1758), one of the greatest men in the history both of America and of the church of Jesus Christ. He was born of Puritan stock in 1703, the son of Timothy Edwards, minister of East Windsor, and grandson of the famous Solomon Stoddard, minister at Northampton from 1669. During his childhood there were several awakenings under Timothy's ministry, but although he was moved at these times it seems that he was not really converted until he had embarked on postgraduate studies at Yale, with a view to entering the ministry. When he returned home in the summer of 1721 his 'mind was greatly fixed on divine things', 'the face of everything was altered' and he felt 'great satisfaction as to my good state'. In other words, he now had an assurance of salvation or, as he termed it, 'spiritual happiness'. So when he did enter the ministry Jonathan did not come under the condemnation of Whitefield as one who preached but did not 'experimentally know Christ'. Indeed, the old-fashioned language must not be allowed to disguise the fact that Edwards was not only an expert on the nature of true Christian experience but also a man of deep communion with God. He records a later experience in the following words:

> Once, as I rode out into the woods for my health, in 1737, having alighted from my horse in a retired place, as my manner commonly has been to walk for divine contemplation and prayer, I had a view that for me was extraordinary, of the glory of the Son of God, as Mediator between God and man, and his wonderful, great, full, pure and sweet grace and love, and meek and gentle condescension. This grace that appeared so calm and sweet, appeared also great above the heavens. The person of Christ appeared ineffably excellent with an excellency great enough to swallow up all thought and conception – which continued, as near as I can judge, about an hour; which kept me the greater part of the time in a flood of tears and weeping aloud. I felt an ardency of soul, to be, what I know not otherwise how to express, emptied and annihilated; to lie in the dust, and to be full of Christ alone; to love him with a holy and pure love; to trust in him;

to live upon him; to serve and follow him; and to be perfectly sanctified and made pure, with a divine and heavenly purity.

EDWARDS' RESOLUTIONS

Something of the character and earnestness of the young Jonathan Edwards may be deduced from these examples from his seventy Resolutions *written in 1722:*

- *Never to do any manner of thing, whether in soul or body, less or more, but what tends to the glory of God, nor be, nor suffer, if I can possibly avoid it.*
- *Never to lose one moment of time, but to improve it in the most profitable way I possibly can.*
- *That I will live just so as I can think I shall wish I had done, supposing that I live to an old age.*
- *To endeavour, to my utmost, so to act, as I can think I should do, if I had already seen the happiness of heaven and hell torments.*

Edwards spent eighteen months as minister of a new congregation in New York but then returned to Yale as a tutor. The next two years were spent in study and illness before he went to Northampton in 1726 to become assistant to his grandfather, Solomon Stoddard. Stoddard's ministry had seen five revival 'harvests', but he was a strong supporter of certain disastrous departures from Puritan doctrine and practice. The so-called 'Halfway Covenant' allowed parents, unregenerate and excluded from the Lord's Supper, nevertheless to have their children baptized. Stoddard went a stage further, arguing that conversion was not necessary for sharing in communion, arguing from the generally accepted belief that men could enter the ministry though 'destitute of a saving work of God's Spirit on their hearts'. All these matters were eventually to cause trouble for the young man who succeeded his revered grandfather when he died in 1729, but that lay twenty years in the future.

Narrative of Surprising Conversions

Jonathan Edwards' ministry attracted little attention for some time, but then in 1731 he was invited to give a public lecture in Boston. Under the title, 'God glorified in man's dependence', he asserted the old Calvinistic doctrines of grace. This caused quite a stir because although the New England ministers were all subscribers to these doctrines, in practice they were, at best, silent about them and, at worst, opposed them rationalistically. As a consequence many began to tremble for the orthodoxy of the church and even unbelievers feared 'that God was about to withdraw from the land'. To meet the needs of the hour Edwards preached a series of sermons on justification by faith, again stressing the sinner's absolute dependence on God. In his *Narrative of Surprising Conversions* he records how 'The Spirit of God began extraordinarily to set in and wonderfully to work among us; and there were very suddenly, one after another, five or six persons, who were, to all appearances, savingly converted, and some of them wrought upon in a very remarkable way.'

One of these conversions was of a pleasure-seeking young woman; it had a tremendous effect on others, and early in that year of miracles, 1735, the whole town was awakened:

> All other talk, but about spiritual and eternal things, was soon thrown by... It was a dreadful thing among us to lie out of Christ, in danger every day of dropping into hell; and what persons' minds were intent upon was, to escape for their lives, and to fly from the wrath to come.

Within six months over 300 out of a population of around 1,200 were, according to the minister's extremely conservative estimate, converted, from a child of four to a man of seventy.

More than thirty parishes on both sides of the Connecticut River were affected before the work gradually died down, leaving behind transformed towns. Edwards wrote,

> Our public assemblies were then beautiful: the congregation was alive in God's service, everyone earnestly intent on the

public worship, every hearer eager to drink in the words of the minister as they came from his mouth; the assembly in general were, from time to time, in tears while the Word was preached; some weeping with sorrow and distress, others with joy and love, others with pity and concern for the souls of their neighbours.

And in November 1736 he could record, 'I know of no one young person in the town who has returned to former ways of looseness and extravagance in any respect; but we still remain a reformed people, and God has evidently made us a new people.'

Before Whitefield arrived in Northampton in 1740 there had been what Edwards calls 'a visible alteration' in the quietness that had succeeded the revival of 1735. More seriousness was apparent among the young people from the spring until Whitefield's arrival in October. The two men spoke together of 'the consolations and privileges of saints, and the plentiful effusion of the Spirit on believers'. Whitefield preached four times and 'good Mr Edwards wept during the whole time' of one sermon. 'The people were equally affected', says Whitefield, 'and in the afternoon the power increased yet more.' The two men were very different in temperament and do not appear to have become intimate friends, but their respect and admiration for each other was unbounded. Edwards warned his young colleague frankly of the dangers of relying on impulses and impressions, as Whitefield was liable to do, but the visitor still wrote in his journal, 'I think I have not seen his fellow in all New England.' His prayer was 'that he might hear that the Lord has renewed his work in their souls, and caused them to do their first works' and within a month, says Edwards, 'There was a great alteration in the town, both as to the renewal of professors and the awakening of others.'

The New England revival spreads

The revival spread from Boston and Northampton throughout New England and then southwards to Virginia. Many churches and ministries were revived and thousands converted. Jonathan Dickinson testified to having 'more young people address me for direction in their spiritual concerns within these three months than in thirty years before'. It has been credibly asserted that out of a population of a quarter of a million in New England some 50,000 were converted. Many new churches were established and ministers and students were converted. (When Whitefield returned to America a few years later there were twenty ministers in Boston alone who attributed their conversion to him.)

The most intense work was during the years 1740 to 1742, but the awakening continued in America for most of the century, as it did in Britain also. Two examples may give something of the flavour of those momentous times. Two days after leaving Edwards, Whitefield preached at Middletown 'to about four thousand people at eleven o'clock'. One of his hearers, an uneducated farmer named Nathan Cole, has left us a graphic description of the occasion. He had heard of Whitefield and longed to hear him, so when he heard that he was coming to preach in the town twelve miles away he dropped everything and went with his wife, 'riding double' on one horse. As they neared the town he saw a fog or cloud and heard a noise like thunder, which he soon discovered to be caused by horses' hooves. 'Every horse seemed to go with all his might to carry his rider to hear news from heaven for the saving of souls.' Ferry boats brought more across the river and Cole joined the crowds who listened to the 'young, slim, slender youth'. As he spoke with 'sweet solemnity', Cole received 'a heart wound and by God's blessing my old foundation was broken up and I saw my righteousness would not save me'. This conviction continued for two years until he was gloriously and lastingly converted.

Not too far away at Middleborough, the minister, Peter Thacher, was in despair after thirty-four unfruitful years with his flock. In May 1741 he wrote to a friend, 'Nothing hath hindered my resigning the pastoral office, but my being at a loss to fix on a farewell sermon.' Then, in spite of being prejudiced against him, he went to hear Gilbert Tennent preach nearby. His prejudice was removed before Tennent had prayed three sentences and he experienced the power of the Word as he remembered it from his youth. Tennent preached for him that evening and though this was without visible effect he did give Thacher this encouragement:

'Oft-times it is darkest a little before dawn.' From that day the people were a little more inclined to hear, but although Thacher invited other ministers to preach and arranged a day of prayer, there was 'no visible success' for eight months. Meanwhile, he heard of the Lord 'carrying on his own work with such a mighty arm in so many places'. Then revival came to Middleborough. After a visiting minister had preached at a service Thacher himself gave an exhortation. 'Many now melted down', he testifies. 'After the blessing people generally stayed, until some cried out with terror, which flew like lightning into every breast; I suppose none excepted. I have written accounts of seventy-six that day struck and brought first to enquire what they should do to escape condemnation.' Within two months nearly 100 were converted and in the following year 170 joined the church, while many who were members already were 'detected of their hypocrisy'. In 1744 Thacher died in peace having, like Simeon, seen God's salvation.

Back in England

It is impossible in brief compass to trace the progress of the revival on two continents so we must content ourselves with a general impression of the future careers of the leaders of the work. When Whitefield returned to England in March 1741 he again found that the situation had changed. Not only had John Wesley taken over the leadership, he had also changed its direction doctrinally. The breach between the two leaders, largely caused by Wesley's opposition to Whitefield's Calvinism and the propagation of his own teaching on 'Christian perfection', is one of the saddest episodes in the eighteenth century, even though it was later healed to some extent. The American, Welsh and Scottish ministers all agreed with Whitefield, and as a result of becoming rather isolated, Wesley concentrated mainly on England. There he laboured heroically, travelling over 250,000 miles on horseback, an instrument in the conversion of thousands and founder of the Wesleyan Methodist movement, which would spread worldwide.

Wesley's journal gives a fascinating account of his travels and the power with which his preaching was accompanied. He concentrated on the great centres of population, preaching mainly to the poorer people. He had more than his fair share of both verbal and physical attacks; he often showed great courage in facing mobs in many different parts of the country. On one occasion he was warned of a mob awaiting him in Plymouth but went to speak there in the open air all the same. Drums were beaten and another preacher was shouted down:

> … by the multitude, who grew fiercer and fiercer as their numbers increased. After waiting about a quarter of an hour, perceiving the violence of the rabble still increasing, I walked down into the thickest of them, and took the captain of the mob by the hand. He immediately said, 'Sir, I will see you safe home. Gentlemen, stand off, give back. I will knock the first man down that touches him.'

In his journal one can trace the progress of the work and the transformation of the land in successive references to certain localities. In 1752 he visited Barnard Castle in County Durham for the first time. He rode 'through very rough roads and as rough weather' and, although he was feeling faint he went out at the appointed time to preach in the street:

> But the mob was so numerous and so loud that it was not possible for many to hear. Nevertheless, I spoke on and those who were near listened with huge attention. To prevent this, some of the rabble fetched the [fire] engine, and threw a good deal of water on the congregation; but not a drop fell on me. After about three quarters of an hour, I returned into the house.

Nine years later all was changed. He 'reached Barnard Castle soon after six. I preached at eight in a ground adjoining to the town. Are these the people that a few years ago were like roaring lions? They were now quiet as lambs; nor could several showers drive them away till I concluded.' After seven more years he records that the commanding officer of the Durham militia freed all his men to attend the evening preaching: 'A large number of them were present at five in the morning. I have not found so deep and lively a work in any other part of the whole kingdom, as runs through the whole circuit, particularly in the vales that wind between these horrid mountains.'

Whitefield also suffered from the attentions of the mob, especially in London, and also from the press who nicknamed him Dr Squintum because of his eye condition. His marvellous voice and powers of description often quieted the crowds in the open air and impressed the nobility who crowded to hear him at the invitation of the godly Countess of Huntingdon. The cultured, but ungodly, Lord Chesterfield declared Whitefield's eloquence to be 'unrivalled'. Listening to the evangelist at the Tottenham Court Road Chapel in London as he graphically compared a sinner to a blind beggar ignorantly nearing a dangerous precipice, the noble lord jumped to his feet shouting, 'He's gone!' In spite of this he was not changed spiritually, but Lady Chesterfield was.

THE COUNTESS AND THE DUCHESS

The Countess of Huntingdon invited the Duchess of Buckingham to hear Whitefield and received the following reply: 'It is monstrous to be told that you have a heart as sinful as the common wretches that crawl on the earth. This is highly offensive and insulting; and I cannot but wonder that your ladyship should relish any sentiments so much at variance with high rank and good breeding.' Nevertheless, she added, 'I shall be most happy to accept your kind offer of accompanying me to hear your favourite preacher.'

Scotland and Wales

As well as visiting America seven times in all, Whitefield went many times to Scotland. He first went to preach there in 1741 at the invitation of the Erskines, Ralph and Ebenezer, who had given him considerable help in his progress towards a clear understanding of the gospel and grace. News of events both in England and America had brought expectancy not only to the Erskines and their friends, who had seceded from the Church of Scotland to form the Associate Presbytery, but also to faithful men who had remained in the established church. When Whitefield refused to limit his ministry to the Associate Presbytery and affirmed that: 'If the pope himself would lend me his pulpit, I would gladly proclaim the righteousness of Jesus Christ therein', they would have nothing more to do with him. Although Whitefield preached in Edinburgh and Glasgow with great power resulting in much conviction and not a few conversions, real revival only came to Scotland after he left.

The Cambuslang revival

The minister of Cambuslang, near Glasgow, was William McCulloch (1691 – 1771), a great admirer of Jonathan Edwards with whom he had corresponded. For about a year he had been preaching on the subject of the new birth in its various aspects and for some months a general concern had been increasing. An extra meeting was requested and this was held on Thursdays. In February 1742 three meetings for prayer were held on successive evenings and after the sermon on the Thursday of that week fifty people came to the minister's house under deep conviction seeking help. After this, numbers seeking the Lord increased daily until within three months over 300 found peace with God. Many people from other parishes visited Cambuslang and were convicted and converted; the awakening then spread to their parishes, notably to Kilsyth. The minister there, James Robe, had been preaching on regeneration since 1740, and on 16 May as he was stressing its importance, 'An extraordinary power of the Spirit from on high accompanied the word preached.' The work spread further afield as the news became known: to Kirkintilloch where a group of children began to meet together for prayer in a barn, to Badernock where the local schoolmaster was God's instrument in the absence of a minister and to many more districts.

Whitefield returned in June to find the work still increasing but also under growing criticism from the brethren of the Associate Presbytery, especially Adam Gib. Whitefield went to Cambuslang where he preached three times on the first day. At the last service he was followed by William McCulloch and the people had to be persuaded to go home at one o'clock in the morning! An estimated 20,000 gathered for a historic communion season and tents and tables were set up in the open air. Whitefield describes how one 'might have seen thousands bathed in tears; some at the same time wringing their hands, others almost swooning and others crying out and mourning over a pierced Saviour. Much prayer had been previously put up to the Lord. All night, in different companies, you might have heard persons praying to and praising God.' Sadly, the seceders, in an official 'heaven-daring paper' (Robe's description) and particularly Gib, in a 'warning' pamphlet, declared the revival to be a delusion, the work of Satan, of whom Whitefield was 'an effectual, though blinded, tool'. It is said that these otherwise great and godly men later repented of their bitterness; the whole is a warning to us all. Happily, the revival could not be stopped.

Calvinistic Methodists

Whitefield's doctrinal position commended him to the Welsh leaders as it had to the Scots, and he encouraged the ministers and societies who were furthering the revival in Wales. Harris led the societies and Rowland, increasingly the leader but supported by many more ministers, went from strength to strength in Llangeitho and far beyond. Whitefield joined with them in their deliberations, mediated when necessary between Harris and Rowland and, in 1743, served as moderator at the first meeting of the joint English and Welsh 'Calvinistic Methodist Association'. Although Howell Harris became estranged from the rest and spent some years in a spiritual wilderness, Rowland continued to lead the work. Harris was restored to his brethren and to usefulness in 1762 and died in 1773. Rowland, 'not tired of the work, but in it', preached on with undiminished power until 1790.

Last days

A host of other men was raised up to support these great leaders, among them were William Williams in Wales and William Grimshaw of Haworth in England. Jonathan Edwards died in 1758, after being, amazingly, dismissed from his pastorate in

Northampton because of his attempt to reverse his grandfather's policy on admission to communion. He retired to Stockbridge to preach to the Indians and write some of his most valuable works before becoming president, for one short month, of the College of New Jersey, the successor of William Tennent's Log College and predecessor of Princeton.

Whitefield, worn out with his exertions, died in 1770 at Newburyport in New England where he lies to this day. He arrived there late on a Saturday, having arranged to preach there the next day. He was exhausted and intended to go to bed early, but a crowd at the door of the parsonage begged him to preach to them. Standing on the landing, halfway up the stairs, he began to preach Christ to them, continuing until the candle in his hand burned itself out. He died during the night at the age of fifty-five. Wesley who lived and laboured on until 1791, preached his funeral sermon at the chapel in Tottenham Court Road, London. After testifying to his zeal, activity, tender-heartedness and charitableness he attributed it all to his 'faith in the bleeding Lord … the love of God shed abroad in his heart, filling his soul with tender, disinterested love to every child of man'. The description that he gave of Whitefield's influence applies in measure to himself and the many others who took part in this great work of God, to whom is all the glory:

> Have we read or heard of any person since the apostles, who testified the gospel of the grace of God, through so widely extended a space, through so large a part of the habitable world? Have we read or heard of any person, who called so many thousands, so many myriads of sinners to repentance? Above all, have we read or heard of any, who has been a blessed instrument in the hand of God, of bringing so many sinners from darkness to light, and from the power of Satan unto God?

Questions for discussion

1. What is the connection between the formation of the 'Religious Societies' and the Great Awakening? What does this tell us about our responsibility today?

2. What are the right and wrong deductions to be made from the fact that both Whitefield and Wesley enjoyed great blessing on their labours? How should we deal with doctrinal differences between godly men? What can we learn from Wesley's funeral tribute to Whitefield?

3. What dangers of eloquence are illustrated by the story of Lord Chesterfield listening to Whitefield? Is it wrong to use the kind of graphic description that Whitefield did?

For further reading

R. Backhouse (ed.), *John Wesley's journal* (abridged), Hodder & Stoughton, 1993.

R. Bennett, *The early life of Howell Harris*, The Banner of Truth Trust, 1962.

* F. Cook, *William Grimshaw of Haworth*, The Banner of Truth Trust, 1997.

** A. Dallimore, *George Whitefield*, The Banner of Truth Trust, 2 volumes, 1970 & 1980.

I. Murray, *Daniel Rowland and the evangelical awakening in Wales*, The Banner of Truth Trust, 1985.

** I. Murray, *Jonathan Edwards*, The Banner of Truth Trust, 1987.

** I. Murray, *Wesley and the men who followed*, The Banner of Truth Trust, 2003.

* J. C. Ryle, *Christian leaders of the eighteenth century*, The Banner of Truth Trust, 1978.

J. Tracy, *The Great Awakening*, The Banner of Truth Trust, 1976.

Enlarge the place of your tent,
    stretch your tent curtains wide,
    do not hold back;
lengthen your cords,
    strengthen your stakes.
For you will spread out to the right and to the left;
    your descendants will dispossess nations
    and settle in their desolate cities.

— Isaiah 54:2-3

Expect great things from God; attempt great things for God.

— William Carey (1761 – 1834)

O Lord our God arise!
    The cause of truth maintain,
And wide o'er all the peopled world
    Extend her blessed reign.

— Ralph Wardlaw (1779 – 1853)

12

Great things for God

On 2 October 1792 twelve ministers met together in Widow
Wallis's parlour in Kettering. There they formed the 'Particular
Baptist Society for the Propagation of the Gospel among the
Heathen'. Their funds, collected in a snuffbox belonging to the
newly-appointed secretary, amounted to £13.2s.6D, and with this
and faith they set out to change the face of the world. The leaders,
not one of them over forty years of age, were Samuel Pearce of
Birmingham, John Sutcliff of Olney, John Ryland of Northampton,
Andrew Fuller (the secretary) of Kettering and William Carey of
Leicester. Of course, this was not the first attempt to take the
gospel to the heathen overseas, but it was the beginning of the
modern missionary movement, which spread the knowledge of
Christ so wonderfully across the world. We have seen John
Eliot's work with the North American Indians and before that
Calvin was responsible for the first missionaries to Brazil. The
Moravians, under the leadership of Count Nicholas Zinzendorf,

had a long and honourable record in missions since their first missionaries sailed for the West Indies in 1732, and the Wesleyan Methodists, in the person of Thomas Coke and others, had begun work in America in 1784. None of these efforts, no matter how commendable and even heroic they were, had the worldwide vision and widespread effect that Carey and his friends had. To understand how this most significant event came about we must retrace our steps. A clue is to be found in the names of the two sons of John Ryland; he named them Jonathan Edwards Ryland and David Brainerd Ryland.

Edwards and Brainerd

Edwards's influence

Jonathan Edwards, after his dismissal from the church at Northampton in America, was himself a missionary for seven years to the Indians around the frontier settlement of Stockbridge, but his influence in other ways was much greater than his example. An extremely foolish attack on the missionaries in 1815 alleged that they had paid too much attention to Jonathan Edwards. In fact, as Andrew Fuller replied, their critics would have done better to pay more attention to him, for Edwards was the inspiration behind their endeavour in three distinct areas. In the first place it was he who wrote the life of David Brainerd and published it together with Brainerd's journal in 1749. This work had a tremendous effect on Wesley, Coke, Henry Martyn, Robert Morrison of China, Robert Murray M'Cheyne and, of course, the men who met at Kettering. They were all moved by the account of Brainerd's godliness and his heroic labours and were stirred to action by the record of his successful but brief work. Indeed, it was recorded that the *Life and Diary* became virtually 'a second Bible' for Carey.

David Brainerd

David Brainerd (1718 – 1747) was born in 1718 and converted twenty-one years later after great convictions and despair, which brought him to depend entirely on God's grace for his salvation and which influenced his later praying and preaching. He 'enjoyed considerable sweetness in religion' in communion with God and entered Yale in 1739 to prepare for the ministry. Of course, these were days of revival and the college was naturally affected. The students, in their zeal, took exception to the new rector's opposition to Gilbert Tennent and George Whitefield, and Brainerd was betrayed into a most censorious criticism, which became generally known and resulted in the somewhat harsh punishment of expulsion. Brainerd acknowledged his fault, but no reconciliation or reinstatement was permitted. He was already showing symptoms of tuberculosis and owing to his overly introspective temperament was thrown into a deep depression. He took refuge in communion with God and wrote in his diary, 'If I had a thousand lives, my soul would gladly have laid them all down at once to have been with Christ.' He began to preach and soon his thoughts turned to the Indian tribes scattered around his homeland. He prayed earnestly for them, and in 1743 he became a missionary to them under the auspices of the Society in Scotland for the Propagation of Christian Knowledge who had been asked by some American ministers to start a work among the Indians.

For the next four-and-a-half years Brainerd endured deprivation, illness and loneliness as he laboured for the salvation of his beloved Indians. After six months, during which he had become reasonably proficient in the language, he moved to a new area, the Forks of Delaware. 'All my concern, almost,' he wrote, 'is for the conversion of the heathen, and for that end I live.' His diary records his excessive self-examination but also his intense longings after holiness and his unceasing intercession for his hearers. Eventually, after another change of place, in 1745 it also records his success.

Success at Crossweeksung

Here at Crossweeksung the Indians listened without objections. His hearers increased from seven to thirty, and then many came from all around. He revisited the Forks of Delaware and found some evidence of fruit, but it was at Crossweeksung that the real work was seen.

His hearers wept as he preached, stressing the majesty of God and the sinfulness of the human heart:

> I stood amazed at the influence that seized the audience almost universally, and could compare it to nothing more aptly than the irresistible force of a mighty torrent or swelling deluge... Old men and women, who had been drunken wretches for many years, and some little children not more than six or seven years of age, appeared in distress for their souls, as well as persons of middle age.

Within a month twenty-five were baptized even though Brainerd's own conversion had given him high standards in assessing conversion. The work continued through 1745 and 1746 until he numbered 150 believers among them. Pagan superstitions and drunkenness were abandoned. Christian marriage, family worship and the Lord's Day were properly recognized and observed, and Brainerd's house was constantly crowded with people seeking 'Christian knowledge'.

Last days

During all this time Brainerd's health had been deteriorating in the terrible conditions; bad weather, long journeys, poor food and sheer hard work in the end forced him to hand over the work to his brother John and leave for civilization. In March 1747 he went to Boston where he read Edwards' *Treatise on the Religious Affections* 'again and again' and in July went on to Northampton where he spent his last days in Edwards' home. The two men had met four years earlier when Brainerd visited Yale, in an unsuccessful attempt to make peace with the college officials, and they had become firm friends. Brainerd had visited Northampton and kept up a correspondence both with Edwards and with his daughter, Jerusha. We do not know just when friendship with Jerusha ripened into love, but Brainerd could write of her, 'It is a little piece of heaven to be in her presence.' They were betrothed, but before they could be married Brainerd's condition worsened still more and Jerusha nursed him for nineteen weeks until he died in October 1747.

Jerusha followed him to the grave a few months later, having caught the disease from him, and was buried next to him. Edwards published the influential *Life and Diary* in 1749.

Andrew Fuller and 'false Calvinism'

The *Life and Diary* was not the only writing of Edwards that was popular on the other side of the Atlantic. His balanced Calvinism as well as his vision of the conversion of the heathen, expressed in his *History of the Work of Redemption*, were welcomed particularly in Scotland but were also partly responsible for changing the theological climate among the Particular Baptists in England. In that denomination the doctrines of grace had been perverted into a cold and barren hyper-Calvinism. This paralysed evangelism and forbade missionary endeavour on the grounds that all men were not commanded to repent and believe in Christ. John Ryland directed Robert Hall to Edwards's *Enquiry into the Freedom of the Will*. This proved to be a liberating influence for Hall and, through one of his subsequently published sermons, for the whole denomination. Carey was helped by the writings of Robert Hall, but it was Andrew Fuller (1754 – 1815), following John Bunyan and Jonathan Edwards, who launched the most devastating attack on what he termed 'false Calvinism'. While still at Soham, before he moved to Kettering, he wrote for his own use, *The Gospel Worthy of All Acceptation or the Duty of Sinners to Believe in Jesus Christ*, which was later published in 1784. This work in no way denied the sovereignty of God in election and particular redemption, in spite of the claims of Fuller's opponents who charged him with Arminianism, but it does insist that men must repent and believe, irrespective of whether they know they are elect or not.

The link with the founding of the missionary society can be seen clearly in the following extract from Fuller's diary at about the time he was writing the book:

I found my soul drawn out in love to poor souls, while reading Millar's account of Eliot's labours among the North American Indians, and their effect upon those poor, barbarous savages. I found also a suspicion that we shackle ourselves too much in our addresses to sinners; that we have bewildered and lost ourselves by taking the decrees of God as rules of action.

He might better have written 'rules of inaction', for this was the inevitable consequence. Carey, on the other hand, drew his own conclusion from Fuller's treatise: 'If it be the duty of all men, when the gospel comes, to believe unto salvation, then it is the duty of those who are entrusted with the gospel to endeavour to make it known among all nations for the obedience of faith.' This he did.

William Carey

The Humble Attempt

There was also a more direct influence from Edwards. During his ministry he was in touch with the evangelical Presbyterian ministers in Scotland, such as James Robe of Kilsyth. In 1744 these men formed a union for prayer for the worldwide extension of Christ's kingdom. This became known in New England and Edwards, having preached a series of sermons on Zechariah 8:20-23, published them under the title *A Call to United Extraordinary Prayer*. This is better known by its subtitle, *An Humble Attempt to Promote an Explicit Agreement and Visible Union of God's People through the World, in Extraordinary Prayer, for the Revival of Religion and the Advancement of Christ's Kingdom on Earth, Pursuant to Scripture Promises and Prophecies concerning the Last Time*. This, in turn, was welcomed in Scotland, and nearly forty years later it formed part of a parcel of books by Edwards that John Erskine sent to John Ryland in Northampton, England. Ryland passed it on to Sutcliff who was so affected that he proposed, at the June 1784 meeting of the Northamptonshire Association, that the churches should set aside the first Monday of each month for special prayer for revival. This 'Union for Prayer' was soon joined by the associations and other denominations and further strengthened when Sutcliff had the *Humble Attempt* reprinted in 1789. Its influence on William Carey (1761 – 1834) is undeniable, and to his work we must now turn in more detail.

The shoemaker

The 'father of modern missions' was born in 1761 at Paulerspury in Northamptonshire. His father was a weaver who later became parish clerk and schoolmaster in the village, but he was poor and, recalled his son, 'unable to do much for me'. William, however, was determined to do much for himself. He had a great thirst for knowledge of all kinds; he read all he could find, especially on science, history and voyages, and collected specimens of plants, animals and insects. School finished for him when he was twelve and after two years as a gardener, which he was forced to give up because of an allergy, he became instead an apprentice shoemaker in the neighbouring village of Piddington.

There he shared an attic with a senior apprentice, John Warr, who, although not yet a Christian, used to argue with both Carey and their master on the relative merits of Anglicanism and his own Independency. Carey had been brought up to attend the parish church and used to sing in the choir but knew nothing of godliness. He tells us, 'I was addicted to swearing, lying and unchaste conversation.' During this time Warr was converted and began to press Carey even harder, thus he began to attend the Independent services and tried to reform. He was convicted of sin through being caught stealing a shilling from his master, and at the age of seventeen and a half gave up 'a lifeless carnal ministry' for an evangelical one. He had been converted and from then on he threw in his lot with the despised nonconformists, although he also owed much to the ministry of Thomas Scott, John Newton's successor at nearby Olney. Scott often visited Carey's new master and later wrote, 'I from the first thought young Carey an extraordinary person.'

In 1781 William married Dorothy Plackett, six years older than himself and able to neither read nor write. Pressed by his friends Carey soon began to preach regularly at Earls Barton, eight miles walk away, and once a month in his home village, to the family's embarrassment. Around this time his baby daughter died of a fever, which nearly killed him also, leaving him bald. While his ideas were still developing he received help from Robert Hall and also heard

Andrew Fuller preach. From reading Robert Hall he also decided he must be immersed, and in 1783 he was baptized by John Ryland who described his future fellow worker as 'a poor journeyman shoemaker'. When his employer died Carey took over both his business and his family responsibilities, and times were very hard.

At this time he was able to borrow *Captain Cook's Voyages*, and reading this 'was the first thing that engaged my mind to think of missions'. This was no mere romantic interest; he began to study as well as preach and run the business, displaying that dogged perseverance for which he was noted.

'I can plod', said Carey later in his life. 'I can persevere in any definite pursuit. To this I owe everything.' The plodding, however, was, in the words of a friend's son, 'the plodding of a genius'. He clearly had a great gift for languages. Even while an apprentice he had been fascinated by some passages in Greek in a book on his master's shelves, a commentary on part of the New Testament, and, with the aid of a failed university student, he had soon mastered the language. Now, in a few weeks he taught himself to read French and Dutch as well as beginning on Latin and Hebrew.

Schoolteacher and Baptist pastor

In 1785 he became lay pastor of a little Baptist church at Moulton, near Kettering, which had been without a minister for many years. To supplement his tiny stipend, as well as doing a little cobbling, he became a schoolmaster. The church began to pick up as people were converted, but the school was less successful. Although Carey's discipline was poor, the pupils did at least learn some geography. Andrew Fuller recalls visiting him at Moulton:

> I saw hanging up against the wall a very large map, consisting of several sheets of paper pasted together by himself, on which he had drawn, with a pen, a place for every nation in the known world, and entered into it whatever he met with in reading, relating to its population, religion, etc.

On the map the Indians were described as 'pagans, vigilant, cruel, warlike', which fits the picture given elsewhere of Carey moved to tears in a geography lesson, pointing to the various lands and crying out, 'And these are pagans, pagans!'

When his school failed Carey made boots for one of Fuller's deacons, Thomas Gotch, who, on learning of his gift for languages, also gave him £26 per annum to help him devote more time to his studies. At this time Carey was only a probationary minister in membership with John Sutcliff's church at Olney, but in 1787 he was ordained as minister at Moulton. Ryland and Fuller took part in the service as well as Sutcliff. Carey now had opportunities to meet and discuss with his fellow ministers in the Northamptonshire Association, which extended from St Albans to Leicester. He was, says Fuller, always talking to his brethren about the possibility of introducing the gospel to all nations: 'His heart burned incessantly with desire for the salvation of the heathen.' It was on one such occasion that Carey proposed for discussion the question whether the Great Commission was still binding on ministers. The chairman was John Collett Ryland, father of Carey's friend, and he is alleged to have told Carey to sit down, calling him 'a miserable enthusiast for asking such a question', telling him that nothing could be done before another Pentecost, when a new effusion of gifts, including the gift of tongues, would fulfil the commission of Christ. Another report attributes to Ryland the following words: 'When God pleases to convert the heathen, he will do it without your aid or mine'. The younger Ryland called the story 'an ill-natured anecdote', but the sentiments were, nevertheless, typical of the hyper-Calvinist opposition with which Carey had to contend.

Carey's Enquiry

Carey set about overcoming such attitudes. His wife had been converted and baptized, but he now had three sons and was 'in considerable straits for maintenance', according to the Moulton Church minute book. So in 1789 he moved to the troubled church in Leicester where he combined dealing with the church's problems with study, preaching and stirring up interest in missions. At the instigation of a Birmingham Baptist, Thomas Potts, he began to write a pamphlet on the subject. In 1791 he pleaded at the Easter association meeting for action, but the difficulties seemed insuperable to the others. Understandably, they regarded the 'unbeaten path', says Fuller, as 'grasping at an object utterly beyond their reach', but they did encourage Carey to finish and publish his pamphlet.

Carey read the finished work to Ryland, Sutcliff, Fuller and Samuel Pearce of Birmingham, and it was published in May 1791 shortly before the association meeting at Nottingham, at which Carey had been invited to preach. Under the title *An Enquiry into the Obligation of Christians to Use Means for the Conversion of the Heathen (etc.)*, he established the doctrinal basis of missions by refuting the idea that the Great Commission applied only to the apostles and then removed practical objections or excuses. Then he dealt with previous efforts, including those of Eliot and Brainerd, and added a statistical analysis of the religious state of the world, whether 'pagan' or 'Mohammedan'. He appealed to Christians to emulate traders, saying, 'It only requires that we should have as much love to the souls of our fellow creatures and fellow sinners as they have for the profits arising from otter-skins, and all these difficulties would be easily surmounted.' He then ended by calling for the setting up of a society to put his plan into effect.

THE NOTTINGHAM SERMON

Three weeks after the publication of the Enquiry *Carey preached his famous 'Nottingham sermon' to the association on the text from Isaiah 54: 'Enlarge the place of thy tent, and let them stretch forth the curtains of their habitations: spare not, lengthen thy cords and strengthen thy stakes.' His two headings were:* 'Expect great things from God; attempt great things for God.' *When the ministers met next morning the matter was not even mentioned and Carey, turning to Fuller, implored him, 'Is there nothing again going to be done?' Fuller was shaken into responding and, being a man of some influence, his support resulted in the passing of a resolution that 'A plan be prepared against the next ministers' meeting at Kettering for forming a Baptist society for propagating the gospel among the heathen.'*

The Society

So the meeting in Widow Wallis's parlour came about and the society was formed on 2 October 1792.

Soon Carey heard of John Thomas, a Baptist and former naval surgeon who had gone out to Bengal in the service of the East India Company and had stayed behind in India preaching the gospel. He was now in England trying to raise funds for a mission to Bengal. He could speak Bengali, had already seen some success in preaching and seemed to be God's provision for their work. The society invited him to return to India as their missionary and Carey offered to go with him. All seemed to be going just as the *Enquiry* had envisaged, but then the difficulties arose. Their funds were very limited and the influential London Association refused its official and financial support. Carey's father asked, 'Is William mad?', when he heard of his plans, and Dorothy Carey, five months pregnant and aware that France had just declared war on England, adamantly refused to accompany her husband.

Also, the East India Company had a business monopoly in India and used it to keep 'troublesome' missionaries out, leaving, in William Wilberforce's words, 'twenty millions of people to the providential protection of Brama'. So the missionaries had to find a captain who was prepared to take them to India without their having a licence to reside there.

Then Carey discovered that John Thomas was deeply in debt and pursued by his creditors. After a long delay and various disappointments, partly because of Thomas' position, Carey secured passages on a Danish vessel. During this period Dorothy's baby was born and she agreed to accompany her husband, together with her sister. Extra funds came in and the party was able to leave on 13 June 1793. They were going to descend into 'a gold mine in India' that promised rich spiritual rewards but involved great danger: 'I will venture down', said Carey to Fuller, 'but remember that you must hold the ropes.' Fuller did remember and held them fast, as secretary, until his death over twenty years later.

It was five months before they completed their journey of 15,000 miles. While on board Carey had conducted services and engaged in personal debate with some of the other passengers but with little success. He also started to study Bengali with Thomas and made good progress. Storms beset them and for two months they saw no other ship. As they neared their destination the winds were against them, and Carey had to be very patient, learning a spiritual lesson that was to be invaluable during his first years in India. 'I hope I have learned the necessity', he wrote in his journal, 'of bearing up in the things of God against wind and tide, when there is occasion, as we have done in our voyage.' Even contrary winds, he had discovered, could be used to make gradual progress with skill and patience.

In India

His first years in India were of almost insuperable difficulty, but progress was made. The first six months were occupied mainly in trying to survive. Everything was much more expensive than Thomas had led them to believe and the articles that they had brought with them to sell in order to raise capital raised very little. Carey left Calcutta in the hope of finding somewhere cheaper to live but soon had to return. He did manage to do some preaching as his Bengali improved and also started to correct Thomas's translation of Genesis. Thomas was no help and resumed working as a doctor to support his family. However, when Carey had the offer of some rent-free land for three years and needed tools he found that Thomas had squandered all the money. He loved Thomas but realized now, too late, that he was utterly 'fickle' and unreliable, 'only fit to live at sea, where his daily business is before him, and daily provision made for him'. Poor Dorothy added to his problems. 'My wife, and sister too', wrote Carey, 'who do not see the importance of the mission as I do, are continually exclaiming against me.' Even worse, Dorothy's mental state gave cause for alarm and soon Carey had to record that she had 'relapsed into her affliction, and is much worse than she was before'.

Carey must have been very low when he wrote to a friend, 'I am in a strange land, alone, no Christian friend, a large family and nothing to supply their wants.' But he could also write, 'Now all my friends are one; I rejoice, however, that he is all-sufficient and can supply all my wants, spiritual and temporal... Everything is known to God, and God cares for the mission.'

Eventually he borrowed some money, at an exorbitant rate of interest, and went to the land he had been offered, which was forty miles or three days' journey away. There, a non-Christian Englishman took pity on them and gave them shelter until Carey could build a bamboo hut for the family. (He was rewarded with the love of Mrs Carey's sister, whom he later married.) Meanwhile, Carey was working with his hands as well as studying the language, spurred on by his confidence in the promises and power of God. He wrote,

> When I first left England, my hope of the conversion of the heathen was very strong, but, among so many obstacles, it would entirely die away, unless upheld of God ... no earthly thing to depend upon, or earthly comfort, except food and raiment. Well, I have God, and his word is sure. Though the superstitions of the heathen were a thousand times stronger than they are, and the example of the Europeans a thousand times worse; though I were deserted by all and persecuted by all, yet my faith, fixed on that sure word, would rise above all obstacles and overcome every trial. God's cause will triumph.

To Sutcliff he wrote, 'When my soul can drink its fill at the Word of God, I forget all', and to Pearce, 'The work, to which God has set his hands, will infallibly prosper.' Although 'almost beaten out in a violent storm', he thought he saw 'the sky begin to clear'.

In the providence of God Carey and Thomas, through a connection of the latter, were offered posts as managers of two indigo factories, 250 miles north at Malda. They took up the posts after a three-week journey by water. Carey was criticized by some living safely in England for 'engaging in affairs of trade', but he had to live. Furthermore, this provided him with a licence, a type of work permit, which made his presence legal, while also allowing him ample time for his missionary labours, especially translation. About this time Carey's five-year-old son died, and this seems to have been the last straw as far as Dorothy's unstable mental state was concerned; she relapsed into a deep depression, probably accompanied by delusions, from which she never recovered. In spite of all this Carey worked on.

A letter home from John Fountain, a new missionary who had arrived much to Carey's surprise, speaks highly of his achievements. By the end of 1796 he had translated into Bengali all but the last few chapters of the New Testament and as far as Numbers in the Old. He had also established small churches, although only among the English residents, at Malda and later at Dinadjpur. Problems continued to multiply. He again had to contend with Thomas, who was once more heavily in debt, and with Fountain, whose letters home were politically indiscreet. 'Mr Thomas has gone away', wrote Carey to the understanding and faithful Fuller in January 1798, 'and my domestic troubles are sometimes too heavy for me. I am distressed, yet supported, and I trust not totally dead in the things of God.'

The Serampore trio

In 1799 the factory that Carey managed had to close down, and then a party of eight new missionaries, plus children, arrived. Owing to a misprint in the local newspaper they were immediately imprisoned as 'papist' missionaries and although they were soon released, they were refused permission to join Carey because they had no licences. Colonel Bie, the Christian Governor of Serampore, a small Danish settlement fourteen miles north of Calcutta, offered them shelter and asked them to set up a Christian mission. Soon Carey was persuaded to join them although it meant sacrificing mission property and his school at Kidderpore. Thus the misprint and the closure of the factory combined in the hand of God to establish Carey's great work, for among the new arrivals were William Ward (1769 –1823), a printer whom Carey had met briefly in 1793, and Joshua Marshman (1768 – 1837). With Carey they formed the famous Serampore Trio and from this point the work never looked back, proceeding under the friendly protection of the Danish colony. Carey, who had arrived at Serampore with his printing-press, type and paper and plans to print a thousand copies of the Bible in Bengali, was much encouraged and wrote to Fuller, 'After all the very distressing disappointments which we have met with, I entertain a hope that day is not far distant, when light will most powerfully break forth and spread over this very dark part of the earth.'

The missionary community settled down happily to work; the division of labour came quite naturally, and as they met together regularly for discussion and prayer relations between them were excellent. As well as translating and printing they preached to the population around them. The Marshmans and Ward, whose wife had died, were a great blessing. Hannah Marshman, as well as helping her husband with the school, which provided useful income, took over many other responsibilities, including disciplining the unruly Carey children! The seventeen-year-old Felix 'seemed exceedingly affected' by her plain speaking and soon, under the influence of the gentle Ward, 'from being a tiger, was transformed into a lamb'. He soon began to take part with others in the open-air preaching, which often encountered violent opposition, and Marshman often returned with his face covered with blood from the bricks that were thrown at them. The first page of the Bengali New Testament was printed on 17 March 1800, a most significant event. Although Carey was quite deliberately making translation his priority, this was not a retreat from preaching the gospel but a necessary preparation for the thorough evangelization of India. It was, therefore, an equally important event which occurred later that same year: the baptism of their first Indian convert.

Carey's first convert

Krishna Pal, a Bengali carpenter, slipped and dislocated his shoulder and the family sent to the mission for help, having heard that a Christian doctor was there. This was none other than John Thomas, who, despite his weaknesses, so often provided the key that opened new doors for Carey. Thomas went to the house, treated the shoulder and also spoke to Krishna Pal of healing for the soul. His words fell on prepared and fertile soil for the Indian had long been aware of his sin and had joined a breakaway Hindu sect in an effort to find relief. The next day Carey visited him and invited him to the mission for further treatment. He went with his friend Goluk and continued to go. After a month both professed faith in Christ and their families were also affected. On 28 December 1800 Krishna Pal was baptized, in spite of opposition and harassment that effectively deterred Goluk and their women-folk. Carey recorded, 'I had the happiness to desecrate the Gunga [Ganges] by baptizing the first Hindoo, viz. Krishna, and my son, Felix.' Sadly Thomas could not be present as he had suddenly become violently mad and had to be confined. However a great crowd, including Colonel Bie and Charlotte Rumohr, a noble lady from Schleswig-Holstein who later became Carey's second wife, gathered to watch the baptism and hear the gospel preached in both Bengali and English. More baptisms, including those of Goluk and Krishna's wife, followed in 1801.

Bible translations

The first complete Bengali New Testament was published in March 1801, which seems to have been the reason why Carey was invited to take up the position of lecturer in Bengali and Sanskrit at the Governor-General's favourite Fort William College in Calcutta. This position provided Carey with a public reputation and useful funds for the mission; it also brought him helpful contacts and facilities, which enabled him to produce grammars, dictionaries and translations in at least seven Indian languages. There was a steady stream of converts also, 500 by 1813, some at the cost of their lives, but it was translation that occupied Carey for the remainder of his life. In all he translated parts of the Scriptures into thirty-four languages, with six whole Bibles and twenty-three New Testaments. His capacity for concentrated work was enormous. He begrudged the time spent on anything else. 'The truth is', he wrote, 'that every letter I write is at the expense of a chapter of the Bible, which would have been translated in that time.' As recorded in a letter to John Ryland, his day began at 5:45 A.M. with Bible reading in Hebrew and continued with prayer, language study, family prayers, translation, proofreading, sermon preparation and delivery at the mission service, visitors, more translation, letters, with meals fitted in somewhere, and ending with more Scripture reading, in Greek, at about 11 P.M.

Trials

Although the work made steady progress all was not plain sailing. The winds still blew contrarily and there were frequent storms. Perhaps Carey's greatest trial, apart from his wife's condition, was the fire of 1812. This destroyed the whole print house with their entire stock of paper and reduced the new Tamil and Chinese type to lumps of molten metal. Worst of all it destroyed all of Carey's uncompleted manuscripts!

At the time of the great fire Carey was at the College in Calcutta. When he returned he stood in the midst of the devastation and said, 'In one night the labours of years are consumed. I had lately brought some things to the utmost perfection I could, and contemplated the mission with, perhaps, too much self-congratulation. The Lord has laid me low, that I might look more simply to him.' A few days later he could write to Fuller, 'God has a sovereign right to dispose of us as he pleases. We ought to acquiesce in all that God does with us and to us.' Such was the character of Carey's Calvinism.

He set to work to replace the lost manuscripts but some projects were never resumed. One result of the fire was publicity in England, and the financial loss was more than restored. Gifts came from many loving sources: £50 from the tiny church at Moulton, £10 from William Wilberforce and an amazing £20 from Mrs Wallis, in whose parlour the work had started.

Carey faced and overcame many other problems. His brilliant son Felix, who had been preaching the gospel in Burma, 'shrivelled from a missionary to an ambassador', representing the King of Burma in Calcutta, although he later returned to the work. There were hiccups in relations with the government, especially after the Vellore Mutiny in 1806 when the missionaries were suspected of being French spies. The worst trouble, however, was a breach in relations with the society in England after the death of Fuller and of Ryland, who succeeded him as secretary. This caused many anxieties for the trio in Serampore and even divisions among the missionaries who had joined them in India, including Carey's nephew Eustace.

In spite of all this Carey pressed on. His vision of a worldwide missionary conference was not fulfilled, but he did succeed in setting up a college in Serampore for Indian students. Although it allowed in non-Christians as day students and included law, medicine and teaching in its curriculum, its primary function was to prepare the way for the evangelization of India by Indians, as envisaged years before in the *Enquiry*. In 1827 the Serampore College was granted a charter by the King of Denmark to confer its own degrees, a notable triumph for the one sneeringly dismissed in his homeland as 'the consecrated cobbler'. Nineteen outstations were set up elsewhere, which, while they added greatly to the financial burden when Carey's Fort William College salary almost vanished in government cuts, produced a steady trickle of converts. His later years were spent completing his various projects, so that he could say that he had 'scarcely a wish ungratified'. He cared for his beautiful garden, which was ruined several times by floods, and about which he joked, 'After I am gone, Brother Marshman will turn the cows into my garden.' More happily still, he made his peace with the society in England and the financial problems were eased.

Henry Martyn and other missionaries

Meanwhile others had not stood still. Although not technically missionaries several Anglican clergymen had been active in India as chaplains sent out by the East India Company. David Brown, who arrived there in 1787, Thomas Thomason, who stood with Carey in the smoking remains after the 1812 fire and especially Henry Martyn, whose life and all too brief labours inspired whole generations of missionaries, were just some of those influenced by Charles Simeon of Cambridge, the leading evangelical Anglican of his day. Martyn arrived in Calcutta in 1806 and at first lived at Serampore where Carey knew him well and wrote, 'As the image or shadow of bigotry is not known among us here, we take sweet counsel together, and go to the house of God as friends.'

On leaving Serampore he worked in various parts of India, already showing signs of the disease that would kill him, but burning, according to David Brown, 'with the intenseness and rapid blaze of heated phosphorus'. Martyn completed a translation of the New Testament into Hindustani (Urdu), which is the basis of the one still in use and was assigned the task of supervising Persian and Arabic translations. His humble character and determined godliness may be seen in his often-quoted wish with which he landed in Calcutta: '*I have hitherto lived to little purpose, more like a clod than a servant of God; now let me burn out for God*'.

He left India in 1811 for Persia where he debated with the most influential Muslims and suffered their contempt. He records,

> Thus I walked away alone to my tent, to pass the rest of the day in heat and dirt. What have I done, thought I, to merit all this scorn? Nothing, I trust, but bearing testimony to Jesus. I thought these things over in prayer, and my troubled heart found that peace which Christ hath promised to his disciples.

He presented a copy of the Persian New Testament to the Shah who praised it and promised to have it read to him. Martyn, already gravely ill, set out to return overland to India but never reached there. He died in the Turkish mountains, alone as far as Christians or even Europeans were concerned. 'I sat in the orchard and thought', he wrote almost at the end, 'with sweet comfort and peace, of my God; in solitude my company, my friend and comforter.' Charles Simeon had a portrait of Martyn over the fireplace in his dining room. He told his friends, 'He never takes his eyes off me and seems always to be saying, "Be serious; be in earnest; don't trifle, don't trifle." And I won't trifle!'

Other missionary societies were founded in the wake of the Baptists: the London Missionary Society in 1795 and the Church Missionary Society in 1799 followed by the American missionary societies. Well before 1820 the world was opened up to missions, with Robert Morrison in China, Adoniram Judson in Burma, John Williams in the South Seas and Robert Moffat in Africa. In 1830 Alexander Duff arrived to represent Scotland in India. And these are only some of the great names; thousands of less well-known men laboured, sacrificed and died to take the gospel to the heathen in a way that had been unthinkable fifty years before.

Carey himself never returned to England. In 1833 he began to have a series of strokes and on 9 June 1834 he died. All these men demonstrated the truth of John Eliot's words: 'Prayer and pains through faith in Jesus Christ will do anything', but none more effectively than William Carey, the plodding genius. According to his instructions only a simple tablet with two lines by Isaac Watts marked his grave:

> A wretched, poor, and helpless worm,
> On thy kind arms I fall.

This indicated very clearly where Carey's hopes lay and where the glory should be ascribed. To Carey?

> Ah no! When all things else expire,
> And perish in the general fire,
> This name all others shall survive,
> And through eternity shall live.
> – *Krishna Pal, translated by Joshua Marshman*

Questions for discussion

1. In view of the work of the Moravians, among others, in what sense is Carey rightly regarded as the 'father of modern missions'? Why was Edwards so important in this respect?

2. Some Reformers shared the view of Carey's opponents that the Great Commission of Matthew 28:18-20 applied only to the apostolic era. Why is this wrong and what effect did it have on the missionary outreach of the church?

3. Is 'plodding' a fair description of Carey's work? What elements of this 'plodding' should we emulate? Is it fair to contrast his attitude with Martyn's words, 'Now let me burn out for God'?

For further reading

** S. P. Carey, *William Carey*, The Wakeman Trust, 1993.

** M. Haykin, *One heart and one soul: John Sutcliff of Olney*, Evangelical Press, 1994.

* S. M. Houghton, editor, *Five pioneer missionaries: Eliot, Brainerd, Martyn, Burns & Paton*, The Banner of Truth Trust, 1965.

J. Sargent, *The life and letters of Henry Martyn*, The Banner of Truth Trust, 1985.

* J. Thornbury, *David Brainerd*, Evangelical Press, 1996.

The Spirit of the Sovereign Lord is on me,
*   because the Lord has anointed me*
*   to preach good news to the poor.*
He has sent me to bind up the brokenhearted,
*   to proclaim freedom for the captives*
*   and release from darkness for the prisoners.*
— Isaiah 61:1

What shall we abolish next?
— William Wilberforce (1759 – 1833)

Take my hands, and let them move
*   At the impulse of thy love;*
Take my feet, and let them be
*   Swift and beautiful for thee*

Take my silver and my gold,
*   Not a mite would I withhold;*
Take my intellect, and use
*   Every power as thou shalt choose.*
— Frances Ridley Havergal (1836 – 1879)

13

The Clapham Sect

Many of the criticisms levelled at evangelicals today have more than a grain of truth in them. One of these charges is that we are not concerned about the physical and mental well-being of our fellow men. We are said to be so occupied with men's souls, or sometimes just with ourselves, that we ignore social conditions around us.

However true this may be of Christians today – and it is true enough to make the theme of this chapter an important one – it was certainly far from true of the subjects of this study. This group of men is known today as the 'Clapham Sect', but in their own time they were known, scornfully but more accurately, as 'the Saints'. They were never a sect, being in fact devoted members of the Church of England, but they were closely associated with Clapham. It was then a village about three country miles from the city of London, of which it now forms a part. There the Saints lived, or stayed with their friends, while they planned and carried into effect an incredible social revolution in the name of Christ.

There is, of course, an opposite danger for the Christian: this is to become so involved in social action that we either confuse it *with* the gospel or substitute it *for* the gospel. The work of the Clapham Sect, arising from the great Evangelical Awakening in the eighteenth century and engaging the cooperation of such men as John Newton and Charles Simeon, never fell into this trap. Indeed, as we shall see, among their many interests they numbered evangelism and missionary work.

The leader, figurehead and best known of them all was William Wilberforce and with his conversion we must begin.

William Wilberforce

His conversion

'If Billy turns Methodist he shall not have a sixpence of mine', said the boy's grandfather. He feared the effect on the young lad from Hull of a stay with his aunt in Wimbledon, in a home visited by Whitefield and other leading evangelicals, or 'Methodists' as they were called. He need not have worried, however, as all this had little effect on Billy, who returned to Hull unscathed and unconverted.

William Wilberforce (1759 – 1833) was born into a wealthy and influential Yorkshire family in 1759. As he grew up he showed that, in addition to these advantages, he had many pleasing personal qualities and especially charm and eloquence that made his success in the world inevitable. After his time at Cambridge University, which he spent in relative idleness, though not indulging in the worst excesses of his fellow students, he became Member of Parliament for Hull in 1780. He thus entered or rather conquered fashionable London society, being known as the friend of William Pitt, the future prime minister. So God prepared a leader with not only the necessary gifts but also the necessary position to do the work he had purposed. As yet, however, the one great thing was lacking. Wilberforce's whole energy was devoted to himself and to his own success. He had already talked with a retired missionary from the West Indies about the slave trade, but it was all, he later confessed, with a view to his 'own distinction'.

All this was soon to change. In 1784 and again in 1785 Wilberforce made the customary tour of the Continent in the company of his old tutor's brother, the Rev. Isaac Milner. At this time Milner, a brilliant thinker, was at least clear about the content of historic Christianity. Wilberforce was conventionally religious and had already made some effort to persuade Pitt to attend church, but he was playing with Socinian, or Unitarian, ideas. Wilberforce regarded the views of his Methodist relations as rather fanatical and enjoyed a running battle of argument with Milner. The two men read and studied together the evangelical classic by Philip Doddridge, *The Rise and Progress of Religion in the Soul*, and Wilberforce who was convinced of the truth of Christianity by the end of the first trip, returned from the second a changed, but not yet a converted, man.

He felt the need of spiritual advice and turned, although with much misgiving, to John Newton (1725 – 1807). He had been enthralled by the old slave trader, whom he had heard during his stay in Wimbledon as a boy, and sought him out again. Newton, now sixty, was rector of St Mary Woolnoth in London. Such, however, was the contempt of fashionable society for evangelicals that Wilberforce took the most elaborate precautions of secrecy and even walked twice round the square before he could bring himself to knock on Newton's door. Patient and sound advice from Newton helped the young man to a true and full experience of conversion; the great change had taken place.

Clapham

From the beginning of his new life William was surrounded by good influences. For a time he attended Newton's ministry and soon after his conversion he stayed with the godly John Thornton, the father of Wilberforce's later comrade-in-arms, Henry Thornton. John Thornton was living in Clapham when Henry Venn senior began his ministry there in 1756 and later, in 1792, paved the way for Venn's son, John, to become rector. From 1797 Wilberforce lived in Clapham for a while, although he later lived in London and only stayed in Clapham as a welcome guest in the homes of his various friends. Around John Venn's evangelical and biblical ministry gathered the men who changed the face of the world. There they found their spiritual food; there they rejoiced in fellowship as they moved freely between one another's homes and there they concentrated their efforts to put their faith into practice.

WILBERFORCE'S TWO OBJECTS

In 1787, soon after his conversion, Wilberforce recorded in his diary, 'God Almighty has set before me two great objects, the suppression of the slave trade and the reformation of manners.' With this determination to devote his life to such great aims (the second, so strange sounding to our modern ears, includes a host of scriptural objectives), he continued his political career. 'My walk,' he wrote, 'I am sensible, is a public one; my business is in the world, and I must mix in the assemblies of men or quit the part which Providence seems to have assigned me.' Around the same time Newton wrote to him, 'It is hoped and believed that the Lord has raised you up for the good of his church and for the good of the nation.'

Both Wilberforce and Newton were clearly right in their assessment of the situation. From our vantage point we can see even more clearly how God in his providence prepared a tremendously powerful instrument for good in the person of William Wilberforce. This, however, was only one part of what emerges clearly as a glorious plan, involving many people and many amazing links. It will not be possible to mention all those involved with Wilberforce, but some, at least, will be seen as we trace God's accomplishment of the two great aims he had impressed on his servant.

The slave trade

We shall never understand what God achieved through 'the Saints' unless we have some idea of the immense power that confronted them. The slave trade was an institution, part of the establishment of the day. It was big business in 1787, when 100,000 slaves were taken from West Africa to the West Indies. The prosperity of England, and especially Liverpool, was, with some justification, regarded as being founded on 'the trade', and all the vested interests of ship owners, as well as plantation owners, were ranged against any reform. The slave was regarded as property. So in a court case where 132 slaves had been pushed overboard for the sake of the insurance the only question raised was one of financial compensation, not of morality at all. To be sure, a few who followed Wesley and others had some humanitarian principles but these were considered only as private ideas that bore no relation to public policy.

When Wilberforce spoke in the House of Commons of the evils of the trade, he was answered with the amazing statement that the slave trade 'was not an amiable trade, but neither was the trade of a butcher an amiable trade, and yet a mutton chop was, nevertheless, a very good thing'. The members apparently found nothing objectionable in this comparison, so it is not surprising that they were ready to accept the assertion by the defenders of the trade that the Middle Passage, the terrible sea trip from Africa to the West Indies, was regarded by the slave as 'the happiest period of his life'.

The situation was made worse by the spread of republican principles. The French Revolution, with the atrocities that followed, made liberty a political swear word and set back the Sect's campaign by many years. The very idea of liberty was suspect; it was regarded as synonymous with revolution and the overthrow of law and order. This was very ironic as the reformers were almost all very conservative men (probably too much so) who had no greater fear than that of upsetting the status quo.

Such was the opposition faced by Wilberforce and his friends when they began their campaign. If they had regarded only man it is doubtful whether they would have started, and certain that they would not have persevered in, their battle. The stage was set in 1788, although Wilberforce was too ill to present his case to Parliament and William Pitt took his place. When Wilberforce took up the struggle in person in 1789 he met with immediate defeat and realized that he had insufficient weapons at his command. When he began his search for facts and figures he discovered more than he was looking for. He found that the Lord had gone before him and prepared an army for him to lead. It was small by comparison with the 'West Indians', as the supporters of the trade were called, but immensely gifted and, in the providence of God, greatly experienced and strategically placed.

'The Saints'

These were, indeed, remarkable men and it is fitting that we should remember them and not just Wilberforce. It is even more important that we should recognize the hand of God and glorify him for his amazing and sovereign working in bringing them together.

Granville Sharp began his life in poverty and was apprenticed to a draper. An early instance of his ability was his successful attempt to establish his master's claim to a barony and win him his title and a seat in the House of Lords. He studied both Hebrew and Greek to enable him to answer opponents of the faith and in 1770 began a legal battle that had momentous results. After two years' research he instructed counsel to contend, against all the experts, that slavery was illegal in England. He won his case with the result that all slaves who set foot in England were declared free.

Thomas Clarkson had already entered the lists. While Wilberforce was on his tour of the Continent Clarkson had read an essay before the Senate of Cambridge University on the lawfulness of making men slaves. What began as an academic exercise ended with Clarkson wandering in the woods, repeating his newly found conviction: 'Then surely some person should interfere!' He resolved that he would interfere by publishing his essay and in the course of doing so met Granville Sharp.

Even more remarkably God brought to the anti-slavery ranks two men who had seen the enemy at first hand. James Stephen was a young lawyer who 'happened' to be in the West Indies at the right time to witness a particularly unjust trial and its barbaric sequel, the burning alive of a negro slave. He returned to England in 1794 to fight against the system that he had come to hate. The other man was Zachary Macaulay. In 1789 he was the overseer of a West Indian plantation, hating himself for enjoying his tyranny.

He gave up a certain and prosperous future in slavery and returned to England. Here, through his brother-in-law, Thomas Babington, he gained treasure in heaven and joined the anti-slavery ranks. So the nucleus of God's army was formed and battle was joined.

The campaign

From 1789 to 1807 Wilberforce put forth motions before the House of Commons almost annually and every one was defeated either by the power of vested interests in the Commons or by the delaying tactics of the Lords. On one occasion he was unsuccessful on the third reading because twelve sure supporters were absent – attending a comic opera! Soon, 'the Saints' realized that argument in Parliament, even with the mass of evidence provided by Clarkson and others, was not sufficient. Public opinion must be educated and brought into the fray; so they began to organize public meetings and petitions and to publish magazine articles. William Cowper's poetry and Josiah Wedgwood's pottery were enlisted. So these Christians were the first to use the means of public agitation with which we are now so familiar, though often used in much less worthy causes. Gradually the atmosphere in the country changed.

Finally, in 1807, after twenty years of unceasing research, travelling, speaking and organizing, the battle was won and the bill to abolish the trade was passed. However, this was only the first stage. Much illicit trading still went on and Wilberforce and the rest could not relax their efforts. Further, slavery itself was still in existence. Abolition of trading must not be confused with emancipation or freeing of those already enslaved. How difficult it must have been to go on with the fight for another twenty-six years until Parliament voted to spend twenty million pounds on compensating the former owners of emancipated slaves, which finally ended the system!

By this time Wilberforce had passed on the leadership in the fight to Thomas Buxton, but he was still able to take part in the battle. On 12 April 1833, just twelve weeks before his death, the frail Wilberforce spoke for the last time in public – on his old subject.

He died, almost in the moment of victory, on the very day that the critical clause about emancipation was passed.

God had richly blessed their labours – and labours they certainly were. They had not been content to feel sorry for the slaves. They were men of constant prayer but did not leave it at that. They spoke and organized, often at great cost to themselves. Wilberforce, who was never strong and often ill, had to be persuaded by his friends to rest lest he literally die under the strain. More than one of these men died in poverty because he had devoted both fortune and efforts to the service of God in the cause of the negroes. Here were good works indeed.

MACAULAY AND CLARKSON

Zachary Macaulay, having been compelled to leave his governorship of the new colony of Sierra Leone because of ill health, spent his convalescence on a slave ship bound for the West Indies in order to gain evidence for the cause. In spite of being almost blind in one eye he was Wilberforce's 'white slave', who could master and reproduce when needed all the facts and arguments that the orator required. Thomas Clarkson's diligence in securing and then spreading information was prodigious. In order to find a sailor who he believed had a vital piece of evidence, but whom he had seen only once, he visited ports and ships all over England and tracked down his quarry on the 317th vessel. Later on, in order to keep the French government under pressure he wrote to Honoré Mirabeau a letter of sixteen to twenty pages every day for a month.

The reformation of manners

At the celebration of the tremendous and, in the end, overwhelming victory, seeing Henry Thornton looking somewhat grave, Wilberforce asked, 'Well, Henry, what shall we abolish next?' Henry replied, 'The lottery, I think.' In fact, 'the Saints' were already committed to doing battle on a number of fronts, all of which would come under Wilberforce's designation of 'the reformation of manners'. They attacked, with some measure of success, not only the lottery but also duelling, drunkenness, bear-baiting and the breach of the sabbath. For many this last cause is a reason for criticizing Wilberforce and his colleagues, but Wilberforce fought for the sabbath as the only way to ensure any free time for the working people of the country. More positively, it made possible the establishment of Sunday Schools where the 'lower classes' could learn to read and thus be taught the Scriptures.

The members of the Sect have often been charged with not caring about the slaves at home and Wilberforce was certainly not perfect. His dislike of the anti-Christian radicals of his day and his built-in fear of revolution probably led him to be too conservative. Nevertheless, his great sympathy with those who suffered the hardships of life was seen very clearly, not only in his attempts to further penal reform but also in his most generous giving to the poor. He ruined his own fortune, partly by refusing to raise rents or even to insist on payment of existing rates. In the famine year of 1801 Wilberforce distributed to the needy £3,000 more than his actual income, a figure that must be multiplied many times to bear any relation at all to current values.

Wiberforce and the gospel

We must also mention more directly spiritual concerns, lest it appears that they were just a group of do-gooders, in the modern sense, concerned only for physical and social welfare. Even if there were nothing else to describe it would not make them purveyors of a social gospel because the evangelical message was always the inspiration of their work and John Venn's evangelical ministry the source of their spiritual power. In fact, it is hard to find any evangelical society or organization founded around the beginning of the nineteenth century that did not directly involve them.

A practical view

Mrs Hannah More had published several books aimed at the reformation of manners in 1788 and 1790, and Wilberforce followed her example by writing an evangelistic book. This was entitled,

A Practical View of the Prevailing Religious System of Professed Christians in the Higher and Middle Classes in This Country Contrasted with Real Christianity. The publisher would only risk an edition of 500, even with the name of its famous author on the title page. Within six months, however, it had sold 7,500 copies, and over the years it was widely used in bringing men, including Thomas Chalmers, to 'real Christianity'. Arthur Young, an eminent agriculturalist of the day, was also converted and later gave much help to Wilberforce in his work. It was widely praised by men like John Newton, although Wilberforce's prose style did not at all match that of his letters and his speeches. It was certainly practical, and its stress on real Christianity, with its suggestion that the religion of the author's contemporaries was false, aroused much opposition. Evangelicals of all denominations rejoiced in the book's appearance and it helped Wilberforce's relations with the Dissenters. This must have pleased him as he had a great love for all believers and desired greater unity among them. Hannah More, supported and subsidized by Henry Thornton, began to issue cheap tracts every month and in the first year sold two million. Others began to contribute money and to write tracts and the work expanded. In some measure this led to the formation of the Religious Tract Society in 1799. Although the Clapham Sect had no direct connection with the actual foundation, within a year Zachary Macaulay became an active supporter, and Legh Richmond, who had been converted when a curate through reading Wilberforce's *Practical View*, became the society's most prolific tract writer.

Moreover, it was at a meeting of the Religious Tract Society committee that Thomas Charles of Bala told the moving story of Mary Jones and her desire and sacrificial effort to obtain a Welsh Bible, which resulted in the formation of the British and Foreign Bible Society. John and Henry Thornton had already given away thousands of Bibles, mainly to soldiers and sailors, and the rest of the Sect had done similarly. It is not surprising, therefore, that they played a large part in establishing the Bible Society. Indeed, one of them, Lord Teignmouth, became president and continued in office until his death. The mention of Lord Teignmouth brings us to another concern of the Sect, which was, in fact, to result in one of their finest achievements.

Missions

India as well as Africa had a share in their concern. The millions of lost heathen, the idolatrous worship and the immoral and cruel practices, such as the burning of widows, all aroused their indignation and prayer and then, characteristically, they acted. The gospel must be sent to India – but how?

In India there was a most powerful enemy of the gospel. The East India Company controlled the country under a royal charter. The company alleged that the preaching of the gospel would upset 'the natives' and cause unrest, which would damage the great god, Trade. Therefore no missionaries would be allowed to enter the country without a licence from the company. In practice this meant that no missionaries were permitted to enter at all. (Carey had succeeded in entering just before this came into force.) So when Wilberforce and his friends attempted to introduce the gospel to India the door was firmly closed.

'Now the slave trade is abolished', said Wilberforce, 'the exclusion of missionaries from India is by far the greatest of our national sins.' The East India Company's charter had to be renewed every twenty years and when this matter came before Parliament in 1793 Wilberforce tried to add a clause empowering and requiring the directors to send out missionaries. This was defeated by the power of commerce and, as Wilberforce put it, twenty million Indians were left to 'the providential protection of Brama'.

This meant that nothing more could be attempted for twenty years! God, however, had already prepared his instruments. If missionaries were not to be allowed into India, then he would raise up Christians within the East India Company itself! Charles Grant began his career in India in the usual extravagant manner and ran up debts of £20,000. In 1776 he was converted after a series of tragedies in his family circle. He soon became friendly with John Shore, another new convert, and together they began to work for missions to India. The army in India was, of course, allowed its chaplains, and in 1786 a young clergyman, David Brown, took charge of a military orphanage in the country. He joined forces with the others and sought to arouse interest in England, contacting both Wilberforce and Charles Simeon of Cambridge, to whom Brown had been curate.

Grant was to become the most influential director of the company, and Shore, later Lord Teignmouth, became Governor-General of India. Shore was able to ease Carey's entry into India while Grant inspired Claudius Buchanan to go out as a chaplain in 1796. Buchanan is a good example of the way God used the members of the Sect and their ministerial friends. He was first influenced by John Newton, sent to Cambridge by Henry Thornton and there cared for by Charles Simeon.

In 1799 Grant and Simeon, together with the rest of the Sect, established the Missionary Society, later to become the Church Missionary Society, but nobody offered himself for service in India until 1802. Then the great Henry Martyn (1781 – 1812) came forward, but the next problem was getting him to India. Though Carey had managed to enter without a licence in 1793 that became a 'high misdemeanour' in the following year and Carey only avoided trouble by taking secular employment. In 1802 not even Grant could gain admittance for a real missionary, so Martyn was compelled to go to India as a chaplain like Buchanan. From there he went on to Persia to 'burn out for God' as one of the greatest missionaries of all time.

Immediately after the failure of the attempt in 1793, 'the Saints', with characteristic foresight, devotion and perseverance, set their sights on the next charter renewal due in 1813. By this time there were nine members in the House of Commons who supported the Church Missionary Society. The same methods were adopted as in the anti-slavery movement and public support was sought and gained.

On 22 June 1813 Wilberforce, in one of his finest speeches to the Commons, lasting three hours in spite of great physical weakness, pleaded for freedom for gospel missions and won the day. He described the work of the Serampore trio, especially Carey, whose college salary was given almost entirely to the mission. 'By the way', he wrote afterwards, 'nothing ever gave me a more lively sense of the low and mercenary standards of your men of honour than the manifest effect produced on the House of Commons by my stating this last circumstance. It seemed to be the only thing which moved them.'

The East India Bill passed with its Christian clause intact and the door was opened for Christian missions. 'The Saints' continued to pray and work for India in the following years in spite of many discouragements, but the central issue had been won.

Summary

It is relatively easy to find fault with Wilberforce and his friends on various counts. Wilberforce was not a Calvinist, although he was very friendly with William Jay and Thomas Scott, who certainly were; the history of his sons, three of whom became Roman Catholics, must cast doubt on his wisdom in certain respects, but in most ways the members of the Clapham Sect are an example to us all. Not only did they have the right ideas about the gospel witness and good works, they also showed extreme diligence and self-sacrifice in pursuing their aims. The time they devoted, the energy they used and the money they expended all condemn our modern ease and self-centredness. Zachary Macaulay gave away £150,000 and ended his life in virtual poverty for the sake of his beloved slaves. Henry Thornton, before his marriage, gave away six-sevenths of his income and afterwards two-thirds.

Even more striking, perhaps, is their perseverance against all discouragements and disappointments. The sheer length of their campaigns, both for the slaves and the Indians, shows this very clearly. Here we see the value of their fellowship and mutual encouragement, and their utter conviction of the justice of their cause and of God's approval. How soon we give up praying and working, and how little we achieve!

Best of all, they demonstrate once again how God chooses, prepares and uses men for the accomplishing of his great and glorious purposes. In the Clapham Sect he drew together men and women with the necessary and varied gifts, abilities, background and experience to do the work he had ordained for them. Wilberforce would have been powerless without the 'white slaves' who laboured in gathering information. They could have done little without his leadership, eloquence and place in public esteem. None of them could have achieved anything but for the God who enables his people by his grace and turns the hearts of kings and parliaments. If our trust is in the same God and our cause essentially the same, the kingdom of God and his righteousness, then we may be encouraged to go out to labour and persevere as they did.

Questions for discussion

1. How important is it to accompany the preaching of the gospel with its social outworking? Should this involve political action? What are the dangers of this?

2. In what ways was Old Testament slavery different from that faced by Wilberforce? How do you explain the fact that many devout believers in the southern states of America owned slaves?

3. What lessons should we learn from Wilberforce's doctrinal weaknesses? While acknowledging the sovereignty of God, can we draw any warnings from the history of Wilberforce's sons?

For further reading

** E. M. Howse, Saints in politics, George Allen & Unwin, 1971.

** D. Newsome, The parting of friends, John Murray, 1966.

* J. Pollock, Wilberforce, Lion Publishing, 1978.

W. Wilberforce, A practical view of the prevailing religious system... contrasted with real Christianity, ed. V. Edmunds, Hodder & Stoughton, 1989.

Oh, that you would rend the heavens and come down,
  that the mountains would tremble before you!
For when you did awesome things that we did not expect,
  you came down, and the mountains trembled before you.

— Isaiah 64:1,3

The Lord would give us great things, if only he could trust us not to steal the glory for ourselves. Not unto us, O Lord, not unto us, but unto thy name give glory.

— David Morgan (1814 – 1883)

When this passing world is done,
  When has sunk yon radiant sun,
When I stand with Christ on high,
  Looking o'er life's history,
  Then, Lord, shall I fully know,
  Not till then, how much I owe.

— Robert Murray M'Cheyne (1813 – 1843)

14

The Fifty-Nine Revival

What is often referred to as the 'Fifty-Nine Revival' in fact covered the years 1857 to 1860 and, moreover, not only had its roots in the preceding years but also affected greatly the subsequent history of the church. This great revival, occurring in various countries on both sides of the Atlantic, was the last general awakening before a general decline set in. It is, therefore, good and even necessary to remind ourselves of these days when God's powerful hand was manifested in the world, when the church was enlivened by outpourings of the Holy Spirit, when great crowds gathered spontaneously to hear the preaching of the gospel, when chapels were filled and public houses emptied, when praying was as natural as preaching and young and old gloried in the reality of knowing Christ. Although England was also deeply affected by the revival we shall concentrate here on America, Ulster, Wales and Scotland.

North America

There is perhaps no more remarkable story in the annals of the church than that of Jeremiah Lanphier's prayer meeting. It would be foolish to regard him as the only human source of the revival for there was already concern in many parts of America over the sad state of the church, where orthodoxy appeared to be dead and even local revivals had ceased. All the same, it is with Lanphier in New York that we can see most evidently the hand of God transforming the situation virtually overnight. Such events encourage us to hope and pray in our own dark and dead days.

In July 1857 Jeremiah Lanphier, a Christian businessman, was appointed as a city missionary in downtown New York by the Dutch Reformed Church. The new missionary was a man of deep spirituality, and when he saw the need his response was not despair but a call to prayer. He distributed a handbill inviting others to join him in a noonday prayer meeting every Wednesday. 'In prayer', he wrote, 'we leave the business of time for that of eternity, and intercourse with men for intercourse with God.' On Wednesday, 23 September the city missionary took his place and awaited the results of his initiative. It was half an hour before anyone arrived, but eventually six people began to pray together. The following Wednesday the six had become twenty and the next week forty met together. After that it was decided to hold the meeting daily.

That same week two other remarkable, but very different, events also took place. First, a financial panic swept the country; banks failed, railways were bankrupted and business came to a standstill. Second, in Canada an extraordinary work of conversion began among the Methodists of Hamilton, Ontario. It was an apparently spontaneous movement beginning among lay people and resulted in 300 to 400 professions of conversion in just a few days. News of this awakening spread throughout North America, and as believers turned to prayer more reports of local revivals were received. In December a Presbyterian convention was arranged to consider the necessity for 'a general revival of religion' and the opening session heard a sermon from the great Dr Charles Hodge from Zechariah 4:6: "'Not by might nor by power, but by my Spirit," says the Lord Almighty.' Thus, as Lanphier had written, the world turned from the business of time to the business of eternity. That, at least, was no longer at a standstill.

In New York itself various areas began to see conversions and in February 1858 the revival began to be reported in the newspapers. After trying to hold three simultaneous prayer meetings on different floors of the original building the leaders began other meetings and soon gatherings for prayer were being held all over the city. At first there was little preaching; they were simply meetings where anyone might pray. They were crowded and earnest but apparently entirely free from fanaticism and false emotion. As the weather improved, numbers at the prayer meetings declined as 'the curious and the spurious' dropped away, but now evangelistic services increased in frequency. Conversions began to be reported from all over the country and figures of 50,000 per week were given in the press. Within six months of that first Fulton Street meeting, writes Dr Edwin Orr, '10,000 businessmen were gathering daily in New York City for prayer, and within two years a million converts had been added to the American churches.' Orr's figures are not just those claimed at the time but based on his study of the permanent growth of the churches; this was no superficial campaign.

Although D. L. Moody began his life's work at this time and Charles G. Finney was active throughout, there were no real leaders. This was pre-eminently a work of God and was seen to be such. The world was compelled to take notice as the Lord of hosts acted by his Spirit. This was not a matter of churches growing steadily but quietly, it was a public event reported in the newspapers. The people of America were amazed to see notices on closed offices: 'Will re-open after the prayer meeting.' Steamer passengers on the Ohio River found the saloon occupied to a late hour by a prayer meeting while conversation on board was dominated by the revival.

Nothing could stop the awakening, not even the Civil War (1861 – 1865) between the north and south. Indeed, an outstanding spiritual work was done in the camps of the Confederate Army. All kinds of churches were blessed, and united prayer meetings were the order of the day. Chicago in 1858 was described as a 'large, wealthy and wicked city', but there great unity and love were shown as black people as well as whites found salvation. One church reported an increase of members from 177 in 1856 to 508 in 1858. Mere statistics, however, can give only part of the picture.

REVIVAL IN KALAMAZOO

Inspired by the news of revival elsewhere, the church leaders in Kalamazoo announced a united prayer meeting. They were apparently somewhat doubtful as to the response they would obtain from the Christians of the town. Their fears were completely unwarranted for the first gathering was well attended. Requests for prayer were invited and received. One was read out at this first meeting: 'A praying wife requests the prayers of this meeting for her unconverted husband.' Immediately a man stood up claiming to be the husband in question, saying, 'I want you to pray for me.' However, another man, seemingly oblivious of the first claimant, made the same confession of need and request for prayer. No fewer than five others followed him, all convicted of their sin and seeking the mercy of God. The whole gathering was filled with the presence of God and a general work of grace began in the town resulting in over 400 conversions.

There were many strong links between America and the United Kingdom, not least with Northern Ireland, and it was not long before the work spread to the other side of the Atlantic. Events prove, however, that this was not just a case of imitation or even of one revival sparking off another. This was God at work and he used various means to bring awakening to the churches of Ireland.

Northern Ireland

Connor, Ulster

In September 1857, before the Hamilton, Ontario, awakening and at the same time as Jeremiah Lanphier distributed his handbill, a small prayer meeting began in the old schoolhouse of Kells, a village in the parish of Connor near Ballymena in Northern Ireland. The inspiration behind it was a young man named James McQuilkin, who had been converted nearly a year earlier. Although he was a very religious man with much knowledge of Christian doctrine he had no personal knowledge of the Saviour. One day an Englishwoman, Mrs Colville, who spent her time witnessing in the area in connection with the Baptist Missionary Society, came to Ballymena. There she visited a dying woman in her home and spoke earnestly to others present, including James McQuilkin. He, full of head knowledge, began to question Mrs Colville about what she believed and especially whether she was a Calvinist. She replied that she wished to be neither more nor less of a Calvinist than Christ was and directed the conversation to the matter of his experience of salvation. He then dropped the subject, but a young woman there took it up and suddenly McQuilkin realized his lost condition. After some weeks of struggling he eventually found peace in Christ and immediately began to witness for his newly found Saviour.

We should not be misled by McQuilkin's interest in Calvinism. In fact he was more of a hyper-Calvinist and only a theoretical one at that. He did not possess an assurance of salvation, did not believe that it was possible to have one and showed by his worldly, pleasure-seeking life that he had no right to one. He was typical of many, then and now, who bring sound doctrine into disrepute by their lack of a genuine experience of Christ and their consequent ungodly ways. In fact the churches of the area were largely orthodox, thanks in no small measure to the courageous stand taken against Unitarianism by Dr Henry Cooke thirty years earlier. As a result of his efforts the Presbyterian denomination had been preserved in the true faith, providing a sound biblical basis for the revival when it came.

As McQuilkin's life changed after his conversion, some of his friends heard that he was professing to know that his sins were forgiven. One by one they joined him in trusting Christ, in rejoicing in salvation and then in praying and studying the Bible together. Thus McQuilkin, Jeremiah Meneely, Robert Carlisle and John Wallace began to meet in the schoolhouse of Kells.

McQuilkin had seen advertised the *Narrative of the Lord's Dealings with George Muller*, and this had led him to begin the prayer meeting.

On New Year's Day 1858 the four young men rejoiced in the news of the conversion of a farm labourer for whom they had been praying, and soon after another was added to the group of believers. Meanwhile news had come to Ulster of the revival in America. A deputation had been sent to investigate the reports at first hand, and not only had they brought back a glowing account, but also two young men from Philadelphia had visited the Ballymena area. They spoke in the church at Connor and even went to Kells to see if anything was happening there because they had heard the name mentioned in a request for prayer at a meeting back home. In the light of all this the Kells gathering turned into a prayer meeting specifically for revival.

Ahoghill and further afield

By the end of 1858 many more had been converted and the number praying together had risen to fifty. One of the latest of these was Samuel Campbell of Connor. On Christmas Day he visited his home in Ahoghill intending to tell his family about his new faith. He pleaded first with his mother and sister and then with his brother, John, to flee from wrath to Christ but with little immediate effect. Later John accompanied Samuel part of the way home and was then left alone by the roadside. There John was overwhelmed by conviction of sin. 'I saw heaven on the one side and hell on the other', he recounts. 'The conviction flashed upon me with overwhelming power that I deserved hell as my eternal portion, and such horror did the thought produce that every joint in my body quaked.' During the night his mother woke the rest of the family, crying out loud under terrible conviction. By morning both she and her daughter had found peace with God, but it was three weeks before John could also rejoice in the assurance of salvation. Soon the work of grace spread to another related family and then to the whole neighbourhood.

Now the tide of revival became irresistible. The brethren from Connor were invited to speak first at Ahoghill and then farther afield to eager congregations. Thus the work of conversion spread to Ballymena, to Belfast and beyond, to all parts of Ulster. Prayer meetings were held at all hours of the day and night; over 100 were held every week in the Connor district. At Portrush great open-air services were held. At one, 6,000 people were addressed by the men from Connor as well as by the noted evangelist, Brownlow North. There were some physical effects due to intense conviction of sin; some collapsed in agony but recovered to enjoy an equally intense joy and peace. A minister from Scotland described the many who were convicted and converted, asserting that there was no deliberate stirring up of excitement, only simple scriptural addresses and prayers.

In April 1858 the Rev. Thomas Toye of Great St George's Presbyterian Church started a prayer meeting in Belfast after news of the American awakening was received. A year later some of the converts from Ahoghill came to speak and the revival took over the city. Within a few weeks 10,000 people were converted. Every morning was occupied by meetings and all the orthodox denominations shared in the blessing, and thus it was throughout Ulster.

The work also extended to the south, although rather more slowly. By August 1859 there were over forty prayer meetings in Dublin and conversions were occurring regularly. Indeed the cross-channel steamer proved such a 'soul-trap' that the Roman Catholic hierarchy protested to the shipping company!

THE CHILDREN OF COLERAINE

There was a remarkable work among the children in Coleraine. One lad had to be sent home from school because he was so upset that he could not work. He was accompanied by another lad, already converted, and on the way the two boys turned aside to pray in an empty house. The convicted lad found peace at last and returned to the school to testify to that fact. Soon, boy after boy quietly left the classroom, and the teacher observed them kneeling separately around the playground. The school was occupied until eleven that night with boys, girls, teachers, parents and neighbours engaged in seeking the Lord.

Crime in many parts of the province was reduced, at least among the Protestant community, and drunkenness was especially affected. A large distillery was put up for sale and one publican gave an unsolicited testimonial to the genuineness of the revival. He was asked whether he thought that the prayer meetings in Belfast were a good thing, to which he replied, 'How can that be good which affects business so much? It has been at a standstill for the last few weeks.'

Naturally such a work aroused opposition and not only from publicans. One nineteen-year-old man took the opportunity at a meeting to mock the converts in obscene language. The minister denounced him and he fell to the ground as if struck by lightning. When he recovered he prayed, 'Lord, save me; I perish', and after finding peace he went about warning everyone never to mock God's cause. In Belfast the Catholics were greatly alarmed by the success of the revival. They regarded it as a kind of plague and sprinkled holy water and distributed consecrated medals to protect their flock from infection. The Unitarians also opposed and mocked.

Old churches were encouraged and membership increased, while many new ones were established. It is estimated that over 100,000 of a population of nine million were converted during the 'year of grace'. Dr H. Grattan Guiness, one of the great revival leaders, testified that although he had been accustomed to seeing tens or even scores converted under the preaching of the gospel, this was entirely different, with ministers dealing with enquirers after the way of salvation until midnight or even three in the morning. Edwin Orr claims with justice that the movement that began with four young men in Kells 'made a greater impact spiritually on Ireland than anything reported since the days of St Patrick'.

Wales

In one way the link between America and Wales was much more direct than in the case of Ulster. The early leader of the revival in Wales was in fact a Welshman who had just spent four years in America. Humphrey Jones (1832 – 1895) was converted at sixteen. He very soon started preaching and records, 'Seventeen souls were convicted under my third public sermon', and 'I have reason to believe that the Lord of his grace blessed my ministry at that time to the salvation of some hundreds of souls.' To his disappointment, however, he was not accepted for the Wesleyan ministry, so he followed his parents to America where he eventually became a free-lance missioner among the Welsh communities.

After experiencing great success in preaching the gospel, both before and during the awakening, he returned to his native Wales in 1858. There he adopted the same methods as in America and by August it was clear that a powerful work had begun. In a letter to a newspaper Jones expressed his conviction that 'Wales is on the brink of blessed things and that revivals will be commonplace happenings throughout the land.' Here he is using revival to refer to a local awakening, but it is nevertheless true that a countrywide revival was beginning.

He preached in one church near his home for five weeks during which the revival spread to neighbouring towns and villages. There were large congregations, much conviction and, on at least one occasion, scenes of holy disorder with scores of people praying aloud such that the preacher's voice was drowned out. In September a godly Calvinistic Methodist pastor, David Morgan, heard him preach and the next stage of the awakening began.

It must not be supposed that the return of Humphrey Jones was the only means that God used in Wales. Many had become dissatisfied with the dead state of the churches. There had been many local revivals in the early years of the century but now all seemed lifeless, no matter how orthodox the churches and ministers might be in creed. Many were troubled but encouraged to pray through the history of God's dealings with the land of revivals. David Morgan was one such man, and as early as 1855 he recorded in his diary a determination to pray for revival. It is said that for ten years before the revival his public prayers always included a petition for an outpouring of the Holy Spirit.

Morgan was at first very suspicious of Jones's ministry, as were other ministers, fearing that this was nothing more than an attempt to work up emotion and produce results. Under the revivalist's preaching, however, Morgan became convinced of his own failures as a minister and went to see the preacher personally. After some discussion he agreed to arrange a prayer meeting because it could do no harm even 'though there should be no more than man in it all'. 'You do that', replied Jones, 'and I will guarantee that God will be with you very soon.'

Morgan's mind was in such a turmoil that he was unable to conduct the service on the next Sunday morning so he went to hear Humphrey Jones instead. In that service an old elder, in response to the preacher's enquiry about the lack of response, said that it was hard to rejoice when the ministry condemned you, and on this public confession the whole congregation was moved to tears. In the evening David Morgan preached himself and announced that prayer meetings were to be held during the week.

It was several days yet before he found that the power of the Spirit was upon him also. On the Wednesday morning he awoke aware of some mysterious change; in some way all his faculties had been enlivened, especially his memory. For two years he was able to remember all the names of enquirers and converts, sometimes praying for as many as 100 in succession by name, mentioning their individual circumstances. At the end of that time the gift left him as suddenly as it had come.

Once convinced of the genuineness of the revival David Morgan threw himself into the work of preaching and counselling. He well knew that, although it is possible to labour in a carnal manner, God in his sovereignty uses human instruments to revive his church. Indeed he had written in 1855, 'As well as praying, we should be doing our utmost to revive the work. So did the godly of old: they prayed and they worked.' We also would do well to follow in these paths.

Morgan now began to preach throughout Cardiganshire in company with Humphrey Jones. There were great scenes of weeping followed by rejoicing; churches were awakened, sinners quickened and the whole land stirred by the news that God had returned to his people. In December 1858 the two evangelists parted amicably, agreeing to work separately from now on. Sadly, it was not long before Jones showed signs of a mental disorder that first altered his methods, then changed his views on revelation and eventually destroyed his ministry. Although he was later enabled to resume preaching to some extent, he was never the same again and the work continued largely without him.

1858 ended with Cardigan on fire; 1859 saw the fire spread to the whole of the principality. Everywhere local ministers of various denominations were used as the Spirit of God moved over the land. Assemblies and association meetings were concerned no longer with ordinary church business but with the revival. Committee meetings were turned into prayer meetings and ordinary services became great evangelistic occasions. All over the country there were multitudes of conversions and great increases in church membership.

David Morgan was by no means the only preacher to be used remarkably, but many of the most striking stories are linked with his name. One day he invited an old stonebreaker by the roadside to go with him to the prayer meeting. The old man rejected the invitation, even though Morgan offered to compensate him for the pay he would lose by attending. So the preacher prayed for him, kneeling on a pile of stones; the heart of the old man was deeply moved and he pleaded for mercy.

In February 1859 Morgan visited Aberystwyth, and after initial difficulties a great work was done and the church there received about 400 new members. One evening a drunkard rushed into the meeting during a prayer. He was halted by the solemnity of the gathering and, dropping to his knees, prayed for mercy. He then began to pray for his equally dissolute wife, Betty: 'Betty is in the house. Go there, Lord, and if the door is locked unship it off the hinges and save Betty, Lord.' Soon afterwards Betty came in and was converted, lastingly, like her husband.

In one village there was a family that was praying for a 'prodigal' son who had left home. They had no means of communicating with him but on the very day that David Morgan was scheduled to preach in their chapel the son walked into the house. No one said anything about the revival but the young man was one of the first to be converted at that evening's meeting. Another convert was a man who went to hear the nonconformist preacher although he was himself an occasional Anglican. Morgan insisted that he must immediately begin family worship in his home. His wife, already a believer, placed a large family Bible on the table after supper. She was, nevertheless, rather surprised that her husband approached the duty with such calmness. She did not know that he had hidden a copy of the Prayer Book in his pocket with the page turned down at a collect that he intended to use when her eyes were shut! However, he first read from the Bible the account of Christ's agony in Gethsemane. The story so moved him that he fell to his knees and poured out his heart in praise. Later, when he undressed for bed, he found the unused book in his pocket.

People from all walks of life and all ages were convicted and soundly converted. One foul-mouthed farmer received a terrible shock one morning; he discovered that he could not swear! To remedy this ridiculous state of affairs he looked around for things to annoy him so that he would be provoked into an oath but nothing worked. In desperation he decided that if he could not swear he would try to pray. This he did, out on a barren hilltop, and we are told that he continued to be a man of prayer all his life.

There was opposition, of course, much of it like Morgan's own early attitude, which was overcome by the evident orthodoxy of the preaching and the equally obvious godliness of the preacher. The opposition of the ungodly was disarmed in a different way. One local squire, who objected to being prayed for by name, threatened to teach Morgan a lesson. A few days later when he was shooting by the roadside his opportunity came as the evangelist approached. As the preacher drew near the squire crouched lower and lower until he was completely hidden behind the hedge. However, something about Morgan's face had utterly destroyed his confidence. We are not told whether he was actually converted but thousands of others were. It is estimated that one-tenth of the population of one million was brought to know Christ during the revival, with many notable converts, many of whom served as ministers or missionaries of great distinction.

Scotland

Thomas Chalmers

The revival in Scotland, though no less powerful than elsewhere, appears to attract less attention today. One reason for this may be that it was preceded by other equally remarkable events so that it does not stand out as much by contrast. The name and ministry of Thomas Chalmers (1780 – 1847) provide a unifying factor for our account of these days. Born in 1780, he had a religious, even orthodox, upbringing, but his interests lay more in the fields of science and mathematics than of theology. Therefore, although he was ordained to the Church of Scotland ministry and given the country parish of Kilmany in 1803, he was more interested in his position as lecturer in mathematics at St Andrews University. He maintained his interest in science, even when he lost his university post, and would often be seen riding off with some elaborate piece of equipment to deliver a scientific lecture. He would assert, as he did in a published pamphlet, 'From the authority of his own experience, that after the satisfactory discharge of his parish duties, a minister may enjoy five days in the week of uninterrupted leisure for the prosecution of any science in which his taste may dispose him to engage.'

Soon events brought a change of outlook. The deaths of his brother and sister, each of whom showed genuine Christian confidence in the face of death, together with his own prolonged illness fixed on his heart 'a very strong impression of the insignificance of time' and of 'the magnitude of eternity'. For four months he was confined to his room and, partly through reading Pascal's *Pensées* and Wilberforce's *Practical View*, he came to see the necessity and sufficiency of Christ's atonement and became a real Christian. His ministry was transformed; previously he had tried, within limits, to improve the morality of the parish with no success, but now as he proclaimed his newly found faith many of the people were transformed also. Science was laid aside in favour of prayer and study of the Scriptures. The church officer commented on the change, saying that whenever he came to the manse now he found the minister at his books, but Chalmers replied that it was all too little.

In 1815 he moved to Glasgow, where he found scope for both his remarkable preaching gifts and his abilities for leadership and organization. His ministry had a profound effect on the whole city, and when he left to take up a university appointment 3,000 people crowded the church for his farewell. He became Professor of Moral Philosophy at St Andrews, where he had a great and good influence on the students. Several students, most notably the outstanding missionary to India, Alexander Duff, joined the infant missionary movement. In 1828 he transferred to Edinburgh as Professor of Divinity and such was his reputation that his inaugural lecture was packed with outsiders as well as enthusiastic students. One of these recorded it for what it in fact was, a turning point in the history of the church in Scotland. It was under Chalmers that many of the most influential preachers of the next generation learned their theology and gained their vision of preaching the gospel in Scotland and the world. This generation changed the spiritual face of Scotland, which at that time was one of deadness going under the name of Moderatism. Among those students in the Divinity Hall from 1831 were Robert Murray M'Cheyne and Andrew Bonar.

M'Cheyne, Bonar and Burns

Robert Murray M'Cheyne (1813 – 1843) had already gained distinction in his arts course and had won a prize for a poem 'On the Covenanters', but it was only the death of his brother in 1831 that awakened him from 'the sleep of nature' and was soon to bring him to Christ. His great friend Andrew Bonar (1810 – 1892), almost three years older, was already a believer and they joined together with others, including Andrew's brother Horatius, the author of many fine hymns, for study, prayer and mutual encouragement in walking the Christian pathway. These men were fine preachers, but it is for godliness that they are chiefly noted today. Bonar's *Diary* and his *Memoir* of M'Cheyne have influenced thousands for righteousness even in our own day. They were marked by an intense love and compassion for souls and a disciplined devotion to communion with God. Another of the young men whom God was preparing, William Chalmers Burns (1815 – 1868), a Glasgow graduate, once ignored his mother in the street. When she spoke to him he explained that he had not seen her because, 'I was so overcome with the sight of the countless crowds of immortal beings eagerly hasting hither and thither, but all posting onwards towards the eternal world, that I could bear it no longer' and he had turned aside 'to seek relief in quiet thought'.

After ordination M'Cheyne settled in Dundee and Bonar eventually became minister at Collace in the country. There they began to preach a message very different from the sterile morality from which Chalmers had been delivered and which still dominated the pulpits of the Church of Scotland. Often the friends met to pray and plead for the Spirit's outpouring on their labours. Soon M'Cheyne began to attract many to hear him preach, but his evident and exceptional godliness made the greatest impression.

PREACHING ON HELL

Bonar tells us that it was M'Cheyne's custom to visit the dying on a Saturday afternoon with a view to being 'stirred up to a more direct application of the truth to his flock on the morrow, as dying men on the edge of eternity'. His preaching was piercing, to judge by the comment of one man awakened under it: 'I think hell would be some relief from an angry God.' Yet he gently rebuked his friend who had preached on hell: 'Were you able to do it with tenderness?'

The friends were particularly concerned for the Jews, and in 1839 M'Cheyne, Bonar and two others were sent on a 'mission of enquiry' to Palestine. During his absence the young William Chalmers Burns, whose departure for the mission field had been delayed, supplied M'Cheyne's pulpit. M'Cheyne's generous nature is shown by these prophetic words:

I hope you may be a thousand times more blessed among them than ever I was. Perhaps there are many souls that would never have been saved under my ministry who may be touched under yours, and God has taken this method of bringing you into my place. His name is Wonderful!

Indeed it was while M'Cheyne was away that great things began to happen.

Burns was preaching at his father's church at Kilsyth, the scene of the revival under James Robe a century before. It was the communion season, unremarkable until the Tuesday when Burns arranged an extra open-air service at 10 A.M. because, he says, 'I felt such a yearning of heart over the poor people among whom I had spent so many of my youthful years in sin.' (He was still only twenty-four.) However, rain compelled them to use the church, where he preached from Psalm 110:3: 'Thy people shall be willing in the day of thy power.' In his application he began to refer to some of the great awakenings of past days. When he came to the outpouring of the Spirit at the Kirk of Shotts in 1630, he was so moved that, like John Livingstone on that earlier occasion, he began 'to plead with the unconverted before me *instantly* to close with God's offers of mercy, and continued to do so until the power of the Lord's Spirit became so mighty upon their souls as to carry all before it, like the rushing mighty wind of Pentecost'. Many cried out and fell to the ground and such was the effect that, with singing and counselling, the service continued until three in the afternoon.

News of the revival at Kilsyth affected the people at Dundee and after Burns's return, the power of God was felt there also. Some had been converted under M'Cheyne's ministry and under Burns there had been signs of increasing concern. This now became overwhelming: 'It was like a pent-up flood breaking forth; tears were streaming from the eyes of many... Onward from that evening, meetings were held every day for many weeks... The whole town was moved.' The awakening spread still further and when M'Cheyne and Bonar came back to Scotland it was to hear of an ever-increasing work. It was a while before Bonar's parish was touched, but meanwhile he helped hard-pressed ministers, including M'Cheyne, who far from exhibiting jealousy of Burns, could say, 'I have no desire but the salvation of my people, by whatever instrument.' Burns himself continued with his evangelistic labours for several years before eventually leaving for China and a very different ministry. Nevertheless, it was the same man and the same message. It was he who declared that places were only distinguished for him by the presence or absence of the Lord and who received the description 'the holiest man alive' from a missionary who had met him in China.

The Disruption, 1843, and beyond

By such men as these, under Chalmers' leadership, God was preparing for a great work of a different kind. For years a conflict had been waged between the evangelicals and the moderates in the Church of Scotland. The central issue was patronage: whether the patrons, usually local landowners, had the right to 'intrude' a minister into the parish against the wishes of the congregation, but the division was essentially between those who believed in the gospel and godliness and those who did not. Over the years the evangelical party gained in strength and by 1833 they had a majority in the General Assembly and they gave the congregation the power of veto. However, the moderates refused to accept this decision and invoked the civil law, thus producing an amazing situation where different ministers were suspended for disobeying either the church courts or the civil courts!

This meant that some areas were left without any ministry; therefore, the evangelicals arranged for several of their number to supply the preaching of the gospel in spite of legal interdicts forbidding them to do so. Although these bans included the open air, men like Dr Thomas Guthrie defied them.

The interdict, he said, forbade him to preach in church, schoolroom and even the churchyard and he obeyed for these places belonged to the state. 'But when these Lords of the Session forbade me to preach my Master's blessed gospel and offer salvation to sinners anywhere in that district under the arch of heaven, I put the interdict under my feet, and I preached the gospel.'

It should be noted that this renewed struggle for the 'crown-rights of the Redeemer' was not some narrow ecclesiastical conflict but involved the very heart of the gospel. It became clear that the church was not to be allowed to run its affairs in obedience to Christ without government interference, so the evangelical party made preparations for a final breach with the state. At a special convocation in November 1842, Chalmers preached to over 470 ministers and detailed arrangements were made for the Disruption at the Assembly in the following May. A further testimony to the genuinely spiritual character of the battle was the presence at this convocation of an ill M'Cheyne, who on one occasion represented the gathered ministers before the throne of grace, seeking counsel from the Lord. He later mentioned the possibility, in the event of the Disruption taking place, of going to preach 'to the many convicts that are transported beyond seas, for no man careth for their souls', but he died before the crucial day arrived.

The estimates of the moderate ministers and members of the government as to how many of the 470 would actually separate varied from between six and ten to a quarter, although one promised to eat all who came out! The assembly was opened formally and then immediately adjourned, and the waiting crowds saw row after row of ministers and elders leaving the hall four abreast, over 400 of them, leaving about a hundred behind. (With the addition of ministers who were not actually members of the assembly, the total was 502, including twenty-one missionaries.) Proceeding to another hall they constituted themselves the Church of Scotland Free, thus maintaining that they were the true successors of the Reformers, and elected Thomas Chalmers as the first moderator.

The days following this impressive act were full of trials: days and even years of suffering. Congregations had to leave their beloved church buildings, ministers gave up manses as well as stipends and missionaries found their support had vanished. Then, under Chalmers' inspiring leadership and with his great powers of organization to the fore, the 'new' church began to re-establish itself. Within a year they had provided nearly 500 churches and a sustentation fund for the preachers. Even more important, the blessing of God on the preaching of the gospel, which had preceded the Disruption, was continuing in many parts of the land. Not all the evangelicals left, but overall there was no doubt where the gospel and godliness were. As one man said, there were still good men and wise men in the established church, 'but the good men who stayed in were not wise, and the wise men who stayed in were not good'! Much was sacrificed for the sake of principle and some thought that the evangelicals were foolish. However, the words of John MacDonald of Ferintosh sum up their convictions:

Had I remained in the old church, I might preach the doctrines I had been preaching for eight and thirty years, but how could I go to the Lord for his presence to accompany my ministrations and render them effectual, when he could cast in my face that I had denied the headship of Christ over the church?

On a somewhat lower level, but making a similar point, was the comment of a man who was asked by a moderate how he was doing with his wooden church. 'Very well', he replied. 'How are you doing with your wooden minister?'

Many of the congregations were not able to have churches because the aggrieved patrons were in some cases the owners of all the available land and used their power to refuse permission for building to try to force the evangelicals back into the established church. Some tenants were forbidden to shelter the homeless ministers and others, in tied housing, were put under great pressure to return to the fold.

The congregation in the mountains at Wanlockhead, consisting largely of miners, met in the open air 1,500 feet up for two bitter winters. They were refused even the use of the empty schoolroom, and they would not stand on planks lying on the ground because these also belonged to the landowner. A tent, which was obtained for the third winter, was soon destroyed by the elements and it was not until 1848 that they were able to erect a wooden building to shelter the determined congregation and their hard-pressed and homeless minister.

Another congregation, numbering 500, had to meet in rain and snow and after two winters had the idea of building a floating church. This was built on the Clyde and then towed to its anchorage about 150 yards offshore. Boats ferried the congregation to the church, which sank one inch lower in the water for every 100 present; on occasions the increase in draught was over six inches!

Scotland in 1859

Nothing, it seems, could drive such people to give up their principles or the preaching of the gospel, and it was to men like these, both in the Free Church and other denominations, that revival came once more in 1859. News of events in America and Ireland had reached Scotland and the godly ministers and their flocks longed to have a share in this new awakening. Saltcoats, on the west cost, experienced it first, and according to a local doctor its arrival followed 'just the track that cholera would have come'. This was no disease, but there does appear to have been a kind of holy 'infection' in this revival, as spreading news was succeeded by spreading power from on high. Andrew Bonar, now in Glasgow, was naturally in the forefront of those looking and longing for revival. 'I have come to this', he wrote in his diary, 'that unless the Lord pour out his Spirit upon the district, nothing will bring them out to hear and attend; and now we hear that this is the very thing which God is doing in the towns of Ireland. O my God, come over to Scotland and help us!' Two months later he was able to record: 'This has been a remarkable week; every day I have heard of some soul saved among us... Certainly this year is a second harvest season to me like that of 1840.'

It was not only established works that were revived; new areas were touched by the gospel and fresh communities deeply affected. James Buchanan, a professor at the Free Church College and a well-known author, used to spend his summer Sunday evenings preaching in the open air in Dumfriesshire. He tells how, after seventeen years during which he saw no 'decided conversion',

> Last year, suddenly and without apparently any human instrumentality to account for it, the whole district was visited with an outpouring of the Spirit of God. Now, in my immediate neighbourhood, I can point to many households where, for the first time, family worship has been established. The whole morals of the district seem to have undergone a complete change … intemperance and profligacy of all kinds have been checked, and the minds of the whole community have become impressed and awed by a sense of divine things.

Brownlow North

It was not only recognized ministers who were used; others, such as Robert Cunningham, a butcher who had lost an eye 'in the devil's service' as a prize-fighter, were able to reach the ordinary people in a remarkable way. Such 'lay preachers' provoked some opposition and criticism, to which the Free Church wisely responded by formally recognizing one of them as an evangelist. This man was Brownlow North (1810 – 1875), grandson of a bishop and great-nephew of George III's prime minister, Lord North. He was born in 1810, the same year as Andrew Bonar (and the year of Chalmers' conversion), but unlike Bonar he lived for many years in pleasure-seeking and ungodliness, thinking only of sport and gambling. The influence of various Christian friends, relatives and ministers sobered him for brief periods, but always he returned to his old life; on one occasion he told an aunt, 'To die the death of the righteous, we must live the life of the righteous and I am not prepared for that yet.' Already, in this clear statement, we can hear the effective preacher of later days.

Those days arrived in 1855. In November of the previous year North was sitting playing cards when he suddenly felt that he was going to die. He went to his room, threw himself on his bed and wondered: 'Now, what will forty-four years of following the desires of my own heart profit me?' Although from that time he was 'a changed man', it was only after a long and deep struggle that he found peace in believing. One night in 1855 he was unable to sleep and rose to read his Bible. As he read Romans 3:21-22 he was struck by the expression: 'the righteousness of God *without the law*', and he records that 'Light came into my soul. Striking my book with my hand and springing from my chair, I cried, "If that Scripture is true, I am a saved man! That is what I want; that is what God offers; that is what I will have."' First in private then in public, North began to seek souls for Christ, gradually becoming a simple and powerful preacher of the gospel. Professor John (Rabbi) Duncan described him as an 'untrained theologue', with the stress, as he said, on 'theologue', for although he lacked formal ministerial training his doctrine was that of the Reformed confessions, unlike so many of the 'lay evangelists' who followed him. Thus he found favour with many of the Free Church ministers and, in May 1859, their assembly recognized him 'as a servant of Jesus Christ, who has received unusual gifts for preaching the glad tidings of great joy and whose work in this department the Lord has greatly honoured'. So when the revival reached Britain Brownlow North was ready to be one of the foremost preachers in Ireland and London, as well as Scotland.

Summary

This widespread revival was quite clearly the work of God; the interaction of news and individuals, coupled with the independent origins of the movements for prayer, speaks of the sovereign hand of the Lord. Although the day of power came suddenly, we should perhaps trace the beginning of the revival to the preparatory days when heresy was defeated, orthodoxy re-established and godly men brought to their knees before the Lord. What better way to sum up this glorious work than the words of David Morgan? One night, after a particularly awesome service, another minister walked home with Morgan. After several miles covered in silence, he ventured to say, 'Didn't we have blessed meetings, Mr Morgan?' 'Yes', replied the preacher, 'and the Lord would give us great things, if only he could trust us not to steal the glory for ourselves.' Then he shouted at the top of his voice, 'Not unto us, O Lord, not unto us, but unto thy name give glory.'

Questions for discussion

1. What, if any, was the relationship between Cooke's doctrinal reformation in Ulster and the 1859 revival there, and between the Disruption and the revival in Scotland?

2. What is the relationship between prayer and the reviving of God's work? Does prayer bring revival or is the fact of prayer itself a sign that God has begun to work? What practical deductions should we make from this?

3. Do the events of 1859 and the work of men like James McQuilkin and Brownlow North justify 'lay preaching'? What does the experience of M'Cheyne and Burns teach us about human instrumentality in the work of God?

For further reading

* A. A. Bonar, *The life of Robert Murray M'Cheyne*, The Banner of Truth Trust, 1978.

** T. Brown, *Annals of the Disruption*, MacNiven & Wallace, 1892.

* E. Evans, *When he is come*, Evangelical Press, 1967.

* K. Moody-Stuart, *Brownlow North: his life and work*, The Banner of Truth Trust, 1961.

* I. R. K. Paisley, *The 'Fifty-Nine' revival*, The Free Presbyterian Church of Ulster, 1958.

T. Phillips, *The Welsh revival: its origin and development*, The Banner of Truth Trust, 1989.

** S. Prime, *The power of prayer: the New York revival of 1858*, The Banner of Truth Trust, 1991.

'Not by might nor by power, but by my Spirit,' says the Lord Almighty.
— Zechariah 4:6

They boast that they have nearly extirpated Puritanism; some of us are described as the last of the race. Have they quenched our coal? Far from it. The light of the doctrines of grace shall yet again shine forth as the sun... The fight is not over yet; the brunt of the battle is yet to come. They dreamed that the old gospel was dead more than a hundred years ago, but they digged its grave too soon... All was decorous and dead; but God would not have it so... A new era dawned. Two schools of Methodists with fiery energy proclaimed the living Word. All England was aroused. A new springtide arrived: the time of the singing of birds had come; life rejoiced where once death withered all things. It will be so again. The Lord liveth, and the gospel liveth too.
— Charles Haddon Spurgeon (1834 – 1892)

O Breath of Life, come sweeping through us,
Revive thy church with life and power
O Breath of Life, come, cleanse, renew us,
And fit thy church to meet this hour.

Revive us, Lord! Is zeal abating,
While harvest fields are vast and white?
Revive us, Lord, the world is waiting,
Equip thy church to spread the light.
— Elizabeth Ann Head (1850 – 1936)

15

Prince of preachers

Charles Haddon Spurgeon

It is possible that no man is more often quoted today in evangelical pulpits than the subject of this chapter, Charles Haddon Spurgeon (1834 – 1892). The nature of the quotation, however, will vary greatly according to the theological convictions, or lack of them, of the speaker. Some persist in regarding him as a humorist, others as a notable orator, but increasingly he is being treated, as he should be, as a serious, God-centred preacher of the whole counsel of God, the outstanding figure in the church in England in the second half of the nineteenth century. His sense of humour need not be denied, but here was a man whose great business was the salvation of souls through the gospel preached in the power of the Holy Spirit, and nothing was allowed to stand in the way of that, neither his own natural humour nor the opposition of men. Here was a man who stood in the line of the Reformers and Puritans, whose works he loved and encouraged others to read, one who lived and ministered through a period when ritualism, rationalism and higher criticism were attacking, defeating and almost destroying the church of Christ. We, who live in the midst of the results of that defeat, must receive instruction from Spurgeon's example but may also take heart from the fact that he is once again in the forefront of Christian minds and in his true colours.

When he was born, in 1834, the church was very prosperous in England. In particular, the dissenting denominations, the Independents, Baptists and Methodists, had experienced great blessing. Although by 1780 the Evangelical Awakening had lost much of its fervour, by the end of the century there had been a tremendous increase in zeal, revivals had spread around the land and many had been won for Christ. The number of chapels and members had increased up to five times; consequently, nearly one tenth of the population had been added to the church, providing a wonderful foundation for the growing missionary movement and social reformation that characterized these years. Then the scene changed. Form and routine took over; doctrine was 'softened' or watered down, preaching refined and the theology and passion of Whitefield became out of fashion. John Angell James, the Congregational minister from Birmingham, wrote in 1851, 'The state of religion in our country is low. I do not think I ever preached with less saving results since I was a minister; and this is the case with most others. It is a general complaint.' James rightly urged his contemporaries to pray for revival, although he was less wise in recommending Charles G. Finney's *Lectures on Revivals*. He died before the general revival came in 1859, but even before then this 'general complaint' was not true at the Baptist Chapel in Waterbeach, near Cambridge. The young Charles Spurgeon had become pastor there in October 1851.

Early years

Spurgeon was born at Kelvedon in Essex, but soon after he went to live with his grandparents at Stambourne, where his grandfather had been the Independent minister since 1810. The influence of this home, both during these four years and on later holiday visits, was clearly very great, not least because of his discovery of an old library of Puritan books, which he loved and read. During one of these later stays at Stambourne the well-known minister, Richard Knill, of Surrey Chapel, London, visited the parsonage. He talked and prayed with the lad, taking him on his knee and saying, 'This child will one day preach the gospel, and he will preach it to great multitudes. I am persuaded that he will preach it in the chapel of Rowland Hill, where I am now minister.' He made little Charles promise that when he did, he would choose the hymn 'God moves in a mysterious way', and so it came about.

Charles owed much to the prayers of his grandmother but also to his godly parents. His father once returned home after setting out to take a service because he was worried about neglecting his children. Entering the house he heard his wife's voice as she prayed aloud, pleading for the salvation of her children, especially Charlie, her 'first-born and strong-willed son'. He went off to preach, his mind at peace.

The son heard *many* preachers, not all of them to his liking. He recalls,

> I have a lively, or rather a deadly, recollection of a certain series of discourses on the Hebrews, which made a deep impression on my mind of the most undesirable kind. I wished frequently that the Hebrews had kept the epistle to themselves, for it sadly bored one poor Gentile lad.

Sometimes he was convicted and tried to pray but found he lacked the power. One sermon shook him and he decided to seek the Lord, but when he went to the afternoon service he heard another 'sermon wherein Christ was not' and felt rejected. Was this one source of his later determination that every sermon should have enough of the gospel for an unbeliever to come to Christ?

By the time he was fifteen he was educated, well-read in the Puritans, knowledgeable in the Scriptures, preserved from open sin but unconverted. In 1849 he went to Newmarket to become a pupil-teacher or usher at a school. An old cook there, an avid reader of J. C. Philpot's *Gospel Standard Magazine*, gave him his 'first lessons in theology', but he continued under the conviction of sin that had gripped him for five years. He listened to the gospel:

> But it was no gospel to me! … I used to read the Bible through, and the threatenings were all printed in capitals, but the promises were in such small type I could not for a long time make them out; and when I did read them, I did not believe they were mine, but the threatenings were all my own.

Conversion in 1850

The young usher was at home for Christmas 1849 and on the first Sunday of the new year snow prevented him from going far to chapel, so he joined a dozen others in the Primitive Methodist Chapel in Artillery Street, Colchester.

There, sitting beneath the gallery, he heard a layman preach on the text, 'Look unto me and be ye saved, all the ends of the earth.' Spurgeon is far from complimentary about this unknown man, whom he describes as 'really stupid', but this, he adds, meant that he was obliged to stick to his text, having little else to say. After ten minutes he fastened his gaze on the young stranger under the gallery and said, 'Young man, you look very miserable and you always will be miserable – miserable in life and miserable in death – if you don't obey my text; but if you obey now, this moment, you will be saved.' Then he lifted up his hands and shouted, 'Young man, look to Jesus Christ. Look! Look! Look! You have nothing to do but to look and live.' Charles said that he:

> Looked until I could have looked my eyes away. There and then the cloud was gone, the darkness rolled away and that moment I saw the sun; and I could have risen that instant and sung with the most enthusiastic of them, of the precious blood of Christ, and the simple faith which looks to him alone. Oh, that somebody had told me this before, 'Trust Christ and you shall be saved.'

He had, of course, heard it before in some form, though not simply or clearly enough. He had also read Baxter's *Call to the unconverted* and Joseph Alleine's *Alarm to the unconverted*, but perhaps even here the multitude of exhortations had obscured the one thing necessary. This element in his conversion experience is, no doubt, what made Spurgeon so rightly critical of all who direct sinners to anything except faith in Christ. He even points the finger at Bunyan for directing his pilgrim to the wicket-gate instead of to the cross.

Nevertheless he was one with the great Puritan: 'I thought I could dance all the way home. I could understand what John Bunyan meant, when he declared he wanted to tell the crows on the ploughed land all about his conversion.' Late into that night father and son talked of how the young lad had found 'salvation' in the morning and, in the evening at the Baptist Chapel, 'peace and pardon'. He returned to Newmarket to resume his duties and attended the Congregational church. He had long had doubts about his father's and grandfather's practice of infant baptism and in May was baptized at Isleham. When he informed his grandfather he received a kindly reply, expressing the hope that 'I shall not be one of the straight-laced, strict communion sort. In that we are agreed!' He soon began to serve the Lord, sending tracts in envelopes to his friends and distributing them from house to house in Newmarket. He also began teaching in the Sunday school, counting 'the letters "s.s.t." higher than M.A., B.A., or any other honour that ever was conferred by man'.

Spurgeon's teacher moved to Cambridge in August 1850 and he went with him to continue his studies as well as his 'ushering'.

In Cambridge he naturally joined the Baptist church, where he soon made his mark. After his first communion at the church he greeted the gentleman with whom he had shared a pew. The man disclaimed his acquaintance, but Spurgeon reminded him that they were 'brothers' and had just shared in communion as a token of that fact! The man accepted the rebuke, exclaimed, 'Oh, sweet simplicity!' and took him home to tea.

Preacher at Waterbeach

Spurgeon's Sunday school teaching soon grew into addressing the whole school and it was not long before he preached his first sermon.

He was asked by the organizer of the local preachers' association to accompany an older man to take a service not far away so that the preacher would have some company on the way. As the two walked there, each discovered that the other was not expecting to preach! The older man encouraged the younger to deliver one of his Sunday school addresses to the 'poor people', which he did successfully, to his relief and to their amazement because of his youth. After this he preached regularly at cottage meetings and then at chapel services. In one village, finding that no one was going to attend the service because of the thunderstorm that was raging, he went around the houses and secured himself a congregation. During this period he heard the great William Jay of Bath in Cambridge and even travelled to Birmingham to hear John Angell James, but it was of the young usher that one of the Cambridge deacons declared, 'Whoever lives to see it, he will become one of the greatest men in England.'

One village where he preached was Waterbeach, where the Baptist church had a chapel and forty members, but no minister. Spurgeon, still only seventeen, agreed to fill their pulpit for a month and continued there for three years. On his very first visit he shared a bed with the son of his host. When the lad jumped into bed without prayer Spurgeon tackled him on the matter, got him out of bed and prayed with him, and that night the youngster was converted. He was so earnest in seeking souls that he pestered his deacons for news of anybody who had been converted and was thrilled to hear very soon that a woman, who had gone home one Sunday broken-hearted, had now found peace. On the Monday morning before returning to Cambridge the pastor was off to see her. It was not long before many others followed. 'It pleased God', writes Spurgeon, 'to turn the whole place upside down. In a short time, the little thatched chapel was crammed, the biggest vagabonds of the village were weeping floods of tears, and those who had been the despair of the parish, became its blessing.' The congregations sometimes numbered 450, and he preached, at Waterbeach and elsewhere, over 300 times in a year. He visited as well as preached and learned to deal fearlessly and wisely with all types of men and women.

THE MAID'S MISTAKE

In 1852 it was suggested that the young preacher should seek formal training for the ministry. At his father's insistence he made enquiries of Regent's Park College, and it was arranged that he should meet the college tutor, Dr Angus, while he was visiting Cambridge. Due to a mistake by the maid he was shown into the wrong room, and the meeting did not take place and was not rearranged. Then as well as later, Spurgeon regarded this as the Lord's providence, confirming his own 'aversion to college' and preventing him from seeking great things for himself. When he later mentioned his lack of college training to the deacons of New Park Street Chapel one of them replied, 'That is to us a special recommendation, for you would not have such savour and unction if you came from college.' This sort of statement should not be used, as it sometimes is, to denigrate theological education and sound biblical scholarship. According to his brother, Spurgeon's intellectual attainments were surpassed by none of his contemporaries and, although he was a non-conformist and excluded from the university, his teacher was sure that he could have graduated at the top of the list.

Spurgeon was content to remain with his 'loving and praying church' at Waterbeach. The chapel was full, with people outside listening at the windows. He had to give up his work as an usher and went to live in the village where he was supported by the church, partly in money, partly by gifts in kind. Here he fought his early battles with Romanism, perfectionism, Arminianism and, especially, hyper-Calvinism.

There were those at Waterbeach who objected to his 'invitation sermons', in which he offered Christ freely to all. One such man, having expressed his displeasure, then went on to comment that the Lord, on the other hand, must be pleased with them, for his son-in-law had been converted and his daughter had gone home in tears under this preaching. 'So', he concluded, 'don't you take any notice of an old man like me', and since that was what Spurgeon was going to do anyway they ended in perfect agreement!

London and revival

Towards the end of 1853 the inevitable happened: Spurgeon's reputation reached London and he received, to his astonishment, an invitation to preach at New Park Street Chapel (1854 – 1860), south of the Thames. The congregation had earlier been served, in other buildings, by such men as Dr John Gill and Dr John Rippon but had fallen on hard times, with 200 people in a building able to hold six times that number. When Spurgeon preached his first sermon there the small morning congregation was so impressed that some of them decided: 'We must get him a better congregation tonight, or we shall lose him.' So they spent the afternoon rounding up their relatives and friends to come and hear him. These included 'little Susie', Susannah Thompson, who later became Mrs Spurgeon. On this occasion she was less interested in the preacher's sermon than in his appearance, which she found rather rustic and somewhat amusing. His ministry thrilled the rest and soon he was invited to supply the pulpit for six months' trial. This period was never completed for after three months the church called him as pastor, and he began his ministry proper in April 1854.

The 'mere handful' to whom Charles Spurgeon began preaching included a few who, as the congregation declined in numbers, 'never ceased to pray for a gracious revival'. Now they carried on praying; the church rapidly filled and the work of conversion began. Indeed, revival had come to New Park Street, as Spurgeon did not hesitate to assert. These were, he says, 'times of revival and of the outpouring of God's grace' and elsewhere he says, 'I do think that many an old Puritan would jump out of his grave if he knew what was doing now.' A distinguished minister from Scotland has left us an account of his visit to New Park Street in 1856, concluding:

> In respect of his power over an audience, and a London one in particular, I should say he is not inferior to Whitefield himself. Mr Spurgeon is a Calvinist, which few of the dissenting ministers in London now are. He preaches salvation, not of man's *free will*, but of the Lord's *good will*, which few in London, it is to be feared, now do.

By the end of 1856 the membership had grown from less than 300 to 860. He tells us that in 1856 he interviewed, 'not less than a thousand who had been converted', and he received thousands of letters.

Some of the conversions were remarkable. One evening a widow decided not to attend worship but to stay at home to pray for her two sons. That very evening the elder son told her he was going to hear the 'odd man' who preached in Southwark, meaning Spurgeon. The woman did not think much of this preacher but was pleased that he should go anywhere near the Word of God. The younger brother went too and later, after praying and feeling that she had 'prevailed', the mother opened the door to her returning sons to be told that both had found the Saviour. After that all three worshipped at New Park Street.

Spurgeon tells of an Irishman who came to him with a problem that his Catholic priest could not answer: how could God be just and yet forgive a sinner? 'He has no right to do that', asserted Pat. A mere mention of the blood of Christ was not enough to satisfy the man; his priest had also referred to that, so Spurgeon used an illustration to make clear the relationship between Christ's death as our substitute and our forgiveness. Light dawned on the man and he said, 'Faith, that's the gospel. Pat is safe now; with all his sins about him, he'll trust in the man that died for him, and so he shall be saved.'

Others came to the chapel by accident or out of curiosity and found, as they thought, that the preacher knew all about them and was speaking directly to them. A man who had just been to purchase his supply of alcohol was convicted when Spurgeon said that there might be a man in the gallery who had come in with no good motive because he had a bottle of gin in his pocket. A prostitute, on the verge of suicide, heard a sermon on 'Seest thou this woman?', which just described her, the worst woman in the city, was melted to tears and saved from suicide and eternal loss.

One Sunday evening Spurgeon opened his Bible during the hymn before the sermon. As he turned to the passage on which he had prepared to preach, a text on the opposite page 'sprang out' at him 'like a lion from a thicket'. As the congregation sang he tried to decide which text to use. He chose the new one and proceeded to preach on it, although, for what he says were understandable reasons, he could not announce his headings in advance. After two points and with no idea what the third should be he was plunged into darkness as the gas lighting failed! Not having to rely on notes he was able to continue preaching and turned to the familiar theme of the child of darkness walking in the light. When light was restored he found the congregation still listening with rapt attention. Later two people applied for membership: one had been converted through the first part of the unprepared sermon and the other through the second!

Soon the chapel could not hold the crowds who wanted to hear the young preacher. It was enlarged and then filled again. Exeter Hall in the Strand, which could hold 4,000, was hired for Sunday evenings and still the crowds grew. The prayer meetings were regularly attended by 500 people and these he always remembered. In later days he reminded his flock of those occasions 'when I felt compelled to let you go without a word from my lips, because the Spirit of God was so awfully present that we felt bowed to the dust'. He exhorted his congregation, 'May God help me if you cease to pray for me. Let me know the day and I must cease to preach.' They did not cease to pray, and when asked later for the reason for his success he was able quite simply and truthfully to reply, 'My people pray for me.'

Attacks

However, all was not sweetness and light. The popular press attacked him with innuendo and cartoons and the religious press with accusations of fanaticism, arrogance, hypocrisy and showmanship. Possibly the worst attacks, because they came from men of undoubted godliness and years in the Lord's service, were those from the hyper-Calvinist Baptists in London who accused him of men-pleasing, of not preaching true experimental, heart-searching religion and even cast doubt on 'the divine reality of his conversion'. The huge attendances to hear the 'Exeter Hall stripling' led to another insult, which must have pleased Spurgeon more than most compliments: 'that the greater part of the multitudes that crowd to his weekly theatrical exhibitions consists of people who are not in the habit of frequenting a place of worship'. So many and varied were the attacks that Mrs Spurgeon had a text printed, framed and put up in their bedroom – the words of Matthew 5:11-12: 'Blessed are ye, when men shall revile you, and persecute you, and shall say all manner of evil against you falsely, for my sake. Rejoice, and be exceeding glad: for great is your reward in heaven: for so persecuted they the prophets which were before you.'

The Surrey Gardens Music Hall disaster

In the autumn of 1856 Exeter Hall ceased to be available and the church arranged to use the Surrey Gardens Music Hall, which held many more people. It was estimated that perhaps 12,000 were there on the first Sunday evening when disaster struck. While the pastor was leading the massive congregation in prayer a panic was caused by cries of 'Fire' and 'The galleries are giving way'. In the stampede that followed this false alarm, seven people were killed and twenty-eight had to be taken to hospital. Spurgeon, a mere twenty-two years of age, was so shattered by this experience that it was feared that he might never preach again. His worst press enemy, the *Saturday Review*, made the most of the tragedy. After sneering at him for preaching 'particular redemption in saloons reeking with the perfume of tobacco', it went on to twist his words about the necessity of having their own building into an intention to 'preach another crowd into a frenzy of terror, kill and smash a dozen or two more'. One can well understand why Spurgeon could later define a true Christian as 'one who loves God and is hated by the *Saturday Review*'.

Spurgeon never forgot that dreadful evening, but he recovered sufficiently to preach a fortnight later. He recalls his experience in his book, *The Saint and his Saviour*, to illustrate 'the love of Jesus, in his delivering grace'. It was the realization of God's compassion and the exaltation of Christ's name that removed his fears and made him preach again. 'Scorn, tumult and woe seemed less than nothing for his sake.' His 'few words' on that Sunday morning were, inevitably, on Philippians 2:9-11: 'Wherefore God also hath highly exalted him, and given him a name which is above every name: that at the name of Jesus every knee should bow.' In fact, this 'great and terrible catastrophe invented by Satan to overturn us' had the opposite effect. Spurgeon, already well known before, became famous overnight. Attacks continued but some rallied to his defence, including some who by no means shared his theology. Services were resumed at the Music Hall but only in the mornings, in the light.

THE CRYSTAL PALACE

Of course Spurgeon was often invited to preach elsewhere, but the most notable occasion of these years was probably the service held at the Crystal Palace on the National Day of Humiliation, attended by 23,654 people. A day or two before the event the preacher went to test the acoustics of the huge auditorium. This he did by pronouncing in a very loud voice the text, 'Behold the Lamb of God, which taketh away the sin of the world.' In one of the galleries was a workman who, not knowing what was going on, took the words as a direct message from heaven. He was immediately convicted of sin, stopped work and went home, where he 'found peace and life by beholding the Lamb of God'. The actual service was an outstanding triumph but imposed such a strain on Spurgeon that he slept through from Wednesday evening to Friday morning.

The Metropolitan Tabernacle

It was, as Spurgeon had said, time that they had their own building, and the church set out to provide one. Funds were raised, a site purchased, plans drawn up and, in August 1859, the foundation stone of the Metropolitan Tabernacle was laid. The cost was to be about £30,000 and there must have been a certain amount of apprehension among the members. When about £10,000 had been raised, a man from elsewhere, concerned that Spurgeon's ministry should not be hindered by anxiety, guaranteed the remaining £20,000, although he was confident that only his intended gift of £50 would be used. Such proved to be the case. While the Tabernacle was being completed,

Spurgeon, who had been preaching, on average, ten times a week for seven years, was given a holiday on the Continent. When he returned the building was not quite ready but meetings were already being held there. The Tabernacle was opened, free from debt, in March 1861. Appropriately, the first service was a meeting for prayer, attended by 1,000 people. The main chapel held over 4,000, but this was soon insufficient to seat even the members and their families. Seventy-two people were accepted for membership at the first church meeting held in the Tabernacle, and by 1879, after twenty-five years of Spurgeon's ministry in two buildings, the membership was 5,066.

Spurgeon in print

Spurgeon's preaching ministry followed the same pattern, more or less, to the end; although the excitement decreased as his position was consolidated, the power of the Spirit continued to rest on his ministry, especially in the proclamation of the gospel. From the beginning of his time in London Spurgeon had other strings to his bow, apart from his preaching, and a consideration of these other spheres of work will help us to take the measure of the man. He was well aware of the power of the printed word and had published a few tracts while at Waterbeach.

Once Spurgeon settled in London he found that his sermons were in demand for publication in various magazines and soon began to issue them himself, at first only occasionally and then weekly, from the beginning of 1855. This continued until his death and then on until 1917. Annual volumes containing fifty-two of these sermons were published as *The New Park Street Pulpit* and then *The Metropolitan Tabernacle Pulpit*, which are still read (and sometimes preached!) today.

THE NEW PARK STREET PULPIT 1855

In his preface to the first volume he wrote,

> *Little can be said in praise of these sermons, and nothing can be said against them more bitter than has*

already spoken... and yet, the printed discourses have for that very reason found a readier sale, and more have been led to peruse them with deep attention.

One thing alone places this book above contempt — and that accomplishes the deed so triumphantly that the preacher defies the opinion of man — it is the fact that, to his certain knowledge, there is scarcely a sermon which has not been stamped by the hand of the Almighty, by the conversion of a soul. Some single sermons, here brought into the society of their brethren, have been, under God, the means of the salvation of not less than twenty souls.

Years later he was able to write about the first twenty volumes of sermons that there were 'discourses among them of which I may say, without exaggeration, that the Holy Spirit blessed them to the conversion of hundreds; and long after their delivery fresh instances of their usefulness come to light, and are still being brought under our notice'. By the end of the century several hundred millions had been published, and the sermons had been translated into twenty-three languages.

Spurgeon reckoned that he had an extra 56,000 'members' who read his sermons each week, corresponded with him and supported his projects, such as the Stockwell Orphanage. As well as ordinary commercial distribution, individuals made the sermons available using a variety of means. One man gave away 250,000 copies; he had some bound and presented them to 'every crowned head in Europe', as well as giving twelve sermons to each member of both houses of Parliament and every university student. A wealthy Russian obtained permission from the censor to print and distribute a million copies of some of the sermons, with the official stamp of the Orthodox Church hierarchy on them! Often they were read in public, in default of a preacher, with great effect; sometimes they were preached unacknowledged, as Spurgeon discovered.

One Sunday, feeling somewhat depressed and troubled as to whether he really enjoyed the things he preached to others,

Spurgeon entered a country Methodist chapel. The service was led by a layman, an engineer, and the sermon moved the visitor to tears, thus confirming that he did enjoy the message he passed on to others. When he thanked the man he had to reveal his identity, much to the 'preacher's' embarrassment, for it was one of Spurgeon's own sermons that he had heard. Spurgeon reassured the apologetic man because this 'accident' meant that it was exactly what he preached that thrilled him.

A lady came to see Spurgeon in the Tabernacle vestry in deep distress about her husband who had deserted her. There was nothing to do but pray for the man, which they did. Some months later she returned with her husband. Far away, on board ship, he had come across one of Spurgeon's sermons, been converted and returned to his wife. Other sermons were printed in an Australian weekly newspaper as advertisements, at great cost to the individual who had the idea. A man read one in a copy of the paper lying on the counter of a public house and was immediately convicted of his sin. Another man was shepherding miles from anywhere when he picked up a single sheet of this same paper, which the wind had blown across the countryside. He started to read, without realizing that it was a sermon, and having begun, had to finish. The sermon caused him to think, so he kept the sheet and reread it many times until he was finally converted. In Syria copies were cursed and burned by the Roman Catholic priests and bishop, but this only aroused interest and created a demand for the sermons.

The editing of the sermons, which had been taken down in shorthand, made great demands on Spurgeon's time, but he always felt it to be worthwhile. He also found time for other writing and anything he produced he was sure to sell, even the massive *Treasury of David*, a commentary on the Psalms with copious notes culled from other authors, which, incidentally, demonstrated his amazing breadth of reading. His writings show great variety, from *The Saint and his Saviour*, published in 1857, to his *Gospel of the Kingdom*, a popular commentary on Matthew. Many have enjoyed his John Ploughman books, aimed at the ordinary man, while his *Morning and Evening* daily readings are increasingly popular in our own day.

Many a minister has used his *Commenting and Commentaries* as a guide to the shelves of second-hand bookshops. Equally popular and useful have been his *Lectures to my Students*, which introduce us to another of Spurgeon's ventures.

The Pastors' College

Early in his ministry Spurgeon was faced with the problem of some young men who, having been converted, were both zealous and effective in preaching in the open air. However, they lacked training and, indeed, basic education and would not have been accepted by the usual colleges. So something had to be done for, as one of them, Thomas Medhurst, insisted, 'I must preach, sir, and I shall preach unless you cut off my head!' This clearly could not be allowed so Spurgeon did his best to help by financing his studies with a minister. In 1857 a second student joined him, and Spurgeon enlisted the aid of the Rev. George Rogers of Camberwell; although not a Baptist, he was ideally suited to the task of training young men for the ministry. Thus began the Pastors' College. The two students soon increased to eight, then twenty and then 100; by 1891, 845 men had been trained and sent out into largely pioneer situations both in England and overseas. At first they used Mr Rogers' house, but when the Tabernacle was built they moved into its classrooms.

The task of deciding whom to accept often fell to Spurgeon. His principle in doing so may be seen from these words: 'I never tried to make a minister, and should fail if I did; I receive none into the College, but those who profess to be ministers already.' This was the Pastors' College, not the Pastor's College. 'Have you won souls for Jesus?' was his first question to all applicants. Thus, although Spurgeon in no way derided learning and sound scholarship he was not primarily concerned with producing scholars who could satisfy the university examiners but preachers of the gospel. The Bible was the basis of all that was taught, but 'As everybody else claims to do the same ... we say distinctly that the theology of the Pastors' College is Puritanic.' George Rogers agreed with him: 'We prefer Puritan to modern divinity.' The college would have nothing to do with that 'idolatry of the intellect', which was contributing to the ruin of the church; nor would Spurgeon and Rogers countenance a 'dead orthodoxy', which merely insisted on conformity to traditional doctrines. 'A man must first know the truth in his own soul before he can effectively transmit it to those who sit at his feet. Knowing it, he must live in the daily enjoyment of it.'

Spurgeon lectured to the students on preaching and related subjects. This gave him ample scope for the humour that he kept out of the pulpit, but mainly he was concerned with more serious aspects. This was certainly true of the addresses he delivered to the annual conference of the Pastors' College. The character of these, some of which were published in *An All-Round Ministry*, may be deduced from titles such as: 'Strength in weakness', 'The preacher's power and the conditions of obtaining it', 'The minister in these times', and, especially, 'How to meet the evils of the age'. These students were going out not only into an alien world but into a church situation that was fast deteriorating and was hostile not only to 'the old Calvinistical doctrines' proclaimed by Spurgeon and taught in the college but even to basic evangelical teaching.

The Downgrade controversy

The battle begins

Spurgeon became increasingly aware of the growth of heresy and utter worldliness, not only in the church in general but also in his beloved and supposedly evangelical Baptist denomination. Eventually he could not be content to teach and warn his congregation and his students; the battle must be taken to the enemy; it must be brought out into the open. So began the 'Downgrade' controversy, which saddened the last years of Spurgeon's ministry and probably hastened his death.

Spurgeon began the warfare in the pages of his monthly magazine, *The Sword and Trowel*, with articles and comments from himself and others. From January 1887 the developing controversy can be traced in its pages, particularly in two articles by Robert Shindler entitled, 'The Downgrade'. As far back as 1873, R. W. Dale of Birmingham, John Angell James's successor, had expressed the opinion 'that Calvinism would be almost obsolete among Baptists were it not still maintained by the powerful influence of Mr Spurgeon'. However, the complaint now being voiced in no uncertain terms was that basic evangelical doctrines were being denied – for example, the inerrancy of the Scriptures, substitutionary atonement and everlasting punishment. Even worse, those who did not deny them openly were either hinting at denial or simply refusing to insist on any test of orthodoxy.

Leaving the Baptist Union

Soon the debate was taken up in the sphere of the Baptist Union, as Spurgeon demanded that some discipline be exerted and that heterodoxy be dealt with, even if only by an unambiguous statement that the Union was 'formed on a scriptural basis'. The details of the struggle need not concern us here; the evasions, ambiguities, compromise and even lies, which Spurgeon encountered in his dealings with supposedly evangelical officialdom, are edifying only in a very negative and warning sense. More positive is the realization that Spurgeon's activity in this matter, like M'Cheyne's in the Disruption controversy, is a necessary consequence of a concern for the prosperity of the gospel and not an unspiritual contention. Many at the time could not, or would not, see the importance of the issue and Spurgeon was left almost in isolation. When his demands were not met he felt compelled to withdraw from the Union, with the deepest regret, although he had from the beginning feared 'that the reform of the Baptist Union was hopeless'. In the end even genuine evangelicals, including many of his students and his own brother, left him to fight alone. History has demonstrated that, whatever the merits of his actual tactics and decisions, Spurgeon was clear-sighted and correct in his diagnosis of the situation; the downgrade continued and the twentieth century saw the virtual destruction of evangelicalism and the triumph of unorthodoxy, secularism and sterile denominationalism.

The bitterness and physical and mental strain took their toll on a man already overworked and ill, and in January 1892 he died at Mentone in France. The memorial and funeral services held in

London were attended by huge crowds as his reputation with the people was undiminished. So the day came to which he had referred in a sermon seventeen years earlier:

> When you see my coffin carried to the silent grave, I should like every one of you, whether converted or not, to be constrained to say, 'He did earnestly urge us, in plain and simple language, not to put off the consideration of eternal things. He did entreat us to look to Christ. Now he is gone, our blood is not at his door if we perish.'

If these words solemnize us, other words addressed to the Annual Conference in 1889 and often quoted in recent years may encourage us: 'For my part, I am quite willing to be eaten of dogs for the next fifty years; but the more distant future shall vindicate me.'

This prophecy is increasingly being fulfilled in our day and should stimulate us not only to follow the example of Spurgeon and the other great men whose work we have considered but also to plead with the Most High once more to remember his people and revive his work in the midst of the years.

Questions for discussion

1. *Why might it be true that it was better for Spurgeon not to meet Dr Angus and go to college? How does this accord with Spurgeon's own founding of a college for preachers?*

2. *Why is it important to remember that Spurgeon was Calvinistic in his theology? How did this influence his preaching, pastoral work and training of preachers?*

3. *How can we account for the fact that many of Spurgeon's evangelical friends, including even many of his students, did not support him in the Downgrade controversy? Has time proved him right and, if so, in what ways?*

For further reading

* A. Dallimore, *Spurgeon: a new biography*, The Banner of Truth Trust, 1985.

** I. Murray, *The forgotten Spurgeon*, The Banner of Truth Trust, 1986.

** C. H. Spurgeon, *Autobiography, Vol. 1: The early years*, The Banner of Truth Trust, 1962; *Vol. 2: The full harvest*, The Banner of Truth Trust, 1973.

We have heard with our ears, O God;
*   our fathers have told us*
what you did in their days,
*   in days long ago.*
In God we make our boast all day long,
*   and we will praise your name for ever.*
But now you have rejected us and humbled us;
*   you no longer go out with our armies.*
Awake, O Lord! Why do you sleep?
*   Rouse yourself! Do not reject us for ever.*
Rise up and help us;
*   redeem us because of your unfailing love.*

— Psalm 44:1,8,9,23,26

Concerned as we all are, or at any rate should be, with a true revival of religion ... we must realize that there is nothing more urgently important than that we should examine ourselves. There are certain conditions in this matter of revival, and God has so ordained it, as history shows us clearly, that before he pours forth his Spirit upon a people, or upon an individual, he first prepares that people or that individual. It is inconceivable that great blessing should be given to a Laodicean, back-sliding, or apostate church without a preliminary work of repentance.

— D. Martyn Lloyd-Jones (1899 – 1981)

16

Following in the footsteps

'And so they all lived happily ever after.' Is that all it is? Is it just a fairy tale or, at least, just a tale? Although not put into words, such is the attitude in practice of many Christians today. The lives of martyrs, the biographies of preachers, the experiences of missionaries, present as well as past, are regarded as interesting and exciting, the evangelical equivalent of popular romantic fiction, but of no relevance to daily life or the testimony of the church. My contention, on the contrary, is that there is nothing more important for us today than a proper understanding of God's activity in the history of the church and in the lives of these great men. We can and must take heart from their convictions and courage. We must rely on their God to work in our situation also. 'Where is the God of Elijah?' on the lips of Elisha was not a complaint but a call of faith to that God, an earnest desire that he would be with Elisha as he laboured for him in his generation. However, we must also ensure that we apply their principles today and by following in their footsteps, know the blessing of their God.

In 1890 John Charles Ryle, the first and great Bishop of Liverpool, wrote, 'There are certain facts in history which the world tries hard to forget and ignore. These facts get in the way of some of the world's favourite theories, and are highly inconvenient. The consequence is that the world shuts its eyes to them.' His words hold good still but with this difference: the world has long since ceased to care, and the contemporary church dislikes these facts of history. As a consequence the modern churchman, although not altogether ignoring the facts, interprets them so that he can use them either to support his own ideas or to justify his refusal to tread in the same old paths.

John Wesley is still in favour with the Methodists, but few of them insist with him that a person must be born again. Baptists honour C. H. Spurgeon, but most follow him only in insisting on believers' baptism. Congregationalists respect the Pilgrim Fathers but twist John Robinson's words to justify getting light from non-biblical sources. Anglicans speak well of the Reformers but regard the Reformation as a 'disaster', whereas Presbyterians glory in the *Westminster Confession* but relegate it to the sidelines with other historical relics.

Of course, there are honourable exceptions, but most modern churchmen follow in the steps of the Pharisees who earned our Lord's condemnation for building the tombs of the prophets, while aligning themselves in practice with those who persecuted and opposed them. Times have changed, we are told; these men were, no doubt, useful in their day, but now we have learned tolerance and love and can see that what really matters is unity and social concern. If the great heroes of the past were alive today, it is said with confidence, they would go along with modern scholarship and sink their trivial doctrinal differences in order to seek the common good against the common enemies of atheism and materialism. And some evangelicals have fallen for it!

The modern critics are right in one matter. Times have changed; things are different and we cannot simply imitate the leaders of the past, speaking and living just as they did. That is both lazy and useless. Nevertheless the basic essentials of man's condition and need, of God's power and gospel, have not changed. The principles on which they worked remain valid, and we have only to apply them in our own situation. It is possible and vital to discover what these men had in common with each other and what we must have in common with them so that we may take our place in the great succession of the footsteps of God.

God's people

They were the true people of God. It is sad that in any age the religious people who make the headlines, whose books are bestsellers and who appear in the media are the heretics, the men who depart from the orthodox line and therefore stand out. They deny the faith and generally display no evidence of an evangelical experience of regeneration and conversion issuing in biblical holiness. It is so today; it has always been so. This book has been concerned with Christianity and Christians in the historic sense, both the leaders and the multitudes who followed their teaching and served their Lord. We have been able to trace the way that they came to trust Christ for themselves or, if that was hidden, we have been able to see the evidence of faith, the activity of love and the steadfastness that comes from hope in their life and service. Here is the real unity of the body of Christ, a unity of truth and faith and holiness, of which the ecumenical movement is not a pale shadow but a denial. These men were all evangelicals, born of the Spirit, trusting in the death of Christ, whatever their background or denominational allegiance. They were, moreover, men of large sympathies and cooperated with one another in love.

We must not be misled by their refusal to work with those who denied the gospel or by the times when they did slip into intolerance of genuine brethren and overemphasize secondary disagreements. On the whole their commitment to the gospel of Jesus Christ, the pursuit of godliness, the salvation of the lost and the glory of God left them little leisure for trivial debates. They were ready to work with the Lord's people wherever they found them. John Calvin consulted with the Anglican Archbishop Cranmer; Whitefield, an Anglican, rejoiced to have fellowship with Jonathan

Edwards; and Spurgeon found many kindred spirits among the men of the Free Church of Scotland.

It was not that they leaned towards doctrinal indifference or thought secondary matters to be of no importance, but differences over externals of worship or sacrament and disagreements over denominational links or lack of them were not allowed to destroy their basic unity of faith and heart. This is the kind of unity that we too must encourage.

God's Word

They accepted the authority of the Word of God, by which they meant the infallible Scriptures. The modern ecclesiastic, of course, will claim the same submission to the Word of God, but when defined this turns out to be a horse of a very different colour. A typical modern view of the authenticity of the Gospel narratives is the following:

> I believe that with all the work that has been put in by saints and scholars and students and critics; with all the discovery of *church additions and changes in tone and attitude from the originals* (all of which have been discovered by devoted study), we have at heart narratives that speak of God in Jesus and are authentic in portraying him, the ways and attitudes of the disciples and *those of the early church* [author's italics].

Similar methods evacuate the rest of the Scriptures of their authority – and then we are told that this is what Calvin, the Reformers and the rest would have accepted if they had lived in these enlightened days! Indeed, sometimes Calvin and others are even represented as being Barthians before Barth, but better-qualified hands than mine have answered this case. I would simply point to the history.

It is not necessary to repeat in detail the beliefs of Wycliffe, Tyndale, Eliot and Carey; their translation labours say it all. Calvin's sermons, lectures and commentaries speak volumes about his faith in the written Word of God. Their devotional lives, their preaching, their debates – all testify convincingly to their commitment to the Scriptures; without the Word of God these men would have been and done nothing.

This was not a superficial, dispensable element in their theology but the very foundation of all that they believed and did. It is quite foolish to imagine that we can remove this feature and then expect to do what they did. In the opposite direction, theologically speaking, we must insist that, for all their stress on the Holy Spirit's work in regeneration and revival, when it came to authority, the testing of doctrine or experience they always went to 'the Word and the testimony'. They encountered, as we do today, those who claimed prophetic and even apostolic authority, immediate inspiration by the Holy Spirit, and they would have none of it. We too must hold to the authority of the written Word of God, neither deserting it for the meagre scraps left to us by the liberal critic nor for the extravagances of the contemporary prophet.

God's gospel

They proclaimed the gospel of God. Everyone claims to do this, but such claims are nothing new to readers of the New Testament. There are many 'other gospels' today, which are not gospels, and there always have been. The men we have been considering had to face this issue and did so quite consistently. Some were clearer than others, especially in the early days when the truth was still being defined against heretical opposition and later when that same truth was re-emerging after the Dark Ages. Augustine, strong on grace, was weak on justification; Wycliffe, clear on predestination and insistent on the work of Christ, was equally unclear on justification. Luther supplied this deficiency and then Calvin supplemented him. Nevertheless, the essence of the gospel was always there, reliance on an objective work of Christ on the cross, even when the technical doctrine of justification left much to be desired. Men were convinced of sin and saved by the grace of God through the preaching of all these men. However, their weaknesses do not justify those who live in the clear light of day since the Reformation but who, while claiming to believe and preach the gospel, evacuate its truths of real meaning.

In this area evangelicals are compromising in a way our fore-fathers would have condemned. Although the church of Rome has not changed its position on justification, some, who used to state the doctrine of justification by faith only in clear, uncompromising terms as the 'article of a standing or falling church', are now urging unity with Roman Catholics because they are better than the liberals. This may be true, but nothing less than the New Testament is good enough. Others, adopting what is known as 'the New Perspective', are amending this crucial doctrine, apparently with the same end in view. Another aspect of the same debate is the tendency to accept the Catholic doctrine of the mass. Anyone tempted to go in this direction should read, or read again, Bishop Ryle's chapter headed, 'Why were our Reformers burned?' and determine not to give an inch in the battle to defend the finished work of Christ. We must either reckon Cranmer, Latimer and Ridley to have been ignorant fools or determine to follow in their footsteps. On the other side of the battlefield we have to insist, against the vague declarations about the death and resurrection of Christ current today, that our Saviour really did suffer wrath and punishment in the place of sinners and that the tomb really was empty. There can be no compromise on these issues if the gospel is to survive and be preached in our day and if we hope to enjoy the same blessing of God on our work that our forefathers had.

God's truth

They were prepared to contend for the truth of God. This is, perhaps, the main ground of criticism against our forefathers in the eyes of those who occupy the headlines today. It is alleged that such an attitude is contrary to the spirit of toleration and the practice of love. We ought to speak in terms of making our contribution, of the evangelical point of view or perspective, not about truth and error. There is no such thing as heresy; anyone who claims to be a Christian is to be accepted as a brother in Christ with no questions asked. Within evangelical circles there are those who have succumbed to the temptation to go with the tide, whereas others ignore error and false ideas, asking only to be allowed to go about their work of evangelism in peace. For some any kind of debate is to be avoided like the plague, as the enemy of evangelism and revival.

How different was the attitude of the great leaders of the past! Because the Scriptures are the Word of God, not of man, and because it is God's gospel, not their own, they did not consider themselves at liberty to pick and choose what they believed or to leave serious error alone to wreak havoc in God's church. There is a contentiousness that is purely negative and destructive and, of course, they sometimes were at fault in this way, but the positive results of their efforts show that usually they were not guilty of that sin. They contended for the gospel against Romanism, formalism, moderatism and modernism so that the truths of salvation might survive and men and women might be saved. It is not enough to go on working in our small corner and allow the rest of the world to go to ruin. Before long the infection will spread even to our 'parish' and our cherished liberty, in practice, will be gone. Our forefathers suffered for their efforts to defend the truth. They were maligned, persecuted and executed so that the true gospel might continue to be proclaimed, so that people in bondage to error might be delivered into the liberty of Christ.

Great discernment is necessary in this area because the devil's target varies from age to age. We need eyes to see which truths are in particular danger at any given point and then courage to defend them.

LOYALTY TO CHRIST

Martin Luther wrote, 'If I profess with the loudest voice and clearest exposition every portion of the truth of God except precisely that little point which the world and the devil are at that moment attacking, I am not confessing Christ, however boldly I may be professing Christ. Wherever the battle rages, there the loyalty of the soldier is proved and to be steady on the battlefield besides is mere flight and disgrace if he flinches at that one point.'

It is in this sense that the old confessions are inadequate. They are not wrong or heretical, but their authors did not have to contend, for example, with men who interpret 'infallible' to mean something different from and less than 'inerrant' in order to allow for mistakes in the Bible. They were not faced with the theory of evolution or the charismatic movement. In their day Romanism did not pretend to believe in justification by faith as it does now in some quarters. Athanasius correctly singled out the deity of Christ as the vital issue for his day and fought for that. Knox rightly saw the mass as the great danger and did battle against it. Many of the old struggles continue today, but we must not be misled into manning the walls at the wrong points while the enemy enters unchecked elsewhere. Resurgent liberalism, as popularized on the television screen, ecumenical compromise and blurring of the issues, as seen in Anglican/Roman Catholic discussions and the dilution of reformed doctrine, in the interests of 'life and joy', these and other trends must be identified, analysed and dealt with as fearlessly in our day as by our fathers in theirs.

Further, they were successful in their efforts. Knox hated the mass and resisted it with all his strength, but this did not prevent Scotland from being transformed spiritually. Luther and Calvin attacked Romanism, but the Reformation was pre-eminently a spreading of the gospel. Whitefield and Wesley had no time for the dead, deistic preachers of their day and said so, but England was transformed. Spurgeon fought against hyper-Calvinism and modernism, but the Tabernacle was crowded with converts. Proper contending for the faith is not opposed to evangelism or the blessing of God. There has never been a Roman Catholic, Unitarian or modernist revival. Let us follow in the steps of those who knew what it was to preach in the power of the Holy Spirit and fight for the truth, whatever it may cost.

God's sovereignty

They believed in the sovereignty of God. Most of the men whom we have described, especially those who lived after Luther, held to Reformation teaching, the doctrines of grace: total depravity, unconditional election, particular redemption, irresistible grace, and the final perseverance of the saints, traditionally, if unhappily, known as Calvinism. The ecumenical men of our day would regard such beliefs merely as an extreme form of outmoded evangelicalism. In fact, they are the only consistent form of evangelicalism, the only truly consistent Christianity and the only viable alternative to Romanism, liberalism and atheism. Only here are God's grace and love seen in their true colours. In every time of great blessing, from the days of the apostles to the last century, this teaching has been present, usually prominent, and it is noteworthy that the decline in belief in the doctrines of grace has been accompanied by a general decline in the fortunes of the church over the last century. It is only since the Second World War that a return has begun to these great teachings that were so dear to Augustine, Luther, Calvin, Tyndale, the Puritans, Whitefield, Rowland, Edwards, Carey, Fuller, Spurgeon and a host of others.

Clearly this teaching is neither the enemy of evangelism, nor of missions nor of revival. These men were not mere scholars, thinkers or theologians, although they were all of these. They were men of action, preachers and evangelists, whom God used to keep the church alive or to bring her back to life. They were his instruments in the winning of souls, the planting of churches, the founding of missions and the spreading of revivals.

Men who believe the same today are often labelled (or libelled) as hyper-Calvinists in order to stir up ignorant prejudice. There is such a thing as hyper-Calvinism, as Fuller and Spurgeon knew well and therefore fought it with all their might, and it is the enemy of evangelism and revival. It is not the same as the glorious New Testament doctrine of sovereign grace, which these men taught in its fullness and which we need today.

It may, however, quite rightly be said that not all of my subjects were Calvinistic in their beliefs. Those in the early days seem to have assumed rather than asserted these truths until Augustine cleared matters up in battle with Pelagius and his followers. John Wesley certainly was not a Calvinist and yet did a great work, Wilberforce was lacking in this direction but achieved much and, since the days of Spurgeon, many non-Calvinists have done sterling work in the service of Christ with great self-sacrifice, devotion, diligence and a host of other Christian virtues. None of this can I, or would I want to, deny. The truth of the doctrines must be established not by a count of heads but from the Scriptures, and if this can be done then we must say that Wesley and others were useful in spite of their rejection of the doctrines of grace not because of it.

However, there is another way of looking at this matter, which is neglected at the present time. It is this: the Arminianism of Wesley was not the same thing that goes by this name today. The popular evangelical teaching is more akin to the Pelagianism defeated by Augustine and popularized by Finney than to Wesley's beliefs. The New Testament teaching on the sovereignty of God is more than the so-called 'five points of Calvinism'. It brings us before the majesty and glory of God. It humbles and convicts in awe and reverence before the presence of the living God. Wesley believed in and preached a great God and the effect of this was evident in the convicting and humbling results of his labours.

Wesley's teaching, with all its faults, had more in common with Jonathan Edwards's sermon on 'God glorified in man's dependence' than with the 'pop-evangelism' of modern man-centred missions. His practice had nothing in common with the superficialities of current evangelicalism, and he and his friends would surely have been appalled by what goes on in the name of Christ today. On the other side of the coin we must observe that merely holding to the 'five points' relating to the way of salvation does not constitute being 'Reformed' when this vision of the greatness and glory of God has gone and when awe and reverence and the fear of the Lord have disappeared.

This is a practical matter as well as a doctrinal one. Knox feared no man because he knew God in his sovereign majesty. Carey persevered in India because he submitted to the will of a sovereign Master. The Covenanters resisted the king because they served a greater King. Where this awareness is abandoned in favour of entertainment, self-expression and gimmicks, the reformed faith is no longer present. What we need today is a recovery of this vision, not only in certain vital doctrines but in the overall concept of the sovereign glory of God who rules in plan and providence, who reigns in majesty and holiness, who upholds and strengthens his humble people and who judges those who rebel against him. Such a concept of God, worked out in practice and experience, can transform us, as it did those who went before us.

God's instruments

They were only instruments in the hand of God. Many of those we have looked at were men of great ability, massive intellect and profound scholarship. All of them were godly men noted for their deep communion with God, their compassion and prayerfulness and their love and zeal. They displayed wonderful gifts of understanding, preaching, teaching and pastoral care. Nevertheless, they were only men, like Elijah, 'a man just like us' (James 5:17). What they did, they did only by the grace of God. Their sufficiency was of God, their power from the Spirit of God. We have concentrated on the leaders and said little about the many individuals who had the same beliefs, contended for the same faith, prayed to the same Lord, witnessed to the same gospel, laboured for the same glory of God and were used, in less public ways, by the same Holy Spirit. By the grace and power of the unchanging God, we may do what they did. A new Whitefield may have been converted as I write. A new Calvin may even now be studying in one of our theological seminaries. A new Spurgeon is possibly serving his apprenticeship in a village pastorate. On the other hand it may be that God will, as so often in the past, do a new thing, so magnifying the infinite variety of his wisdom and his grace, using a different kind of man or many different men. Whatever he does, it is our responsibility to fit ourselves, by his grace, to follow in the footsteps of our great predecessors. Our trust must never be in men, however great, however gifted, but in the living God. He alone delivers his people in their hour of need. He alone can revive his work. We must pray to him alone and to him alone will be all the glory.

> O'er the gloomy hills of darkness
> Look my soul; be still, and gaze:
> All the promises do travail

With a glorious day of grace:
Blessèd Jubilee!
Let thy glorious morning dawn.
— *William Williams (1717 – 1791)*

Questions for discussion

1. *What is the place and function of creeds, confessions, doctrinal statements or a basis of faith? What new elements, or errors, ought to be covered in a modern confession? What particular areas are under attack today?*

2. *In the light of history how would you define the biblical gospel? Is the first mark of a true church the belief of the truth or the preaching of the gospel?*

3. *In the light of these chapters, how do you see your own responsibility today? How can we contend for the faith without becoming cold and hard? What help does history give us?*

For further reading

** J. Blanchard, *Whatever happened to hell?*, Evangelical Press, 1993.

** P. H. Eveson, *The great exchange*, Day One Publications, 1996.

M. Haykin, *Defence of the truth*, Evangelical Press, 2004.

H. R. Jones, *Only one way*, Day One Publications, 1996.

* D. M. Lloyd-Jones, *What is an evangelical?*, The Banner of Truth Trust, 1992.

** I. Murray, *Evangelicalism divided*, The Banner of Truth Trust, 2000.

* F. Schaeffer, *The church before the watching world*, Inter-Varsity Press, 1972.

** D. F. Wells, *No place for truth or whatever happened to evangelical theology?*, Inter-Varsity Press, 1993.

Appendix:
The use and abuse of
church history

Perhaps I should add a third element to my title – disuse – because, in fact, many Christians simply ignore church history altogether. They would join with the car maker, Henry Ford, who said, 'History is more or less bunk.' They would probably also add, in the words so beloved of schoolchildren, 'It's boring'. Some see all mention of 'men of the past' as distracting from the great task of evangelism in the present. I feel sorry for anyone in this position. Not only are they missing out on one of the most wonderful, thrilling and profitable privileges of being Christians, especially British or American Christians who have a glorious

This is an abridged and adapted version of the present author's contribution under this title to the *1989 Congregational Studies Conference Papers*, included by permission of The Evangelical Fellowship of Congregational Churches, PO Box 34, Beverley, East Yorkshire, Hull UK HU17 8YY from whom that booklet may be obtained.

heritage, they are also likely to be less effective in this great and honourable aim.

Others 'misuse' or 'abuse' church history. Hegel, the nineteenth-century philosopher, is often credited with saying, 'History teaches us that history teaches us nothing.' This sounds too illogical for a famous philosopher, so let us quote him more exactly: 'What experience and history teach us is this: that people and governments never have learned anything from history, or acted on principles deduced from it.' This is rather different. He makes two points. First, it is not that there is nothing to be learned, but, for various reasons, people have not done so. Second, even when they do deduce principles they do not act on them. Both of these abuses will concern us shortly.

What, then, is the proper use of church history? Is there such a thing? For this we must stop quoting men and turn to the Scriptures. Except for one important qualification, what the apostle Paul writes about the use of Old Testament history applies to us also: 'These things happened to them as examples and were written down as warnings for us, on whom the fulfilment of the ages has come' (1 Cor. 10:11). There are lessons to be drawn from the Scriptures, both examples and warnings, and the Bible frequently draws on them. Deuteronomy and the Psalms (i.e. Ps. 44, 77, 78, 105, 106) constantly look back to God's dealings with Israel and deduce principles that can be applied and practised in the later period. We can and should follow that pattern.

The qualification is that church history does not have an infallible interpretation attached to it. Hence it is easy to make mistakes; one man's truth is another man's heresy, just as one man's liberty is another man's license. We must beware of using history without discrimination. Only the Word of God is perfect and we must test what has happened by that standard before we take it as an example rather than as a warning.

Church history, therefore, must be of interest to a Christian. It can also be of profit to a Christian if it is used with due biblical care because it is the story of God's truth, of God's people and of God's work. I want to look at our subject under these three headings, dealing with abuse and use in each case.

The history of God's truth

Abuse

The abuse of church history in this area occurs in two opposing ways, both of which fall into the trap of being unhistorical (i.e. lacking a sense of history, not seeing the past properly in relation to the present).

1. The first error sees us as superior and the past as really beneath our notice.

We have learning and scholarship; we are enlightened and sophisticated; therefore, these men of the past have nothing to teach us. This is particularly the error of liberals, the children of the Enlightenment, but not exclusively. Every minister comes across the person who dismisses the past as beneath his notice. Those who hold to this opinion should read a little of one of John Calvin's commentaries on the Bible.

2. The other mistake is the dangerous absolutizing of the past.

This is more likely to occur in evangelical circles. In this we adopt an uncritical attitude to the teaching of men such as Augustine, Wycliffe and Luther, as if they had all the benefits of centuries of Reformed study and teaching. In fact, both Augustine and Luther held to baptismal regeneration and Wycliffe was by no means clear on justification. A lack of historical perspective leads to an uncritical admiration of things that should be rejected. It is good to honour the courage and principles of the Pilgrim Fathers, who left their land in search of religious liberty, but essential also to realize that when these early independents reached the New World they were most intolerant of any other form of even evangelical Christianity. Of course the doctrine of the Scriptures has not changed, but man's understanding of it has developed with the centuries and we must recognize this fact.

This is true even of the great confessions. Although we may not commit the first error, of despising them, we must not regard them as infallible and therefore sacrosanct on all issues. Further, the great seventeenth-century confessions are inadequate for today. There is no mention in them of modernism, Barthianism, the kenosis doctrine, dispensationalism or the charismatic movement. Such omissions are as inevitable as they are regrettable because these errors have appeared relatively recently.

Use

Bearing all this in mind we can still gain great profit from the teachers and confessions of the past. Let me simply list some positive benefits of knowledge of the history of Christian doctrine.

1. The first positive gain is humility.

When we realize how clearly our forefathers understood the Scriptures – without our modern advantages – and how deep their grasp of Christian doctrine was, we can only be amazed and deeply humbled. The outstanding phenomenon of the past in this respect is that in the seventeenth century the Presbyterians, Congregationalists and Baptists were so agreed on the truth that their three confessions – the *Westminster Confession*, the *Savoy Declaration* and the *1689 Baptist Confession* (not forgetting also the *39 Articles* of the Church of England) – differed on only a few minor points. There was no problem over the person of Christ, atonement, the doctrines of grace, sanctification or eternal punishment. All the subjects we have to be tactful about and make allowances for so that we do not wreck our fragile evangelical unity, they asserted without hesitation or apology. They deliberately adopted the same wording as far as possible to show their unity. Compare this with the difficulty that we have today in getting agreement to the most basic and minimal statement of faith and you have some idea of how far we have come down the road of theological decadence.

2. From the study of history we learn what our forefathers really believed, which is sometimes contrary to what tradition tells us.

Anglicans can learn how different their modern beliefs and practices are from Reformation Anglicanism. The historic confessions refute the common claim of the ecumenically-minded modern free-churchman that Baptists and Congregationalists 'don't have creeds'. The Congregationalist fathers were not only convinced paedo-baptists but were also wedded firmly to reformed theology and the doctrines of grace. Again, look back to the seventeenth century and you will find that, far from boasting of the democratic processes of the church meeting, they believed in elders, who were to rule the church. Going a stage further we find much teaching on synods and their authority. You will find, indeed, that they preferred to be known as 'Congregationalists' because they rejected the isolationist and separatist implications of being called 'Independents'.

3. We can learn from the errors of the past.

If we may adapt the words of the Preacher of Ecclesiastes, we may say that 'there is no new heresy under the sun'. Heresy, like history, repeats itself and an awareness of this can save much time and labour. Although Scripture must remain the only arbiter of sound doctrine, the knowledge of how the church condemned various errors on the doctrine of the trinity in the early centuries and united behind Augustine to condemn Pelagius's doctrine of free will, will save us from having to go through the whole process once more. In fact, people do not know, and we have to go through it all again and sometimes the ill-informed come to different conclusions! It is well said by George Santayana that, 'Those who cannot remember the past are condemned to repeat it.' Once Pythagoras has proved his theorem, we do not have to prove it over again from scratch for ourselves. We simply teach the children how it is done. One example of this is a dispute that divided the evangelical constituency but which would easily have been dealt with if those concerned had had any knowledge of a man called David Sandeman, who, among other errors, held to a deficient definition of faith.

4. Put in another way, this provides us with a short cut.

We should feel no obligation to investigate, and so waste time on, every new idea that crops up. When you are told that you cannot have power to win souls unless you are baptized with the Spirit and speak in tongues, the simple recollection that men like

George Whitefield, Jonathan Edwards and C. H. Spurgeon had no need of this will preserve you from a wild-goose chase. Let me illustrate this from the ministry of Martyn Lloyd-Jones:

> Commenting in later years on what had kept him detached from associations with which it was often assumed that he would be identified, Dr Lloyd-Jones spoke of two principles by means of which he had sought to determine his decisions: 'First, my understanding of the Scripture and, second, my reading of the Calvinistic Methodist revival of the eighteenth century. These things governed me and when anything presented itself to me, if it did not fit into that framework, I had no difficulty over my duty. When I saw something which was so different from the high spirituality of the Methodist Fathers I did not have a struggle over whether to follow it or not' (Iain H. Murray, *D. Martyn Lloyd-Jones – the first forty years 1899 – 1939*, The Banner of Truth Trust, 1982, p.195).

5. History, involving as it does the experiences of men, helps to flesh out doctrine, to show its relevance and power, and perhaps to make it clearer.

It is all very well to read the definition of justification by faith in the *Shorter Catechism*, but what can compare with reading the life of Martin Luther, with the account of all his struggles with the idea of God's righteousness until he found freedom through the dynamic concept of Christ's righteousness counted as ours? We may read of a similar process in John Wesley's *Journal* for 1738.

The history of God's people

Abuse

Once again there are two opposing tendencies.

1. The first fault is merely to be interested in the past.

There are those who have an antiquarian interest in old books, who take great pride in possessing all the old volumes that they can collect but they never read any of them. Others simply like to delve into the past or – and this is worse in some ways – use Christian biography as a form of escapism. This is just a historical version of the missionary slides syndrome! The stories of God's people in the past are just entertainment. An amazing extension of this problem that I have encountered is the attitude that says, 'I don't understand why I have problems. I've got all the right books'!

Such a detached attitude to the men of the past leads to other forms of abuse. We can sit in judgement on them, either admiring uncritically or denigrating according to our pleasure. We must resist the modern overreaction against hagiography, which leads to efforts to find all a man's faults and lower him in the eyes of the Christian public. Iain Murray once said that he had learnt to speak of the dead as carefully as if they were alive or, we may add, as if they could sue us for libel. Equally we must resist the tendency of the past to hero worship (or saint worship!) as with John Calvin, C. H. Spurgeon and, more recently, Martyn Lloyd-Jones, where the great man can do no wrong and his opinions are quoted as ending all argument.

2. The opposite error is imitation.

Imitation is often referred to as the sincerest form of flattery, but in this connection it is a serious fault. Imitation is not the same as learning from their example and applying it in our own lives and circumstances. What I am referring to is the undiscerning, direct and wooden copying of the past. How many 'little Puritans' have filled our pulpits in recent years, aping their manners, their speech and their methods in totally different settings and with little of their life and power. Let me quote Martyn Lloyd-Jones on this subject:

> There are men who seem to me to be using the Puritans and their writings as a substitute for thought. Let me expound that. A man once came to me after listening to an attempt of mine to preach a sermon in which ... I had made a detailed analysis of a certain condition and given the reply to it in a number of propositions. He was a preacher himself and asked me: 'Did you find that list of questions in one of the

Puritans?' He revealed to me thereby that that was what he did himself! I must confess that I was rather amazed and alarmed at the thing, but I can see the possibility. Now if you do that, you are using the Puritans as a substitute for thought. You are not working the thing out yourself and putting yourself through the process and discipline of thought, but you are taking ready-made divisions and thoughts... This applies equally, of course, to the misuse of any other writers (D. Martyn Lloyd-Jones, *The Puritans: their origins and successors*, The Banner of Truth Trust, 1987, p.32).

If you imitate Joseph Caryl, who spent ten years expounding Job, you may end up with a tenth of your congregation as he did! If you write to your maiden aunt using Samuel Rutherford's letters, with their use of the language of love from the Song of Solomon, she will probably refer you to a psychiatrist! And if you copy Billy Bray, the great Cornish Methodist, and dance around the vestry carrying your minister, he will get a shock!

Use

Please do not allow the abuse to put you off the correct use. The reading of Christian biography is one of the healthiest ways to spend the afternoon of the Lord's Day and the easiest way to learn the history of the past so that we may profit from it.

1. In order to profit from Christians of the past we must first see them as Christians like ourselves.

Christians are essentially the same in any age, and we can learn much from these great men and women. J. I. Packer wrote in his 'Foreword' to the 1958 Puritan Conference papers,

> We look on the Puritans as our fellow-Christians, now enabled to share with us, through the medium of their books, the good things which God gave them three centuries ago. We study their teachings on the topics which took first place in their own thoughts and writings... We study the history of their doings as a commentary upon their

convictions (J. I. Packer, *A goodly heritage*, Puritan Conference Papers, 1958, p.5).

Earlier in that 'Foreword' he pointed out how the Puritans differed from us, not merely in the externals, which we have to take into account, but in the basics of godliness. Thus we can test ourselves by comparison with them:

a) Whereas the Puritans demanded order, discipline, depth and thoroughness in every department of the Christian life, the modern Evangelical temper is rather one of casual hap-hazardness and restless impatience. We crave for stunts, novelties and entertainments; we have lost our taste for solid study, humble self-examination and unspectacular hard work in our callings and in our prayers...

b) Whereas the Puritan outlook had God and His glory as its unifying centre, and was in consequence a broad, balanced, biblically-proportioned whole, its modern Evangelical equivalent has a different centre. It revolves round the individual man, as if he were the real hub of the universe (Packer, *A goodly heritage*, p.4).

2. We must see how they applied the Bible, not by slavish copying, but by noting their principles.

To continue J. I. Packer's words, 'The question which we ask is not simply the historical one: "What did they do and teach?"... Our questions are rather these: "How far is their exposition of the Scriptures a right one? And what biblical principles does it yield for the guiding of our faith and life today?"' (Packer, *A goodly heritage*, pp.5-6). Thus we see how their doctrine worked out in their practice. It is sometimes a failing of historical and biographical works that they fail to do this. For instance a book review in the *Banner of Truth Magazine* (No. 296, May 1988) says that, 'It would have greatly enhanced the value of the book, if it had shown what kind of Christianity motivated these men and the church that was to suffer such severe trials.' When we read about the great men of the past we need to understand what it was that made them tick, what it was that made them great. It was certainly not modern pseudo-Christianity or neo-evangelicalism.

Listen again to the words of Martyn Lloyd-Jones on the dust jacket of the 1953 reprint of John Calvin's *Institutes*:

> The most urgent reason why all should read the *Institutes*, however, is to be found in the times in which we live. In a world which is shaking in its very foundations and which lacks authority, nothing is so calculated to strengthen and to stabilise one's soul as this magnificent exposition and out-working of the glorious doctrine of the sovereignty of God. It was the 'iron ration of the soul' of the Reformation martyrs, of the Pilgrim Fathers, the Covenanters and many others who have had to face persecution and death for Christ's sake.

This procedure of the application of principles, rather than lifting their methods directly into the twenty-first century, is most important because their situation differed from ours in many ways. We may read Richard Baxter's *The Reformed Pastor* with great profit, provided we remember that he was the minister of a parish and that everyone recognized his right to visit and to require them to attend for catechizing. Try to do the same thing in the same way today and you will soon learn something about historical relativity! Similarly, when a somewhat discouraged listener at the Puritan Conference expressed his despair of ever matching the Puritan devotion to prayer and meditation, Dr Lloyd-Jones simply reminded him that 'they had servants in those days'!

3. Another benefit of this historical study is tolerance.

Or at least it should be; however, too often it is not. It can do only good for Congregationalists to be reminded that Adoniram Judson's becoming a Baptist on the way to the East to become a Congregationalist missionary did not ruin his ministry in Burma. It can only do Baptists good to realize that most of the great men of history before the twentieth century were paedo-baptists, whom the Lord did not exclude from his communion and service. It can only do good for consistent Calvinists to know something of the godliness and effectiveness of the saintly Arminian John Fletcher of Madeley, not to mention the Wesleys, whereas nonconformists in general will do well to remember that most of the great men of the eighteenth-century awakening were ministers in the Church of England. For instance, revival broke out at Llangeitho in Wales while Daniel Rowland was actually reading the Anglican Prayer Book Litany!

> An overwhelming force came upon his soul as he was praying in those most melting and evangelical words ... a sudden amazing power seized his whole frame and no sooner did it seize on him, than it ran instantly, like an electrifying shock, through all the people in the church, so that many of them fell down on the ground they had been standing on in a large mass together, there being no pews in the church (Eifion Evans, *Daniel Rowland and the great evangelical awakening in Wales*, The Banner of Truth Trust, 1985, p.50).

The moral is to read as widely as possible about men of every persuasion, to be aware that not all the truth and godliness lies in any one camp. Samuel Taylor Coleridge put it like this: 'If men could learn from history, what lessons it might teach us! But passion and party blind our eyes.'

The history of God's work

Abuse

All that we have considered in the previous section applies here also, but we can add to it.

1. There is a danger of prejudice arising from denominational bias.

This results in some strange interpretations of history, such as the tendency today to regard the Waldensians as evangelical Baptists or primitive Plymouth Brethren, when in fact they were rather unclear about the gospel. The same desire to claim everybody for our party leads to a somewhat romantic view of Augustine and

Wycliffe. In an age when Congregationalists are regarded by most evangelicals as the lowest of the low because of their recent liberal history, it is, no doubt, good for morale to remember that the Congregationalist John Owen is still the greatest of English theologians. However, they will do well to make sure that they agree with him before placing much stress on this fact! In a different direction this abuse leads to a refusal to see anything wrong with those who are without doubt of our party; for example, the frequent attempt to justify Calvin's treatment of Servetus in every respect.

2. There is also a great danger of seeing history merely in terms of men, movements and trends and forgetting God.

We must not neglect to consider properly the means that God uses so that we may learn our duty from them, but we must take care to glorify God. It is difficult to keep the balance here, but the key is to see them within God's purposes at all times. Thus Psalm 44:3 says of the fathers, 'It was not by their sword that they won the land, nor did their arm bring them victory; it was your right hand, your arm, and the light of your face, for you loved them.' Similarly Psalm 77:19-20 keeps the balance: 'Your path led through the sea, your way through the mighty waters, though your foot-steps were not seen. You led your people like a flock by the hand of Moses and Aaron.' This gives due attention both to God and to his instruments.

3. Further, there may be a tendency to become stereotyped in our attitude to revival in a way that effectively, at least in our minds and prayers, limits God.

I am referring to the frequent desires and prayers for 'another Whitefield' or 'another Spurgeon'. If God had worked like that in the past we would not have had Whitefield or Spurgeon but only a succession of Pauls, who would not have been suited to the situations with which the Lord actually dealt. (Of course, one may argue that Paul, Whitefield and Spurgeon, great men that they were, would have adapted themselves and their methods to the different situation.) One lesson of history seems to be that God, almost invariably, does a *new thing*, not in the current charismatic sense but in the sense of his unfailing wisdom and power to deal with any and every situation.

An extension of this fault is the feeling that if we reproduce the pattern of a previous awakening then we shall necessarily enjoy the same blessing. Thus because two old ladies prayed in an isolated cottage and revival ensued, we must look for two old ladies. Because Jonathan Edwards preached on the sovereignty of God in justification and revival came, if we follow him we, too, shall be successful.

Use

The usefulness of church history from this angle can hardly be overstated. As someone has said in a totally different connection, 'The history of art is the history of revivals.' So it is with the history of the church. Viewed as a continuation of the story of God's people recounted in the Scriptures, it encourages us to serve and glorify God in our own day as our forefathers did in theirs.

1. The history of the past shows us just how low we have sunk.

To hear people talk of the great things that are happening, of the strength of the evangelicals in the Church of England and of the popularity of Christian Unions in the universities and colleges of our land you would think that all was well with us today, that is, until you read something of the great days of the past.

This is true not only of light and superficial observers but also of those who, quite rightly, rejoice in the progress of sound doctrine as evidenced by the increased popularity of certain reformed ministers' conferences, with up to 300 or 400 present. But do we realize that in 1662, the year of the Great Ejection, with a population far smaller than today, there were nearly 2,000 reformed ministers prepared to sacrifice everything for the sake of the gospel and be ejected from the Church of England? The equivalent today would be approximately 30,000 reformed ministers!

We need the dual perspective of Ezra 3:12: we find great rejoicing over the laying of the temple's foundation, combined with sorrow from those who had seen the former temple in its glory and realized just how far they had to go before they achieved anything similar. We must be glad and glorify God for all that has been done in recent years but be aware of just how little it is in what the economists call 'real terms'. Our complacency must be shattered if we are to be strong and strive for a great work of God in our own day.

2. Further, the study of the work of God in the past can convince us of the possibility and reality of things that we have never experienced for ourselves.

If we were limited to our own lives and times we would not know that there is such a thing as deep and general conviction of sin, that whole communities can be changed and that the most desperate situation can be completely reversed. When we look at our towns with nearly empty churches and chapels, do we realize that once upon a time, with much lower populations, these buildings were both necessary and sometimes full?

Can you imagine a situation in which your town was like Richard Baxter's Kidderminster? He records that when he first arrived there, 'There was about one family in a street that worshipped God and called upon his name, and when I came away there were some streets where there was not past one family in the side of the street that did not do so.' Paul Cook comments, 'During that time – under fifteen years – hundreds had been converted and the church had had to be enlarged to hold the crowds. And Baxter was only one among many' (Packer, *A goodly heritage*, p.17). If that kind of work happened in our towns, where would we put the people? Could we use two or three football stadiums every Sunday? Our eyes need to be opened to what is possible under God; our children and young people must be informed as to what we are looking and praying for.

3. The example of the past will also stir us to work.

There were giants in past days and our stress on the activity of God should not be allowed to blind us to that fact. By comparison we are only pygmies. Think of the hours that Luther must have worked merely to produce his written works; it takes almost a lifetime to read them! Remember Calvin slaving away to teach the Word of God, in spite of suffering from almost every known illness, and when his friends pleaded with him to ease off, answering, 'Would you have my Lord find me idle when he comes?' Read of those who were ready to be burnt at the stake for the sake of the gospel. Consider William Carey and his colleagues going boldly where no man had gone before, without the example and encouragement of generations of successful evangelical missionaries. We need not limit ourselves to the distant past. Read of Hudson Taylor going to inland China when almost all others were confined to the treaty ports. Notice their labours, their prayer and their sufferings. All this must stir us to action!

4. Last, the study of the history of revivals will lead us to pray in hope.

Read Bishop Ryle's account (J. C. Ryle, *Christian leaders of the eighteenth century*, The Banner of Truth Trust, 1960, pp.13-14) of the state of religion in England before Whitefield and Wesley and realize that even our spiritual decadence and moral decline can be reversed. On a more local level read the account of Peter Thacher's ministry in Gillies's *Historical collections* (John Gillies, *Historical collections of accounts of revival*, The Banner of Truth Trust, 1981, pp.401-405). He despaired after thirty-four years with an unresponsive flock and then revival came to New England and to Middleborough in particular. Within two months nearly 100 were converted and the following year saw 170 joining the church.

There is, of course, no substitute for the Word of God itself – heard, read, understood, believed and put into practice – but accounts like this, and thousands more, cannot fail to enlighten, encourage, move and stir us to action. Truly, we have a goodly heritage. Let us make a right and proper use of it.

A wide range of excellent books on spiritual subjects is available from Evangelical Press. Please write to us for your free catalogue or contact us by e-mail.

Evangelical Press
Faverdale North, Darlington, Co. Durham, DL3 0PH, England
email: sales@evangelicalpress.org

Evangelical Press USA
P. O. Box 825, Webster, NY 14580, USA
email: usa.sales@evangelicalpress.org

www.evangelicalpress.org